Family History in Black and White

Social Fictions Series

Series Editor

Patricia Leavy (*USA*)

International Editorial Advisory Board

Carl Bagley (*University of Durham, UK*)
Anna Banks (*University of Idaho, USA*)
Carolyn Ellis (*University of South Florida, USA*)
Rita Irwin (*University of British Columbia, Canada*)
J. Gary Knowles (*University of Toronto, Canada*)
Laurel Richardson (*The Ohio State University (Emerita), USA*)

VOLUME 42

Family History in Black and White

A Novel

By

Christine Sleeter

BRILL

SENSE

LEIDEN | BOSTON

All chapters in this book have undergone peer review.

Library of Congress Cataloging-in-Publication Data

Names: Sleeter, Christine E., 1948- author.
Title: Family history in black and white : a novel / by Christine Sleeter.
Description: Leiden ; Boston : Brill Sense, [2021] | Series: Social
   fictions series, 25428799 ; vol. 42 | Includes bibliographical
   references and index.
Identifiers: LCCN 2021007390 (print) | LCCN 2021007391 (ebook) | ISBN
   9789004462830 (paperback) | ISBN 9789004462847 (hardback) | ISBN
   9789004462854 (ebook)
Classification: LCC PS3619.L446 F36 2021 (print) | LCC PS3619.L446
   (ebook) | DDC 813/.6--dc23
LC record available at https://lccn.loc.gov/2021007390
LC ebook record available at https://lccn.loc.gov/2021007391

ISSN 2542-8799
ISBN 978-90-04-46283-0 (paperback)
ISBN 978-90-04-46284-7 (hardback)
ISBN 978-90-04-46285-4 (e-book)

ADVANCE PRAISE FOR
FAMILY HISTORY IN BLACK AND WHITE

"Set in Northern California, Christine Sleeter's follow up to *White Bread* (her first novel), *Family History in Black and White* stitches together poignant examples of the real and realistic struggles of educators trying to do the right thing while confronting their own implications in a broader racialized history. Her protagonists, Ben and Roxane, show us that racism is both intimate and universal, dispiriting while providing the condition for a refusal of despair. Weaving together stories of love and heartbreak, family life and institutions, Sleeter not only engages our politics but stokes our imagination for a better education and a more just future."
– Zeus Leonardo, Professor, University of California, Berkeley, and author of *Race Frameworks: A Multidimensional Theory of Racism and Education*

"*Family History in Black and White* is a primer for anyone who wants to learn about history, race, gender, school dynamics, teaching, curriculum, ethnic studies, urban school reform, and so much more. This novel is full of intellectual ideas but does what a university textbook, academic book, or research article cannot. It offers a provocative, page-turning plot that will pull you in, even as it teaches you about some of the most intractable problems found in society and schools today. I cannot wait to use this in my graduate course!"
– Keffrelyn D. Brown, Professor and Distinguished University Teaching Professor, The University of Texas at Austin

"It's hard to say which narrative twist is more compelling: the one in which Christine Sleeter genre-jumps with inspiring finesse and dexterity or the one that darn near jumped from the page in the second

half of *Family History in Black and White*. Read this book and, like me, enjoy both twists at once."
– Paul Gorski, Ph. D., Equity and justice educator, writer, and activist, and author of *Reaching and Teaching Students in Poverty*

"Christine Sleeter, a trusted voice in educational research, uses the art of the novel to center critical issues in education. Through Roxane and Ben, relatable characters who come from different backgrounds, but whose lives are surprisingly intertwined, the reader is reminded of the costs of personal ambition in a system that doesn't always play fair. Through stories revealing the complicated nature of their present and past lives, the book critiques the inequitable systems we all live within; takes on gentrification and bias, and lays out a history absent from most of today's classrooms. All at once, Family History in Black and White, reveals the need for historical literacy, the lasting impact of generational trauma, and serves as a reminder of our pasts while offering hope for our future."
– Yolanda Sealey-Ruiz, Teachers College, Columbia University and author, *Love from the Vortex & Other Poems*

"Christine Sleeter's brilliant novel takes up issues of trust, educational leadership, and racism in America's public schools –topics that usually appear only in educational texts. It makes a compelling case that we need trust. With racial dynamics engrossing the world's imagination, this riveting novel will forever shift your views on race and education."
– Muhammad Khalifa, President of the Culturally Responsive School Leadership Institute, and Professor of Educational Administration at the Ohio State University

"In *Family History Black and White* Christine Sleeter effectively and brilliantly examines the complexities of leadership within contemporary contexts and intersecting issues of race and class. Using a fictional approach and storytelling Christine captures some of the tensions that practitioners and academics are wrestling with. The work is unique in its approach and focuses on an area that needs to be critically

examined. In this book, Christine courageously tackles pressing issues in education leadership and schooling in an unconventional manner. It will greatly benefit educational leadership scholars, students and professionals."
– Ann E. Lopez, Director of the Centre for Leadership and Diversity, Ontario Institute for Studies in Education, and author of *Culturally Responsive and Socially Just Leadership in Diverse Contexts: From Theory to Action*

"This novel, by a nationally well-respected education scholar, Christine Sleeter, is ostensibly about a Black female principal and a White male principal competing for the same superintendency of a racially diverse district. While we see family dynamics at play for each, it also has race and racism interwoven throughout, both within education and within each principal's and their families' personal lives. In addition, it has surprising plot twists and an unexpected and provocative history of each family's prior racial connections in the Jim Crow South, drawn from Sleeter' own family history. If you want to learn from fiction about education and race or if you are teaching about the same, this book would be an excellent choice."
– James Joseph Scheurich, Professor, Urban Education Studies Doctoral Program, Indiana University – Indianapolis (IUPUI), and author of *Anti-Racist Scholarship*

"Christine Sleeter's latest novel, *Family History in Black and White*, confronts difficult issues of systemic racism and how to right past wrongs head on. As two San Francisco Bay Area high school principals, one Black, one White, compete for a school district superintendency, conflicts arise around how they approach their principal jobs in diverse school settings and what they want for their families. While Sleeter digs into controversial topics such as racial justice and neighborhood integration, she includes a historical story, reminding readers that no matter how diverse we feel, we all have a past that intricately weaves us together."
– Mary Smathers, Educator, educational entrepreneur, and author of *In This Land of Plenty*

CONTENTS

PREFACE

Family History in Black and White grapples with race and racism in the context of today's rapidly shifting demographics. The novel's main premise is that racism shapes how white people and people of color experience and see the world, with differences on sharp display during competition. But differences in perspective and experience, rather than dividing us, represent our intertwined relationships that have long historical roots.

The novel traces two urban high school principals as they compete for the position of school superintendent. Ben, a white man who had been bullied as a child, craves recognition of his expertise. But, unsure whether he can trust today's competitive process to be fair to a white person, he wrestles with compromising his own integrity to get what he wants. Roxane, a Black woman who has navigated racism all her life, craves recognition of her humanity. But she can't be sure which of the professionals around her are actually trustworthy, including her chief competitor, Ben.

This novel, like my previous novels, engages with family history. Germs of this novel emerged as I dug into my mother's roots. That was how I discovered that I descend from slave owners. Not big plantation owners, but still, my great-great-great grandparents in east Tennessee owned a Black family. They considered it acceptable to own people and profit from their labor. I had to sit with that for a while as I pondered the fact that practices once considered acceptable, and profits accrued from slavery, do not simply disappear with the next generation.

Digging through records in Monroe County, Tennessee, I came upon a deed of sale that intrigued me. Sometime after the Civil War, the grandson of my slave-owning ancestor drew up a deed involving farm animals he was buying from a man I assume was a sharecropper on or near his land. As I studied the deed, I could only conclude that it documented a clever way for my ancestor to extend a loan to a proud, formerly enslaved man. I found myself trying to reconstruct the story behind the deed as I wondered: Was that ancestor the kind of person one might regard as a "good white"? What does it mean to be a "good white," anyway, and how does that differ from being an ally? What had my ancestor absorbed from his grandparents' stance on slavery that remained with him?

As I plowed around in my family history, another white historical figure caught my attention: Benjamin Franklin Butler, a former Union army General during the Civil War. I am not related to him, but an ancestor named a son after him. Butler was among the first to free fugitive slaves during the Civil War. As General in charge of the North's occupation of New Orleans, he promoted literacy for Black residents. Was he an anti-racist figure? Although the more I read about him, the murkier that designation became, stories about him served as grist as I developed one of the main characters, Ben.

And what of Roxane? Where did she come from? When I picture Black women in education leadership roles whom I have known over the past four decades – principals, superintendents, deans, thought leaders – Roxane stands among them. But rather than describing her from the outside, I had to get to know her from the inside. How well I did that, only Black women readers can judge. However, the process sharpened my appreciation of everyday experiences of women like Roxane.

Most of *Family History in Black and White* is set in 2018. As I write this preface in 2020, we are witnessing a white retreat from about two months of solidarity with Black Lives Matter protests against police brutality. When the protests were first organized following the police killing of George Floyd, I and many others were struck by the large numbers of white people joining the protests. In fact, some protests were virtually all-White, but in clear solidarity with Black Lives Matter. While many white people continue to maintain that solidarity, others have peeled away, I think due mainly to the intransigence and pervasiveness of society's negative images of people of color, and to fairly shallow relationships most white people have with Black people. Coalitions can be fraught and dissolve as people compete for control, or as stereotypes, like gasoline, are hurled onto the fire by a president who repeatedly uses a politics of division.

Readers who enjoyed my previous novel *White Bread* will be pleased to see a return of one of its main characters, Esteban Ayala. No longer a fifth grade teacher, Esteban is now a high school principal in the same school district, which now has a name: Cypress View Unified School District. Readers may also wish to read my second novel, *The Inheritance*, set in Milford Elementary School where Esteban taught fifth grade, and featuring some of the characters from *White Bread*.

I hope that *Family History in Black and White* will prompt readers to reflect on the embeddedness of racism in their own lives and work. As a social construction, I believe racism can be dismantled. But that will not happen unless we examine the roots of our own beliefs. And for white people, challenging racism will entail what Sonia Nieto, in a 1995 talk to the Graduate School of Education at the University of California Berkeley, termed "arrogance reduction." *Family History in Black and White* can be used to prompt discussion and reflection in education leadership, ethnic studies, and sociology courses. School leaders may see some of their own struggles reflected in Roxane's and Ben's work, and may gain ideas they might try. In addition, *Family History in Black and White* can be used, in conjunction with my Critical Family History blog (see https://www.christinesleeter. org/critical-family-history), to engage readers across the disciplines in researching their own family histories, and learning to situate their families within a broader context. Or, *Family History in Black and White* can simply be read for pleasure.

CHAPTER 1

AN OPPORTUNITY

Coffee in one hand, iPad in the other, Ben Harris scrolled through *New York Times* headlines. News addicted him like cigarettes addicted other people, although he was tired of the repetition from day to day. What else went on in the world outside Washington's Beltway?

"Trump finally fired that Manigault woman. She seems to have been a disaster on wheels," he commented to his wife Lisa as she fixed breakfast.

"Yeah, but at least she was one of the few women in a White House that's fueled by testosterone," Lisa replied. "Unfortunately, that's one less female voice we'll be hearing."

"Good point. She was also one of the few Blacks there. But still, she was pretty incompetent."

Lisa slid his eggs onto a plate with buttered toast, which she set in front of him.

"Ever hear about World Tsunami Awareness Day?" He picked up his fork, pausing to read. Now, here was something different, a story you didn't run across everyday. "Seems to be a big deal in Asia. Over a hundred schools there have a program to train kids in evacuation techniques."

"Nope, never heard of it," she replied as she retrieved a box of cereal from the cupboard. "But I have heard of Christmas, and we need to get our tree up this weekend."

"Right." Ben smiled at the thought. Christmas was less than three weeks away, and he always enjoyed setting out lights and hoisting up the tree.

He shoveled down the eggs as he skimmed the op-eds. His eyes fell on one that touched a nerve. "Now, how did David Brooks get to be an education expert? Here he is, spouting off about schools, as if he knows what he's talking about. Why do people go to him rather than someone who's actually there, doing the work?"

He felt genuinely piqued. As a high school principal, Ben had put in long hours learning to lead a school successfully. He could tick off countless improvements he had made over the last three years that had good results. Student achievement scores were up, the graduation rate was up, relationships between his school and the tech world were strengthened – he knew how to get things done. Yet the news media seemed to overlook people like him.

Lisa shook her head as she set the table for the boys' breakfast. "You mean someone in the trenches like you?"

He looked up at her. After thirteen years of marriage, he still felt a flutter when her nose crinkled, as it did now. Years earlier, before the boys were even toddlers, certainly before he was a school principal, that look on her face would have prompted him to lead her back to bed for a quick snuggle before work. He wondered if she even remembered those days.

He shrugged. "Could be me. Could be a lot of other people as well."

"*You* try writing an op-ed," she said. "That'll get you noticed. Okay, I'm heading upstairs to rouse the boys."

Ben wolfed down his toast, poured the remaining coffee down his throat, and grabbed his backpack and coat. When the boys were younger, he made a point of not leaving home until he greeted them and ruffled their hair. But the older they got, the harder it was to get them moving in the morning. Nine-year-old Jason was probably already awake, but his twelve-year old brother Evan, a night owl at heart, could sleep through anything, particularly in the morning. As principal, it was important to be the first administrator in the building, so, faced with San Jose traffic, he no longer waited around for his sons to emerge. It was okay if he didn't see them until dinnertime.

Twenty minutes later, he pulled into his parking space at Richford High School. While walking to his office, he quickly scrolled through his email to see if anything needed immediate attention.

His secretary Carmen was just arriving. Ben greeted her, held the door for her, then continued scanning email as he unlocked his inner office door. A message from Mitchell Andersen caught his attention. Mitchell was an old acquaintance. The two had grown up in Seattle's Ballard neighborhood, although to consider Mitch a childhood friend would be a stretch. Ben had been one of those kids who other kids bullied until he learned to use martial arts to fight back. As soon as Ben won his first fight, Mitchell switched from tagging along with the neighborhood bully, to being Ben's greatest cheerleader. After high school, the two lost contact until last year when they ran into each other at a regional conference for school administrators. Mitchell had just been hired as math and science curriculum coordinator in Cypress View Unified School District, northeast of San Jose.

The subject line read "Urgent." Ben was about to open it when Carmen stepped in. "Just a reminder that Mrs. Hardy will be here to see you in about fifteen minutes."

"Thank you, Carmen." He sighed. Mrs. Hardy was a helicopter mom with two daughters at Richford. The girls, both good students, were forever devising tactics to get around her rules, so she haunted the one place where she had the least control over them – the school. Ben gave up trying to get her to back off and give the girls some space. The only way he knew to cope with her was to keep meetings as brief as possible.

He turned back to his email. Mitchell had written that Cypress View's superintendent had just announced his impending retirement at last night's school board meeting. A search for a new superintendent would be underway soon. Ben should apply.

Mitchell wouldn't know this, but Ben liked to picture himself at the helm of San Jose Unified School District. He imagined himself as its superintendent, capably leading its schools toward academic excellence, and shifting more money into the district's instructional program, even while strengthening its financial solvency. Heaven knew solvency was a challenge. Schools were drowning in a tidal wave of expenses, as the newspaper put it. San Jose Unified was a large, complex urban district with an on-and-off history of attempts to desegregate, thousands of students from homes in poverty, a high population of students from immigrant households, and never enough money to do all that was needed.

Cypress View, much smaller but facing similar demographics and challenges, just might provide Ben with the perfect training ground for the larger platform he sought. Move over, David Brooks!

***

"Mama, pass the sugar. Please." When Roxane Bedford felt rushed, she tended to forget her manners. She caught herself just before reaching across the table.

Her coffee sweetened, Roxane gulped it down as she took her mug to the counter to make lunch for herself and her daughter Imani.

"That girl needs to learn to take shorter showers," she grumbled as she listened to water gushing through the pipes. "We've got a drought going on here. We should be getting rain now that it's December, but all we've had is a trickle. Water's expensive."

Her mother looked up from reading the morning paper. "Child, you sound just like me twenty years ago." She flipped the page and frowned. "Now here's a story about an immigration official complaining about a tsunami of people crossing the border illegally. Tsunami? Please. That man needs a different job."

"Sounds like the die-hards on my staff," Roxane said. A handful of white teachers and parents were always questioning her competence, challenging her every move, and undermining her in ways only they thought were subtle. Just last week someone managed to "lose" the Spanish version of her monthly parent newsletter. She knew it wasn't lost – Terry, her vice principal, had intercepted it when it came back from the printing office. She couldn't imagine how she had managed to acquire a vice principal who believed immigrants would not learn English unless it was the only language they encountered.

"I guess bigots are everywhere," her mother said as she continued reading. She frowned. "Omarosa was fired, did you hear? Some people are saying she quit, but everyone knows that man fired her."

"I can't see how she stuck with him as long as she did. Or why. I bet she has a tell-all book in the works."

Her mother grunted in agreement. Roxane couldn't understand why an intelligent Black woman like Omarosa Manigault would have tried to defend the president, even going so far as to say he wasn't racist. She figured reality was catching up with the woman.

"Now listen to this," her mother continued. "'Solutions to the nation's problems already exist somewhere out in the country; we just do a terrible job of circulating them.' This man is writing about good leaders making good schools."

"Someone wrote an article about that? They actually put something so obvious in the newspaper?" Roxane paused her lunch preparation.

"Mm-hmm, someone named David Brooks wrote it. Let me see. Ah, here's what he says good principals do. 'They build a culture.'"

Roxane laughed. "Mama, I hope that man didn't get paid for writing that. Who is this writer? What did you say his name is?"

Her mother skimmed to the end of the article. "David Brooks. He's a columnist for the *New York Times*. Listen: 'Today's successful principals are greeting parents and students outside the front door in the morning.'"

Roxane rolled her eyes. "Mama, I could have written that. What do people think I do when I get to school every morning?" Turning in the general direction of the stairs, she hollered, "Imani, I'm leaving. Pick you up at four-thirty, okay?"

"Bye, Mama," came a voice from upstairs. "Love you!"

"I love you too, Baby." Roxane circled back to her mother and kissed her cheek. "We'll be home usual time. I have a meeting tonight, so I'll be bolting down dinner pretty fast, but you'll have Imani with you for the evening."

"You have a good day, Baby. I'll be busy with that writing class I'm taking," she said with reference to an adult education course on memoir writing she had signed up for.

Roxane flew out of the house to the car. A half hour later, as she left the freeway to turn toward Taylor High School outside Stockton, her cell phone rang.

"Hello?" she said while changing lanes.

"Glad I caught you," came a familiar voice.

"Hey there, Esteban. I'm driving to work, maybe we can talk later?" Esteban Ayala was a high school principal in a small school district northeast of San Jose. The two had become good friends in their administrative credential program a few years back. They jokingly referred to each other as "partners in crime" as they backed up each other's ideas about how schools could best serve Black and brown students.

"For sure," he replied. "I just want to give you something enticing to think about. Last night our esteemed superintendent Al Cordero announced his impending retirement. I want you to consider applying for the job."

"Why don't you apply for it?" Roxane chuckled. "You're already there, you know the district. You'd be a shoo-in."

"Frankly, I don't want the job. I don't go to sleep at night dreaming about being a superintendent."

"Me neither," she replied. What she did dream about was returning to Oakland to lead its schools. Although her family left had Oakland almost twelve years ago after losing their rental house to gentrification, she still considered the town to be home.

"But just think about us teaming up to transform a whole school district. Cypress View is small, only one high school, a couple middle schools, and half a dozen elementary schools. It's manageable. You could take everything you're doing now, and move it to a larger scale. Just think about it. We'll talk." With that, he hung up.

By the time she pulled into her parking space, Roxane realized she couldn't stop thinking about Esteban's proposal. She loved many of the people at Taylor High and was excited about the initiatives she had started. She even enjoyed cheering on the Taylor Cougars in basketball.

But there were days. It was difficult being around Terry and his ilk who seemed to fear drowning in a sea of people who simply looked different from them.

Cypress View would have some of the same people, of course. But working with Esteban, maybe she could get more done there than at Taylor. It was worth exploring.

CHAPTER 2

AMBITION

"Good morning, Joaquin, 'morning, Sam." As Ben greeted students on a chilly March morning, he wondered if he would miss them. His job application for the Cypress View superintendency was in and he felt confident. Who wouldn't want to hire Dr. Ben Harris for a position like this? He was smart, experienced, and knew how to get things done. Just last week, Mitchell told him that he was one of the top contenders for the job. Maybe *the* top contender. Mitchell wasn't supposed to know that, and he certainly wasn't supposed to spill it to Ben, but he did anyway.

Ben couldn't wait to be called for an interview. He pictured himself skillfully fielding every question, wowing the committee with the same blend of expertise and humor he had used to win over his students when he taught math a few years back.

"Michael, the hat, please." The kids knew not to dodge him, but some always tried. Richford's dress code prohibited wearing hats in the building, as well as gang colors and professional sports logos. Ben suspected that most kids appreciated the safe climate the dress code fostered, but there were a few rebels in the crowd.

Many school administrators wouldn't insist that all kids adhere to sensible rules like this one. A lot of principals wouldn't even be out in front of the building day after day, making sure things got off to a good start. What would happen to Richford after Ben left? Would standards begin to fray like a house that isn't well kept up? Too bad he couldn't choose his successor.

As the river of kids slowed to a trickle, he turned to Chad Hernandez, the school security officer standing next to him. "Any plans for spring break?" Still two weeks away, conversations about spring break were beginning to crop up like California poppies.

"I'll be taking a couple of vacation days since the kids will be around," Chad replied. "We might head to over to Pismo Beach for a long weekend."

"Pismo Beach. Both times I've been there, it was socked in with fog." Ben pictured his own kids' disappointment last summer when the family arrived, beach gear in tow, only to find a cold fog blanketing the whole beach. "By the way, I've wondered, what does the "L" in your name stand for?" He pointed to the name badge: L. Chad Hernandez.

Chad laughed. "My parents saddled me with the first name Lautaro, my mom's grandfather's name. As soon as I entered school, I dropped it. Everyone was always mispronouncing it, so I started using my middle name. I would have dropped the "L" entirely, but Mom would have taken that as an affront to her side of the family."

"Names are funny," Ben said. "My middle name, Daniel, and my first name go back generations in the Harris family. I haven't tried to trace them, but it seems every generation gets some version. I passed them on to both our boys as middle names. My wife got to pick their first names."

After the last stragglers arrived, Ben walked briskly back to his office, thinking of his first summer after college. Newly arrived in San Diego (better weather than Seattle), he had found a part time job as a computer specialist in a Boys and Girls Club. The director put him in a tiny room off the main office that had probably once been a closet. The isolation suited his introverted nature, and it protected him from his discomfort with the racial and ethnic diversity of the club's youth. Having grown up in Ballard, he was accustomed to seeing people of color around the edges of his world, but not interacting with them in its center. The Black kids, in particular, had felt intimidating as they noisily claimed space with a style of speaking he could barely understand. There had been times in high school when he felt small, boring, and resentful of those bussed-in intruders. San Diego, with all of its racial diversity, threw him back into that earlier disequilibrium. He was happy to retreat to the relative quiet of his workspace, especially when he shut the door.

But all of this changed on the day that Antwon, a tall ninth grader, walked in and asked Ben to teach him computer skills.

"They teach computers in the schools here, don't they?" Ben asked, thinking of Ballard's gleaming new high-tech high school.

"In middle school, we went to computer lab once a week. Period," Antwon replied. "We got some computers here, but in summer kids mostly play games on them. I was hopin' you could teach me spreadsheets and stuff like that."

Spreadsheets? Antwon didn't look like a budding computer geek. Nevertheless, Ben agreed to give Antwon lessons in basic computer applications. Within two weeks, several other kids had joined them. To his surprise, over computers Ben's introverted nature and insecurity around urban youth faded. He discovered that he could connect with kids just like those who had been bussed in to his high school, at least when he had something to offer that they wanted. They even laughed at some of his jokes! He was actually teaching them things and watching them catch on, right before his eyes. What an intoxicating experience! He began to visualize himself as a teacher.

Who would have thought that sixteen years later, Ben would be greeting hoards of Black and brown youth every day as their school principal? Who from his adolescent days would have imagined that the nerdy, scrawny, acne-faced boy with a lisp he had once been was becoming a force to be reckoned with?

After taking the call he was summoned for, he spent much of first period putting out fires – a parent calling about her son who was rushed to the hospital with a broken arm, another parent calling about her chronically absent daughter, a new substitute having trouble with students, a girl who had just vomited on the way to class.

Then he had Carmen set up phone conferences with representatives from three large tech companies. In Ben's opinion, the district's schools did not use their location in Silicon Valley as well as they could. He wanted to expand apprenticeships in the tech sector for juniors and seniors, and add coursework that would prepare high school graduates for semi-skilled technology careers. There was no reason the United States should import tech workers from other countries when it could invest time and resources preparing them right here. Even someone with only a high school diploma could find work in web design, tech support, or tech repair, if they had technology skills. A college degree only added to the possibilities.

But most of Richford students didn't seem aware of these opportunities, nor envision themselves in the tech world. So Ben worked with math and science teachers to talk up tech work, and with computer companies to make sure all Richford's students had ready access to laptops and tablets. He even managed to secure donations for college scholarships to promising students who intended to major in computer science.

He figured this creative work with the tech sector would give him an edge over other candidates for Cypress View's position. He couldn't stop thinking about it.

But Cypress View? Ben still wasn't sure it would be the right career move. Would spending a few years over there actually propel him toward becoming San Jose's superintendent and a noted expert in urban education? One could describe Cypress View as "urban-lite." Parts of it resembled inner city San Jose, but other parts seemed rural, bumping right up against farmland.

On the other hand, because it was small and relatively simple, running the school district would be good practice. To Ben, organizations were like machines. He loved tinkering with them – oiling and calibrating to make them run smoothly and predictably. It was a challenge he was good at, one he enjoyed. As a middle school teacher, he had figured out how to get his math classes to run smoothly while many of his colleagues flailed. Part of the secret was convincing students that you get what you work for, and running the classroom accordingly. That was the American way, after all. Ben's whole life was a testament to the system. Born into a working class family and saddled with a frail physique and a funny-looking face, he had learned to succeed.

The bell rang between classes. Ben had just stepped outside his office when Gerald Smith, an energetic second-year science teacher, appeared.

"Can I speak with you a minute, sir?" Gerald asked.

"Sure, come on in. What can I do for you?"

"I'm sorry to have to tell you this, but I've just accepted a job over near Fresno," Gerald said, brow wrinkled and eyes sad. "I love my job here and I love the students, but my wife and I just can't afford a house where we can raise our kids."

Ben froze. Gerald's was the third resignation this year by someone who couldn't afford to live in San Jose. While the other two teachers were not among his favorites, Gerald was a rising star, a mentee he valued.

"Anything I can do to make you change your mind? If you'd like to earn extra money coaching ..."

"No, thank you, sir. I thought about that. But in Fresno, we can get double the house we have here, for less money. And our kids will have an actual back yard. I've enjoyed working with you here. You were the one I most dreaded telling, but, well ..."

Gerald looked almost guilty. But the cost of housing wasn't his fault and it wasn't Ben's. Ben draped his arm across Gerald's shoulder. "We've been lucky to have you here. You're one of the finest teachers I've met. Thank you for telling me."

Gerald nodded, turned, and left.

Ben didn't have an answer to the housing problem, but it was one he would need to figure out. Nor did he have an answer to the eroding pay of classroom teachers, not just in California, but all over. Even West Virginia's teachers had just finished striking for higher wages and better benefits. Would San Jose's teachers follow suit?

On the other hand, with the normalcy of staff turnover, Richford folks would probably take his own departure in stride. A paradox of working as a change agent is that the moment you get a useful innovation going, you're in high demand elsewhere. But when you leave the innovation you started, it often falls apart. Ben worried that his staff, especially those who appreciated his keen sense of organization and his work with the tech world, would feel abandoned when he left. Particularly those he had actively mentored. But then, Gerald was one of those mentees, and Gerald was leaving.

He shrugged. Coming and going was part of life in the public schools. His own possible departure was not something he should feel guilty or worried about. He needed to look out for himself and his family, first. Gerald had just reminded him of that truth.

***

Letter to the editor: Struggling for affordability

 I am a middle school teacher who is struggling to afford to live here. I'm in my second year teaching many of your kids. I'm a pretty good teacher for a beginner and according to research on teacher effectiveness, by the time I complete my third year, I'll have a very good handle on what I am doing. I love teaching your kids, and I want to stay here to become better and better at what I do. But there's a problem.

 This school district has to replace about one out of seven teachers every year who are driven out by the high cost of housing. I don't want to be one of those deserters who will be replaced by another beginner. But I'm struggling. If it weren't for my two roommates, all my take-home pay would go toward rent. Right now I can make it, but barely. Any rent increase will leave me with the options of getting a third roommate, moonlighting, or moving somewhere I can afford that's a two-hour commute away – options that will cut into the time and space I currently use to prepare the next day's lessons.

 We have to come up with a solution. Your children deserve it!

Letter to the editor: Don't dismantle good neighborhoods

 San Jose needs more affordable housing, don't get me wrong. But the solution is NOT to build it right in the middle of well-established residential neighborhoods of highly educated people. My family and I moved here specifically because we appreciate the quality of life our neighborhood affords us and our children.

 Now the school district is proposing building affordable rental units in different neighborhoods, one of which is mine. I'm sorry, but opening the floodgates to low-income workers will change this neighborhood, and not for the better. We bought our home here because it's a safe place to raise our children. We're told that the units will be reserved for teachers, but there's no guarantee of that, and even teachers don't have the education of most of my current neighbors. Teachers need housing, yes, but not at the expense of some of the city's highest taxpayers.

***

Ben pulled into the driveway of the family's modest two-story home, thinking about the two letters to the editor he skimmed earlier. He looked around. He and Lisa wouldn't have been able to afford this house on his teacher's salary. No, it took him becoming an administrator during a housing market slump, and the couple's combined income.

This was a good place to live, Ben thought as he scanned the tree-lined street, washed in late afternoon sunlight despite the dinnertime hour. As Ben stepped from the car, he smiled at the cluster of laughing children skateboarding down the sidewalk. They looked so joyful, so carefree, certainly more than he ever was at their age. He figured Evan would still be playing baseball in the park at the end of the street.

Evan had just turned thirteen. Tall and athletic, with auburn hair and a huge smile, Evan had none of his father's awkwardness and much of his mother's natural beauty. Sometimes it seemed like the world was arranged to benefit boys like Evan. For Evan's sake, Ben hoped it still was. Sometimes he imagined Evan as a successful business entrepreneur, maybe a political office-holder. State senator, governor, even.

Not so Jason, now ten. Jason reminded Ben of his own childhood self, although thankfully Jason had not inherited his father's overbite and speech impediment. But Jason was small for his age, and awkward around people he didn't know. Although his mind worked like a computer when it came to math, by nature he was dreamy and forgetful, a sweet-natured boy, but one who could easily be conned. Gullible. He would need his parents' guidance more than Evan would.

Ben wondered if Lisa would thrust on him another one of her ideas about where they should live. About six months earlier, she started coming up with one neighborhood after another where they should move. Why couldn't she be content right here, like he was? If this neighborhood wasn't good enough, maybe no neighborhood would do for her.

He found Lisa in the kitchen, putting a pan into the oven. "Hi, Sweetheart," he said as he tossed his bag on a chair. "What's for dinner? Where's Jason?"

"Chicken and potatoes with roast vegetables," she replied. "Jason's in his room doing homework. Or playing video games. Evan's doing bat practice as usual. I told him to be home by six."

Ben glanced at his watch. Evan still had five minutes, by Lisa's count, but Ben knew his son wouldn't think to look at the time. He was about to stroll down the street to retrieve Evan when Lisa stopped him.

"I found a house I want you to see," she said. She picked up a flier from the counter. His heart sank. He must have grimaced because she continued, "I know you aren't that interested, but let's think about what's best for the boys."

"I'll look at it if you want, but the boys seem perfectly happy right here," Ben said. This was becoming an old argument. Lisa worried about the security of the neighborhood, although she had not experienced anything to disrupt her sense of safety since long before the couple bought the house they now occupied. Almost twenty years earlier, when she was an undergraduate in San Diego, she and her roommates had been terrified by a break-in to their apartment. But that was before she met Ben, who she saw as her protector. And it was before they moved to San Jose.

Lisa was a worrier. Since an apartment complex went in a couple of blocks away, she worried that the neighborhood demographics were changing too much. She worried that the boys might take up with the wrong kinds of kids. When he tried to pin her down, out came a laundry list of concerns: Did any of the neighborhood kids deal drugs? Shoplift? Drink? Despite knowing all the families within a two-block radius, she still worried. It was ridiculous. The neighborhood kids were more or less like those Ben worked with every day, although more were white and from middle class families. In any case, they weren't budding criminals, they weren't losers, they were just kids. But to Lisa, a financial analyst for a car insurance company, they were liabilities.

"The boys are happy, but they're too young to evaluate influences on them. The families on this street are fine, but then you have those apartment buildings over there. You know what I'm talking about," she said.

No, I don't, Ben said to himself. Kids from the apartment buildings were also just kids. But to Lisa, they were suspicious, especially those who called out to each other in Spanish or Vietnamese.

"And you know that as the boys get bigger, we just need more space," she continued. "This house doesn't have much room for them to entertain their friends, and their stuff keeps getting scattered all over. I get tired of picking up after them."

She handed him the real estate flier. "Look at this. It has a full rec room, wouldn't that be great? And look at the size of the master bedroom and master bath." She flipped a page. "A three car garage, so when the boys start driving there will be space for their car as well as yours and mine. And this yard. We could even put in a pool if we want. And – now I know this is important to you – it's within the San Jose school district."

Ben glanced at the flier, then at Lisa. "Why would we do this?" he asked. "This is more than we can afford, and besides that, you know I've applied for the supe position at Cypress View. What if I get hired there?"

"Well, you could commute," she said, frowning. "It would only be about an hour's drive each way. A little more maybe when traffic is bad. And with a superintendent salary, we can certainly afford it."

Beneath the determined look on Lisa's face, as Ben knew, lay a well of vulnerability. He had left San Diego to take a job in San Jose. She had followed him to escape a fear that she was being hunted by a drug dealer connected with the break-in, a roommate's boyfriend who she could identify if asked to do so by the police. A weird story to Ben, but real to Lisa.

But that was so long ago. Since moving to San Jose, no one had come looking for her, no one had threatened her. Yet, she still worried. Ben had come to realize that anxiety was part of Lisa. Past experiences only triggered it, they did not cause it.

"And the middle school in that neighborhood is better," she added.

"We'll look at it this weekend, okay?" he said. "But Lisa, you have to understand that I won't saddle myself with a house above our means or a long commute. And I can't just move into an all-white enclave, if that's what this is, and maintain any integrity as a leader in urban education."

Lisa kissed his nose lightly. "All I want you to do is look. Who knows, this place might excite you as much as it does me."

It won't. Ben said to himself. *I'll look at it, but I already know it won't.*

***

Most Fridays, Ben looked forward to the weekend. The best thing about weekends was hanging out with the boys. While Evan accepted his parents' company only when he lacked other options, Jason hadn't yet reached that age when parents are an embarrassment.

But the worst thing about weekends was Lisa's pressure to attend to something that, for her, took on crisis proportions. Then she was relentless. Case in point: Viewing this house her mind was set on. Ben not only wasn't interested – the thought of it churned his stomach.

So he figured he would take his time getting home. As usual when the last bell rang, he made himself visible during the kids' explosive exodus from the building. After the last stragglers headed down the steps, he returned to his office to finish a couple of reports before leaving. He was just signing off on one of them when his cell phone rang. Mitchell. He picked it up.

"How's life?" he asked while tidying the papers strewn across one side of his desk.

Ben had been expecting this call. Earlier in the week, he had asked Mitchell what he knew about the superintendent job competition. He knew he shouldn't ask for insider knowledge and felt slightly guilty about it, but heck, he figured, everyone does that these days. If Mitch wanted to see Ben get the job, he might help out.

Mitchell was easy to manipulate. Not skilled at accomplishing things himself, he had always latched onto capable others. Ben had learned that about Mitch when they were children. Mitch rode other people's coattails. That was how he got ahead. That was probably how he got his current job. Ben knew Mitch didn't tell him about the opening out of the goodness of his heart. No, Ben suspected he did so in hopes of gaining a better salary and more influence within the school district if Ben were to be hired.

Knowing this about Mitch, Ben simply requested that he alert him to anything that might help him win the job.

"Things are getting interesting," Mitchell replied. "Do you know a principal over near Stockton named Roxane Bedford? Ever meet her?"

"The name doesn't ring a bell," he said. "Should I know her? Is she someone I'm going up against?"

"Damn straight. She's your main competitor. I managed to get a copy of the short list. You and she are at the top."

"I don't want to know how you got that list," Ben said. He knew he should feel guilty for probing into confidential information like this, but didn't most people who got ahead do such things?

"Well, Google her if you're at your computer," Mitchell said.

A few seconds later, Ben had opened Roxane Bedford's official Taylor High School principal's page. "She seems kind of young," he remarked.

"And kind of Black," Mitchell said.

Ben thought so, too. He thought back to his first application for a high school principalship. At the time, only two of San Jose's seven high school principals were not white, a situation the local NAACP and LULAC were concerned about. When Ben lost the job to a Filipino American administrator, he felt stung. In his heart, he believed his qualifications exceeded his competitor's, but his whiteness seemed to work against him. Then the district's math curriculum coordinator left unexpectedly, so Ben took that position for a year while he began his doctorate. By the following year, when the position at Richford opened up and he secured it, three principals were of color. He figured three out of seven must be the magic number in San Jose. He wondered what it was in Cypress View.

Mitchell continued, "So I did some nosing around this afternoon to get an idea of who this woman is. If you just look at her resume, she seems pretty good, although she's only been doing admin work for six years, which is pretty thin for an incoming supe, even in a tiny little district like Cypress View. She'd be better as deputy. Anyway, I think what the search committee likes about her is that she's Black and has a lot of energy for getting things done. Compared to some of the stodgy old folks in the pool, she looks interesting on that point."

"Uh huh."

"But here's the thing. This is mostly a minority district, and it has a terrible track record educating minority kids. Only about 20% of the kids are white. The rest – Latino mainly, plus a Black population, a small but growing Filipino population …"

"Mitchell, I already know that," Ben interrupted, "I studied up on the district before I wrote my application letter."

"Right, you did. Well, from what I understand, you and this Ms. Bedford have the strongest track records of bringing up minority student test scores, as classroom teachers and as school administrators. And that's the number one thing the school board is honing in on."

He did indeed have that kind of track record. It was his record as a math teacher that had brought him to the attention of San Jose's deputy superintendent several years ago, the first person to encourage Ben to earn his administrative credential. It was his record that had bolted him into the district's math curriculum position, then on into his current position.

"So this Ms. Bedford looks good on paper, with the exception of her thin administrative experience. And she'd be the first Black superintendent in a district that serves mainly minority kids. If anyone in the pool can beat you, she's it.

"Okay, well, thanks for the heads up. Assuming I get called for an interview, knowing who I'm up against will help me prepare," Ben said.

"I'm not done. Cypress View is one of those districts with a history of white parents agitating to secede and create their own school district. Hear what I'm saying?"

Ben was familiar with the issue, although he didn't know it affected Cypress View. In numerous communities around the country, as schools were desegregated, white parents petitioned to withdraw and create their own school district. About seventy-five new districts had been created this way since 2000, and many more were in the works. Ben knew that school boards generally tried to keep the district together, which sometimes involved taking steps to appease white parents.

"Okay, so what does this have to do with the job?" Ben asked.

"I did some digging around, and found out some things about Ms. Bedford that would add fuel to the fire, so to speak. Things about her personal history that white parents in this district would find mightily disturbing. I don't want to get into this over the phone. Can you meet me for a quick beer? I want to show you what I found and get your take on what we should do with it."

What might things about her personal history have to do with her work as a school administrator? Ben checked his watch. Lisa wouldn't necessarily expect him for another hour or two, and he was in no rush to get home.

"Can you give me a clue what you're talking about? I've got something on my desk I'm trying to finish up before the weekend," he said.

"It's about her daughter, her dad, and something from her past. Something she wouldn't want to have splashed all over the news, something the white parents here would jump on," Mitchell replied.

"And you're thinking of doing just that?" Ben asked.

"No, not necessarily. I'd like to strategize with you how to use this material if we need to. Let's say she does a dynamite interview. Shouldn't the search committee know the full Ms. Bedford and not just what she chooses to reveal?"

Ben felt as though he had suddenly been dropped into a crime drama where a blackmail scheme was being cooked up. He didn't like the sound of Mitchell's proposal. But then again, he didn't know exactly what Mitch was referring to.

"Let's get a beer and at least let me see what you have," Ben acquiesced. "But I'm not in favor of doing something dishonest or underhanded. So if that's what you have in mind ..."

"Nothing of the sort," Mitchell said.

They agreed on a time and place.

Traffic on a Friday afternoon could be horrendous. He decided to take Interstate 880 for just a few miles, then exit onto side streets where he could avoid the worst of it. As he drove, a jazz station playing in the background, he worried about finding another science teacher as strong as Gerald. Since Gerald had joined the faculty, it seemed as though the quality of the whole science department had been elevated. Gerald was not only a strong teacher in the classroom, but he was also a damn good team player. He could have lorded his successes in the classroom over less capable teachers, but he didn't. Instead, he listened to them, supported them, and if asked, helped them.

Traffic on the exit ramp was slow, but Ben anticipated losing some of it once he started heading northwest. The SUV in front of him had slowed to a crawl.

Suddenly a loud boom startled him. It was followed by a series of cracking noises. The exit ramp jerked, then dropped. The car behind slammed into the rear of Ben's car. As he pitched forward into the airbag, Ben pictured Evan playing ball down the street with his friends and Jason playing a computer game while waiting for his dad to get home. What would the boys do if he never made it? Would Lisa mourn, or simply activate her plans for the new house she dreamed of? Everything went black.

CHAPTER 3

ASPIRATION

Since January, Roxane had been second-guessing the wisdom of her decision to apply to become Cypress View's next superintendent. Despite Esteban's encouragement, she wasn't sure she could even get the job because she didn't have enough experience. And did she really want it? This would be a career leap that hadn't been on her radar.

But meetings like the one she just led on safety procedures suggested she might be good at it. This was despite Terry's scowl when she sided with the counselors against initiating lock down drills in the wake of the mass shooting in Parkland, Florida. She figured Terry was probably a Trumpite with a MAGA hat in his closet, just waiting for her to brandish her #BlackLivesMatter T-shirt. She had one, of course. She also had a Kaepernick T-shirt, but she didn't wear them to school.

Roxane shook her head as she hurried down the hall. Three school shootings already in March, not counting those in universities, and the month wasn't even over yet. Why did so many mass shooters target schools? Perhaps because school was where they learned they were not valued? Why were a majority of mass shooters white males? Black and brown youth might be stereotyped as violent, but white youth were most likely to charge into a school building, armed for killing.

She was proud of the students. During the meeting, and with the leadership team's blessing, about half of them took to the sidewalk in the second annual March for our Lives protest against gun violence. It lasted precisely seventeen minutes, one for each life lost in Parkland, Florida, the previous month. She was convinced that young people needed to learn to advocate for what they believed in, and she championed them when they did so responsibly.

Esteban enticed her by stressing how much she could accomplish as a superintendent. But did she really see the Cypress

View job as an opportunity to make a larger difference than she could as a school principal, or simply as an escape from Taylor's mean-spirited people? On the other hand, her mother was right: there would always be people who couldn't deal with the leadership of a Black woman, especially one who advocated for students of color. She drew heart from Stockton's recent election of a young Black mayor. She found it ironic that while many white people had come to accept Black leadership, a vocal segment worried about being crushed by a wave of brown people and in the process, losing something they felt entitled to. How much did that fear underlie mass shootings by white perpetrators?

Just yesterday, she was following up on several Black student complaints about Hank Garrett, the veteran health teacher who students said repeatedly belittled them. Hank had glared at her when she tried to point out that his students would treat him with respect if he reciprocated.

"I don't teach Black literature, Ms. Bedford, I teach health," he declared as though that mattered. "Stay in your own lane." Her own lane? That could – and probably did – have multiple meanings. If people like him would just focus on what the students needed rather than on themselves, there wouldn't be so much petty friction.

The school security meeting having run overtime, she was now late to a classroom observation of Chandra Dhupam, a first-year teacher. Some principals designated their second in command to this task, but Roxane enjoyed being in the classroom and supporting novices as they struggled with many of the same things she had, years earlier.

She recalled her own rocky trajectory learning to become the teacher her adolescent self had wanted but didn't have. Growing up, Roxane had had a few Black teachers who seemed to get her at a personal level, but their work in the classroom left her intellectually asleep. It had been mainly her parents' support rather than her teachers that got her through school. Her parents had believed in her like they believed in the Oakland Raiders. One couldn't ask for better fans. But not having attended college themselves, they couldn't coach her on college preparation. She had to piece together what she needed as best she could.

In her first Black Studies course at San Francisco State University, Roxane finally had a teacher who knew how to cultivate her intellect along with her Black identity. That teacher – Professor Wilkins – became the role model she wanted to emulate. So, three years later as a student teacher, Roxane imagined herself as a younger version of Professor Wilkins, ready to grab her middle school Language Arts students by their rhetorical hands and lead them into literary analysis, where they would blossom under her tutelage.

But they didn't. Her cooperating teacher, a white woman named Madeline Hall, loved chatting with students about their favorite music and TV shows. But her casual, laid-back attitude toward academics grated on Roxane. For her first lesson, Roxane intended to walk students through an analysis of one of Gwendolyn Brooks' poems after providing some background on the poet. But not five minutes into the lesson, students began squirming, whispering and surreptitiously tossing things at each other. Roxane quickly ditched the background presentation and told students to read the poem, first silently then out loud. They complied, but only a handful seemed to take the poem – and her – seriously.

Later, Madeline cautioned Roxane against expecting "these kids" to act like honors students. The kids in this school, with their low reading levels, scant experience with serious poetry, and impulsive thought processes needed something simpler. And Roxane needed to lighten up. Inwardly, Roxane chafed, but her poetry lesson had clearly flopped.

A month later, when she took over Madeline's classes for two weeks, she tried her best to combine Madeline's approach with what she wanted hers to be. She was stricter than Madeline, and demanded more; by then her relationships with the kids helped. Things went better. But she still couldn't bring forth the analytical thinking and word play she knew the kids were capable of.

When she overheard some of them picking apart a TV show with all the literary dexterity of a critic, she asked why they didn't apply that same level of thinking in the classroom.

"We just talkin' about TV, Ms. Bedford," one boy replied. "TV ain't like poems or books. It's just TV."

"Yes," Roxane replied, "but you're digging into that show thoughtfully. You're making arguments about why you did or didn't like it. About the characters, the plot ..."

The kids looked at each other as though Roxane had sprouted a second head.

"Have you ever watched *Degrassi*, Ms. Bedford? Like, a whole episode?" asked another boy.

"Well, I've seen some of it," she replied.

"This season?" he continued. "They messing with the story in a way that don't work."

Roxane listened to the kids go back and forth about the pros and cons of a new character and a twist to the storyline. Finally she said, "Now, this is what I want to see you do with a piece of literature."

"Aw, Ms. Bedford, you gotta understand, TV is for home. It's just for fun. It ain't serious, like school."

Roxane completed student teaching with an elaborated vision of the teacher she aspired to become, but without a well-furnished toolbox to get there. It seemed as though kids had learned to survive school by limiting their investment in it. As a kid herself, she had done exactly that. How could she encourage kids who had been beaten down by school to take risks, to trust the process, and most of all to trust her, a symbol of the school's power over them?

Now as principal, she found many beginning teachers facing much the same problem, and they didn't want mandated classroom observations to serve as evaluations of their teaching. Instead they wanted help.

Chandra's biology class was already underway when Roxane arrived, so she slid into a chair in the back of the room. Chandra had worked for ten years as a medical technologist before enrolling in a teacher preparation program designed for working adults who wanted to change careers. Without such a program, she wouldn't have been able to enter teaching.

Roxane enjoyed visiting Chandra's classroom. As a mother, Chandra was used to setting bounds and expectations, something beginners often struggled with. Her main challenge was learning to trust her extensive knowledge of biology. She depended too much on the textbook, using it like a script for a play.

During their debriefing afterwards, Chandra, already aware the textbook got in the way but unsure what to do, took Roxane's suggestions enthusiastically. As they wrapped up, she remarked, "You have a knack for making complicated problems seem solvable, Dr. Bedford. I know some people around here seem to enjoy making life difficult for you, but most of us think you're wonderful."

"Thank you, Chandra. I just think of it as doing my job," Roxane said, a bit flustered.

Chandra looked steadily at her. "You don't just do your job. You do more, you look for ways to make things better. And that inspires me. When I quit my job as a med tech, I was nervous about becoming a teacher. Would I actually like handling class after class of kids? Would I have a boss who respects what I'm capable of learning to do? I really worried about these things, just ask my husband. But the tone you set here, the belief you have in us as teachers, well, every day I'm convinced I made the right decision. The help you gave me just now is an example. I wanted you to know that."

"Your words mean a lot to me, Chandra. Thank you." Roxane felt herself blush. To her, helping teachers was an enjoyable part of her job, a part she valued.

Listening to the sounds emanating from open classroom doors as she walked back to her office, Roxane thought about how everything in a school is connected, sometimes smoothly and sometimes not.

"… and you can see how a couplet was used here …"

"The Internet isn't really a source, you need to ask yourself, who published …"

"What does xy stand for in this equation, Marcus, can you …?"

That stream formed a kind of braid, a tapestry that students experienced as a whole. The tapestry might make sense to them, but just as easily, it could confuse or even alienate them. The tiny bit of help she just gave Chandra would enable her to link the content she knew with the textbooks she was given and the students in front of her. Maybe, on a larger scale, Roxane could learn to weave together the multiple strands of schooling – the different subject areas, teachers' diverse points of view, students' even more diverse points of view, tests that didn't necessarily fit any of this. Might a leader make the thread of school life less random and more meaningful, particularly to students? Perhaps she could learn to translate what she knew into the work of a superintendent.

An important part of that tapestry, a part of her vision for education, connected schools with their communities. Schools in impoverished communities of color could become a resource for community empowerment. Too many educators saw school as a means of enabling young people to escape, but Roxane saw it as a means for learning to uplift the community. She had seen her own students learn to do just that, and she knew her teaching contributed. Esperanza, a former student, was just finishing law school, intending to return to Oakland to practice civil rights law. Daryl, another former student and community activist, was in dental school at the moment. He combined stints of volunteer dentistry for those who couldn't afford dental work otherwise, with advocacy for a dental clinic in an area that lacked one.

As a teacher, Roxane had prompted her students to mine their communities for wisdom, and to see themselves as intellectually capable people with valuable cultural identities. She once assigned students to collect old community newspapers from their elders. That's how the *Oakland Post*, northern California's largest weekly African American newspaper, had surfaced in her classroom. While some students knew about it, most didn't. How did the *Post* treat news topics compared with mainstream sources? What kinds of news sources did other local communities of color produce? What did these news sources indicate about wisdom within the community?

Teachers like Chandra were invested in the community. The Hanks and the Terrys – well, Roxane wasn't sure what their vision was, but it wasn't hers. But whether she stayed at Taylor or went elsewhere, she would always have to deal with such people.

She remembered, during her first year as an English teacher, noticing that the few teachers of color were assigned lower-level classes, while the more experienced white teachers gave themselves the upper level, Honors, and AP classes. Kids were sorted in roughly the same color scheme. When she mentioned this to her department chair, she was told that teaching assignments were based on seniority, not race; it was coincidental that most teachers of color were new.

That was the American system for you, in a nutshell. What white people knew and thought became the official basis of everything. As people of color gradually fought their way in, they were evaluated on their ability to function like white people. Those who didn't measure up were slotted into the lower levels of schooling and life. Persistently unrecognized was the fact that people of color knew a lot of things that white people didn't know. So when kids of color underachieved, it was them rather than the system that was blamed.

Convinced the system produced racist effects, Roxane began to consider how she could subvert it by redesigning her lower-level classes. Bonita Cruz, who worked with the immigrant students, gave her the key.

Roxane had mused, "Would I be crazy if I retooled 'Bonehead English,' as I've heard it called, into college prep? Not by changing who the kids are, but by changing what they get."

Bonita regarded her friend. "Interesting idea."

"Yeah. I mean, you get assigned to this class and automatically you aren't going to college. Even if you thought maybe later you wanted to, you aren't getting that kind of preparation," Roxane continued.

"What happened? Did one of your students ask about college?"

"No. I just see myself at their age. I wasn't in remedial classes, but I also wasn't treated as though I had much potential. I never had college prep, so I'm not even sure what it looks like. I wonder what goes on in Alan Greerson's Honors ninth. I could ask him for his syllabus, but I doubt he'd give me much. He seems to think that since I teach remedial classes, I must be remedial myself. Anytime I ask him something, he blows me off."

Bonita grinned. "I can get anything you want from him. He has some of my English learner kids, even a couple in Honors. Every time I ask what I can do to support them, he at least gives me a copy of the assignment. Let me have a couple days."

Greerson's Honors syllabus turned out to be exactly what Roxane sought. It showed her what college-bound students were being taught, and how. She also saw improvements she could make. Greerson assigned mainly white male authors, but how students learned to analyze and interpret literature didn't depend on which specific pieces they read. That, she could change.

"When you compare the reading list for his Honors class with the one I'm supposed to follow in my so-called bonehead class, it's like the difference between a dress from J.C. Penney and one designed by Dior. Or Laura Smalls," she remarked. Seeing Bonita's puzzled expression, Roxane clarified, "Smalls is a Black fashion designer."

Within two years, her students were achieving at considerably higher levels. One would think Roxane would earn praises. But no.

Her department chair, while grudgingly crediting Roxane for her students' learning, didn't like her bucking the system – especially the system of the English department. One day out of the blue, her chair confronted Roxane. "I want to talk to you about Wally." Blue-eyed, red-headed, second-year teacher Wally could have jumped right out of a *Where's Waldo* puzzle. Roxane had been Wally's mentor during his first year of teaching. "Wally seems to have developed your habit of reaching into the eleventh grade curriculum for his tenth grade lessons, and then when students get to eleventh, they're bored."

"And you'd like me to tell him to stop?" Roxane asked.

The chair bit her lip. "I will, but I believe he got that from you. What he also seems to have gotten from you is permission to make his English curriculum resemble sociology. This week I believe they've been analyzing racism in popular film, and as department chair, I'm the one that gets complaints."

"Complaints?"

"Yes. From Alan Greerson. A group of students in his English twelve who were in both your classes actually took it upon themselves to analyze the English twelve textbook for racism and sexism, then create a petition to stop using it. Of course Alan's ignoring their petition, but this kind of disruption is unnecessary."

Roxane had to chew the inside of her cheek to keep from laughing. The students had learned well. Good for them! But why was the chair of the English department so determined to defend tradition when students were obviously capable of more?

And that was the heart of what led Roxane to envision herself as a superintendent. Students were capable of more. And education could nurture tools to defend and revitalize communities like the one in which she had grown up. Leadership mattered.

After returning a couple of phone calls, replying to several emails, and organizing material for Monday meetings, Roxane was about to leave when the phone rang. "Dr. Bedford speaking," she answered distractedly.

"Roxane Bedford? This is Jayne Brown. I'm a news reporter with KTOP."

Jayne Brown? Good heavens! Roxane had seen her on TV countless times. "Yes. How can I help you?"

It turned out that Jayne wanted to do a feature on Roxane as an outstanding classroom teacher of urban youth who was now a school principal. One of her former students, Hugo Lattimer, who now worked at KTOP, brought Roxane to Jayne's attention. Would she be available for an interview and camera shoot next week? Could she put a few more former students in contact with Jayne?

Oh my, Roxane said to herself after accepting the invitation. What an honor, and what a responsibility to her community. But if she was already a target for resentment and jealousy, what new headaches would a news item featuring her bring about?

***

An hour later, Roxane burst through the front door. "Mama, you'll never guess what just happened."

Ada Dwyer Bedford was in the process of putting pork chops and rice in the oven. Judging from the open computer and the clutter on the kitchen table, Roxane surmised that she had been browsing the Internet in search of bits about the family's history. Her mother enjoyed collecting any information she could find about the family. She kept her findings in a large box of envelopes with labels such as "Family Reunion in 1994," "The Watson line" (her maternal grandfather's family), "Chattanooga Dwyers," and "Grandma's letters to Mother." Recently she had enrolled in an adult education course on memoir writing, with the intention of adding her family's story to Black history writ large. Roxane couldn't see her mother's writing ever contributing to the academic discipline of Black history, but figured it would make a good gift to Imani.

"What's this?" Roxane asked, startled, as she picked up a computer printout that displayed a familiar face.

"Shhh, Imani's upstairs doing homework. This is something I found about her father in the *San Francisco Chronicle*," Ada whispered.

Imani was the fruit of an intense love affair between Roxane and an Oakland community activist, Richard Sellers. They met at Oakland's Liberation Food Bank, where both volunteered, when Roxane was twenty. A high school drop out, Richard was a master organizer and orator. He was the main one who procured food donations from groceries and wholesalers, and he recruited most of the volunteers that bagged food and distributed it to families. Richard also led one of the grassroots campaigns opposing many of Mayor Jerry Brown's urban redevelopment initiatives.

Roxane was immediately drawn to him the first time she heard him speak before a group in a community center.

"We all know Oakland has major problems," Richard's voice had boomed. "The town's segregated, the town's broke, and our kids aren't getting the education they deserve. The mayor says he's fixing all that. Now, I know some of you voted for him. Others of you didn't. But let's look at the record."

Murmurs of "Amen" and "You right, man" rippled through the audience.

"'Elegant density.' Mayor Brown's term for urban renewal. Let's think about who he sees as elegant, and what happens to the folks that aren't elegant, at least in his view. Now, probably everyone in this room knows someone who got pushed out of downtown, and we've all seen the spanking new high rises built for rich white folks who are meant to replace people like us. Some of you might have believed the mayor was going to fix this town. And if you're a rich investor, I suppose he did. But if you're Black or brown, and you're poor, well, elections are coming up and we need someone who will represent us."

Richard was gorgeous, inspirational, and quickly attracted to Roxane. But he was wary of her pursuit of a bachelor's degree in English Literature. "Why you reading those white stories?" he asked one day after glancing inside her book bag where Oscar Wilde and Virginia Woolf had taken up temporary residence.

"Not all the authors I read are white," she pushed back. "I'm also minoring in Black Studies, and read plenty by Black authors. And besides, I love reading. I open a book and pretty soon I'm off in some other time and place, thinking about what I would do in someone else's life."

"What's wrong with your own life?" he asked.

"Nothing. But when I read literature, I can experience ten different lives. Twenty different lives. I can try on someone else's point of view, feel how they felt, crawl into how they think."

Richard looked at her askance. "You can do that watching TV, girl. Our community doesn't need someone who sits around dreamin' 'bout someone else's life. We need folks who can do things for us."

"With my degree, I could become a lawyer," Roxane replied. "Or a journalist. Or a teacher. Or maybe I could set up a food bank that works directly with the schools, making sure all the kids get good meals." She thought about her father's work serving meals to kids when he was a Black Panther, back before her parents married.

"And you need English Literature for that?" Richard asked, eyes twinkling. At the time, she had no idea what she planned to do with her degree, but she knew two things. She loved reading stories and analyzing how authors played with words, and she fully intended to complete her studies.

Roxane kept the relationship from her parents for as long as she could. Her mother, who had urged her to apply to San Francisco State, worried Richard would derail her. "You're the student in this family, Roxane," her mother would say. "Tanisha never liked school. She's doing alright working at Macy's, but that's the best she'll be doing. Michelle, well, she seems to like driving a bus although I can't see why. But you, you always persisted. You have Dwyer in you. You can be the one who moves this family ahead."

"Don't worry, Mama. Richard won't stop me. Besides, he's proud that I'm getting a good education. He teases me about it, but he's in my corner."

As things turned out, he was in her corner only until he learned she was pregnant. Then he disappeared, initially just from her life, then from Oakland and her radar screen entirely.

She decided to keep the baby despite her parents' distress. At Imani's birth, however, that distress evaporated; they were smitten. Roxane's mother, cooing over her tiny hands and button nose, began humming lullabies. Her father, may he rest in peace, strode proudly about, Imani curled into his arm, her head resting on his shoulder.

Roxane was never entirely sure what happened to Richard. When she asked around after Imani's birth, she heard he was sent to prison after shooting a convenience store owner in southern California. She tracked down a brief newspaper story about his arrest. She assumed there was a trial, but couldn't locate information about it. Was he guilty or not? All she could find were rumors, so she just stopped looking. She was so disappointed – no, angry, really – for his having abandoned her and their child, that she shoved him out of her mind.

She and her parents decided simply to tell Imani that her father had passed. Imani didn't need to grow up wondering why her father rejected her by disappearing rather than caring for her. She certainly didn't need to know she was fathered by a prisoner and possible murderer.

Across the top of the printout was the heading "No Parole for Sellers," and below it, a grainy photo of him, older looking and thinner but still striking.

"Mama?" Roxane repeated into her mother's silence.

"Baby, I wasn't even looking for Richard, but there was his face, tucked away near the back of yesterday's *Chronicle*. You read it, then toss it out. This isn't anything Imani needs to see."

It wasn't. But seeing his photo, Imani's face reflected in his, reminded Roxane of how it had felt to soar into the heavens with love, even if that love had long since burned out.

She skimmed the short article. It confirmed that he was convicted of murder and sent to prison. She learned he was in a federal prison in Minnesota. Apparently he had scrapped with one of the guards, which led to denial of his request for parole.

Bucking the guards was so like Richard. When she first met him, Roxane had been attracted to the confidence it took for him to stand up to the white establishment. She had admired how he channeled his anger at racism into advocacy for the Black community. But gradually she had recognized that he would challenge anything and everything associated with white supremacy, even when the only conceivable result would be harm to himself. For a time, she had hoped he would learn to control his anger better. But he didn't.

Maybe it was best for her and Imani that he left.

As Roxane closed her eyes, she felt her mother's arms embrace her. She also heard movement upstairs.

"Done with this?" her mother asked, taking the printout.

Roxane nodded. As her mother tore it up and threw it in the trash, Roxane quickly rearranged her face for her daughter. By the time Imani entered the kitchen, Roxane was able to smile as though she had not been transported momentarily back into Richard's world and into the dreams she used to have for the shape that world might take.

"I swear, girl, you grow inches the moment you're out of my sight," Roxane said as she hugged her daughter, now almost her own height. "Pretty soon you'll be borrowing my clothes."

Imani's eyebrows lifted as if to say, *get real.* "I don't want to look like I'm fifty, Mama."

"Fifty? You think I'm fifty?" Roxane tickled her daughter. Age was a running joke between them. Imani spoke of fifty as being near death. To Roxane, fifty was about fifteen years away, and to her mother, fifty was a memory.

"Dinner will be ready in about twenty minutes," Ada announced. "Roxane, you were about to tell me something when you came in, but we got sidelined."

"Oh my god," Roxane whooped, then told them about Jayne Brown's phone call.

"You're gonna be on TV?" Imani sounded incredulous. "Does that mean you're famous or something?"

"Not famous," Roxane replied. "It's 'or something.'"

"Well, does that mean …"

Roxane's phone rang, interrupting them. Esteban. She answered.

"Are you watching the news?" he said without preamble.

"No, I was about to turn it on. Say, next week …" she began.

He interrupted her. "This is important, Roxane. Do you know who Benjamin Harris is? A high school principal in San Jose?"

Puzzled, she replied. "I've heard the name. I don't know him. Why?"

"You and he are the top candidates for the supe position. I'm not supposed to know that. He was just in a car accident. Turn on the news."

Already in the living room, Roxane flipped on the evening news in time to hear a reporter say: " – two confirmed fatalities at this time, a number that is likely to rise since another car is buried under the concrete. A rescue team is working as quickly as possible to locate survivors. Three drivers of other cars and one pedestrian have been airlifted to local hospitals. One of the confirmed survivors is Dr. Benjamin Harris, principal of Richford High School in San Jose. His wife, who has been notified, is at the hospital awaiting news of his condition."

The reporter explained that the entrance and exit ramps for that section of the freeway were overdue for reconstruction, and a minor earthquake was all it took to dislodge crumbling supports. Images showed a crew attempting to raise teetering blocks of concrete from a crushed vehicle. Off to the side was an ambulance, ready and waiting. As the camera panned, a white sedan, pitched downward and front end badly buckled, came into view. "This is the car Dr. Harris was rescued from," the reporter said.

Roxane dropped her phone. That could be her. She knew the exit, she had driven past it a week earlier. Another high school principal – it could be her, she though irrationally. Her legs gave way and she sank into the couch.

CHAPTER 4

SURVIVAL

The last thing Ben remembered was the car's airbag smashing into him as everything pitched forward. The suffocating pressure on his chest was now gone. Waves of pain rushing in and through him were slightly muffled as though coming from the next room.

Dull light penetrated his eyelids. Easing them open, he saw a grid of perforated ceiling tiles. He let his eyelids slide shut again as he slowly stretched an arm.

"I think he's coming to," someone said.

Footsteps shuffled. Ben cracked his eyes open, this time seeing a woman clad in green looking into his face. She smiled.

"Do you know where you are?" she asked.

"Hospital?" he croaked through parched lips.

"Yes, Good Samaritan Hospital. Can you give me your full name?"

"Benjamin Daniel Harris."

"Date of birth?"

"October 16, 1979."

"Good. Do you know what year it is?"

How long have I been out? he wondered. "2018?" he asked uncertainly.

"Good. We think you've had a mild concussion, but you're doing fine with my questions. Let me just take a quick look at your eyes." Slowly she spread back the lids of one eye, then the other. "Pupils equal and reactive. Look at my hand. Now follow it," she commanded, moving one gloved hand slowly across his field of vision. He complied, then clamped his eyes shut.

"Dizzy," he said.

"Any nausea?" she asked.

"A little, yeah."

"You might have that for a few days. We'll monitor it," she told him. "Now tell me how much pain you're having, on a scale of one to ten. You should be having some pain, but we don't want you too uncomfortable."

What number to choose? Not 10, not 1, somewhere in between. "Maybe 5?" he ventured. "Could I have some water?"

She put a wet sponge in his mouth. Then she rustled around, adjusting something behind him. When she removed the wet sponge, Ben asked, "Nurse, can you tell me what happened?"

"You were in an accident and airlifted here earlier today. You have some broken bones, they've been set. A CT scan shows bruising of your spleen, but a laparoscopy found no internal bleeding. Your doctor will be in shortly to check on you, and he can give you more details. Right now it's about midnight. Your wife is here. Shall I send her in?"

"Yes," he breathed. He was alive and Lisa was here. After those two facts, nothing else mattered.

Over the next day, Ben drifted in and out of sleep. Sometimes when he opened his eyes, Lisa was holding his right hand. Sometimes she was gone but a nurse was there, checking vital signs. Sometimes he was alone. Dizziness came and went.

During lucid moments, he learned that a minor earthquake had triggered a collapse of the Cedar Street ramp from the freeway, and four people had died. Luckily, when the pavement broke, his car pitched downward into another car, but didn't sail off the ramp. The airbag saved him from careening head-first into the windshield. But given the lopsided pitch of the car, he slammed against the door, cracking the radius in his left arm and breaking his left fibula. His right foot, caught under the pedal, sustained a fracture. The impact had also bruised his spleen and cracked a couple of ribs. Quite a trauma to the body.

Ben tried to remember where he was going when the accident happened. It had something to do with Cypress View, a meeting perhaps. He thought he took the exit to avoid traffic, but couldn't quite retrieve the details.

Opening his eyes, he saw Lisa studying his face. As his eyelids fluttered, her pensive expression relaxed.

"You were mumbling," she said. "Should I call the nurse?"

"No, I was just trying to remember what happened. You're not at work. What time is it?"

She smiled. "It's Sunday morning. I'll have a couple days off this week." Ben thought she looked exhausted. She wasn't wearing make-up, and her hair, usually carefully styled, was twisted up into a rough topknot. He gripped her hand.

"And the boys?" he asked.

Their next-door neighbor was looking after them at the moment. Lisa would bring them as soon as he had more stamina. Her face showed deep concern, but he seemed to remember anger. Had they been quarreling? He couldn't remember. Something about a house.

But she was here, and that's what mattered.

He had met Lisa in San Diego. She was the cute little red-headed barista with a wild tangle of copper curls, who worked in the coffee shop down the street from the middle school where he student taught. All his life, pretty girls like her had ignored Ben unless they needed help with homework. But for some reason, she seemed pleased to see him every afternoon. He learned that her name was Lisa, she had grown up in Sacramento, and she was taking business courses in a community college.

Then she disappeared.

Ben didn't see her again for almost a year. One day, he ran into her (literally) as he was racing down the stairs of the university library. He dashed around a corner just as she was turning to walk up. They collided. This time, he made sure to get her phone number.

In the hospital room, as Lisa stroked Ben's hand, he marveled at the fact, not for the first time, that she loved him enough to marry him and raise children with him. She could have had anyone, but she chose him, someone most women didn't look twice at. He felt his face melt into a smile.

She released his hand. As his eyes fluttered open, he caught her frowning. The doctor said he would live and walk again. That should be good news. Was he damaged in other ways? Had they quarreled?

***

By the next afternoon, Ben felt more alert. He still hurt, especially when sitting and walking, one leg in a cast, the other foot in a boot. But the dizziness and nausea were receding, and his brain was chugging back into gear. He could participate in short conversations without nodding off every few minutes.

"Dad!" Jason burst into the room, making a beeline for his father.

"Careful now, be gentle." Lisa entered, followed by Evan.

"Whoa, this place looks like a Hallmark store," Evan said as he took in the array of cards and balloons Lisa had arranged in the cramped space.

"Can I write on your cast?" Jason pointed at Ben's left arm. "Mom, do you have a marking pen?"

"A nurse may have one," she said to Jason, then to Ben, "How are you feeling this afternoon?"

"Better."

"Hey, Dad, can we see where they cut you?" Jason interrupted.

"I'll go ask for a marker at the desk by the elevator," Evan volunteered.

"Evan, just sit," Lisa said. "Sorry, maybe I should have brought them one at a time."

"That's okay," Ben replied, glad to have them there. With his right hand, he drew back the blanket and shoved aside enough of the hospital gown to show three tiny laparoscopic incisions, now thin red hyphens. "What do you think?"

"I thought there would be stitches," said Evan dubiously.

"I thought they cut you open," said Jason. "How could they get anything through those little holes?"

"They pumped air in through one of them so they could see, and they inserted a camera through another one to check for internal bleeding," Ben explained. "There wasn't any. I passed."

"A camera?" Jason held his hands in the shape of a small Canon.

"Not that kind." Evan looked at his younger brother with exasperation. "We've seen them on CSI. They stick a tube through the hole and have the camera hooked up to a computer, so they can see what's going on inside."

"Eeew, gross. Did it hurt?" asked Jason.

"I was asleep when they did it." Ben flipped the blanket back over his abdomen as Lisa said, "Now that's enough. Just sit down, both of you."

"Aw, Mom," Evan grumbled as he picked up the remote and turned on the TV.

"Keep the volume down," Lisa said. She looked apologetically at Ben. "I'll come back in the morning when they're in school. Maybe I should have left them at home, but they couldn't wait to see you."

Ben smiled. "I'm glad you brought them, I've missed the pandemonium."

She looked down at her lap, then back up at him. "I thought when we leave here, we'll swing by that house you and I were doing to take a look at on Saturday. See what the boys think about it."

Ah, no, not this again. Lisa's dream house was the last thing Ben wanted to think about. "Lisa, I wish you wouldn't rush this thing," Ben said. "I know this is something you're all excited about, but I'm not. And lying here, it isn't something I want to worry about."

"No, of course not. But I thought you agreed …" she began.

He took a deep breath as he felt his blood pressure rise. Lisa could be so controlling at times, and her attempts to control him felt particularly aggravating. She had been an only child to doting, aging parents, who had given her whatever she wanted whether her desires were sound or not. Halloween candy for breakfast? Why not? Her own set of keys to the family car before she had her driver's license? Yes, of course! She got used to being at the center of others' attention. Ben could usually ignore her when she went into her control mode. But now, flat on his back in the hospital, he couldn't do much at all.

"I agreed to go look at it with you. And I will when I'm mobile again, but that won't be right away. Look, we haven't even agreed that moving's a good idea. And I'm still waiting to find out about Cypress View."

"Cypress View?" Lisa raised her eyebrows. "You're in the hospital, you can't even walk, and you're still aiming to be superintendent over there?"

"I haven't ruled it out. And I'm in no condition to make big decisions right now, one way or the other. Not about anything, not the job, not a different house. Let's just – Look, Lisa ..." Ben sank back down into the pillows, suddenly exhausted.

"I'm sorry, I didn't mean to upset you, I really didn't." She planted a kiss on his cheek. "Just get some rest. You're alive and that's what counts. C'mon, boys, time to go home. Evan, turn off the TV." Lis began shooing the boys toward the door. "See you in the morning?"

"Of course. I love you and I'm glad you all came."

Sometime later that afternoon, Mitchell came to visit while Ben was dozing.

"I won't stay long, I just wanted to check on you. I've felt rather guilty about the accident, since it was me you were on your way to see." Mitch approached the bed hesitantly.

"Sit," Ben motioned toward the chair next to the bed. "Why would you feel guilty? You didn't vote against the road repair measure, I assume."

As Mitchell folded his lanky frame into the chair, Ben took a close look at him. Mitchell wasn't aging gracefully. Like Ben, he was thirty-nine, but unlike Ben, what was left of his thinning blond hair was now turning white.

"Road repair's one tax I always support, along with school bonds, of course," Mitchell replied. Looking around the room, he remarked, "You have a lot of friends, I see. You could open a card shop."

"That's what my son said a while ago," Ben replied.

"Look, Ben, I really feel awful about what happened to you. You know how excited I was about the possibility of you taking the driver's seat in Cypress View, and now, well ..."

"Well, what? Someone with a few broken bones and a bruised spleen is ineligible?"

Mitchell blinked. "You're not withdrawing? How do you plan to interview when you're ..." He waved a hand vaguely at Ben's body.

"On crutches, I imagine," Ben said. "One thing you can do is spread news that you've seen me and I'm healing. I'll bounce back from this."

"Like surviving the Titanic," Mitchell joked.

"Like surviving the Sultana," Ben echoed softly.

"The what?"

Ben hadn't thought of the Sultana in years. Back in high school, while working on a family history project, he acquired from his uncle a folder of papers about some of the Harris ancestors. Daniel Harris, a Union soldier from east Tennessee during the Civil War, had requested that his gravestone read: *Survived the Sultana.* Wondering what it meant, Ben had done some investigating. He learned that in 1865, a Mississippi riverboat named *Sultana* was carrying Union prisoners of war north from a Southern prison camp, when it blew up. Of the roughly 400 men from east Tennessee, only 68 survived. Had Daniel not been among the survivors, Ben wouldn't be here.

"It was a riverboat that exploded. One of my ancestors managed to survive." As Ben talked about the Sultana, he realized that he had a chance to do some things over. The easiest, most immediate do-over would be to extricate himself from Mitchell's sleazy plan. After all, if he hadn't listened to Mitch a few days ago, he wouldn't be lying here in the hospital.

"Look, Mitch, I've been doing some thinking. I'd rather compete for this job fair and square. Whatever information you have about – what was her name?"

"Roxane Bedford."

"Right. Well, not to be superstitious or anything, but my accident might be the universe giving me another chance, and with it, I'd rather keep things above board."

"Suit yourself. You don't even want to hear what I learned?"

"No, I'd rather not."

Mitchell stroked his chin. "Okay, then. That stays quiet. I'll blab around that I visited you, and found you on the mend, feisty as a bull in the ring." Mitchell stood.

"Good. I'd appreciate that. And thanks for coming. If I get a call for an interview, I'll let you know."

As Mitchell left, Ben sank back into the pillows. Daniel had survived the Sultana, and now Ben survived the Cedar Street exit collapse. Why did some people get to live while others perished? Why had Daniel lived when two of his brothers-in-law died?

Ben drifted off after Mitchell left. He awoke, imagining himself flailing about in the frigid Mississippi River after the explosion. Something was tugging at his arm. He tried to pull free.

"Ben?" a voice said.

Opening his eyes, he saw a nurse holding a blood pressure cuff in one hand, his thrashing arm in the other. "I'd like to check your vitals." Her nametag read *Alma*.

"My vitals – ah, I was having a bad dream," he gasped. "I was drowning and couldn't tell if you were saving me or keeping me from freeing myself."

"Should I come back in a few minutes?" she asked. "You'll need to calm down before I can get a good reading."

"Alma, do you know anything about the people who didn't survive the accident I was in?" he asked.

"Yes, I've seen stories on the news," she replied. "Is that what you were dreaming about?"

"No, another catastrophe that killed hundreds. But I'd like to know about the people who died in the bridge collapse."

"Well, let me see." Alma thought a moment. "There was a young woman from New York visiting her grandmother who lives here. They were both in one of the cars that was crushed. I can't tell you their names. But it happened so quickly I don't think they were even aware of it."

"Any others?" he asked.

"Another was a man who owns a local Starbucks franchise. He was an immigrant from Pakistan who had moved here with his family some time ago. He was the only one in the car. I think he was on his way home."

A family had just lost their father, a wife was suddenly widowed. They had probably come to the U.S. for a better life, and now this.

"Any more?" he asked.

"Just one. A university student. She was very pretty. I think she was studying architecture or something like that. Some other people were injured, but of the survivors, your injuries were the most serious."

Ben nodded, then held out his arm for the blood pressure cuff.

After Alma left, he thought about the four people who had perished. Why had he lived while others died? Ben wasn't a religious person. Normally he didn't respond to tragedies by asking what God's plan might have been. Yet right now, it was difficult to think of life and death and his own survival as simply random. A young woman's visit with her grandmother cut short. Who did she and her grandmother leave behind? An immigrant businessman who had come for opportunity, most likely, whose life was suddenly crushed. What would happen to the family now? A university student with a whole future unfolding before her that now would remain unlived.

And here he was with manageable pain, bones that would heal, a family checking in on him, a job he would be able to return to. Did he owe the universe something? Did he owe anything to the people who had perished? Did he have a debt to repay?

He would never know. But at least he could live with integrity. He had just taken a step toward that goal when he dismissed Mitchell.

Integrity. Certainly his steadfast support for public education counted as that. He saw public education as battered, not as badly as his body, certainly not yet on life support, but still far from thriving. Once viewed as fundamental to a democratic society, many people were now giving up on it. Loss of faith in public education was evident in school funding cuts, abbreviated programs that certify teachers, the growing number of families deserting public schools for privates, and now a Secretary of Education who showed little interest in supporting public schools.

He worried about the burgeoning influence of wealthy venture capitalists. Mark Zuckerberg, for example, would have software practically replace teachers, while Ben would add it to a rich toolbox professionally-educated teachers had at their disposal. Now really, what did Zuckerberg know about teaching? Or take the Waltons. Recently he had attended a presentation by a Walton Family Foundation associate about their network of privately-run, publically funded charter schools. At first blush, the schools sounded exciting – innovative, resource-rich, and freed from constraints of regular public schools.

Including the constraint of responsibility to the local public, and there was the rub. He pictured the Walton family rather than an elected school board running schools. The teacher inside him gagged. While he had no great love for some school board members he had worked with, at least he understood them as locally-elected people, many of whom had kids or grandkids in the schools. However much he might disagree with individual board members, he respected the fact that local folks voted for them. As a school administrator, he believed in answering to parents and voters rather than hand-picked appointees or private foundations.

Maybe public education was the cause he had survived to champion. Maybe that's why he was still alive.

Why else would he have worked so hard to learn to appear comfortable before an audience? He had always been shy, too self-conscious. But then came an opportunity that changed things. One day as an undergraduate working in the university admissions office, the charismatic senior who usually showed prospective students and their families around had been out sick, so Ben's supervisor asked him to fill in. Initially he was terrified. But as he interacted with the families, he discovered an ability he hadn't known he had to charm people. By cultivating that ability, bit by bit Ben created an engaging public persona.

That persona served him well as a math teacher. Within a few years, he had learned how to raise math achievement in his school, partly by using his persona to engage the kids. Now as a principal, he was hitting many indicators of success, which he regularly commended his faculty on. Graduation rates at Richford were going up, test scores were up, truancy was down. These were forward steps that he knew how to make happen.

He was aware that test scores alone don't equate with becoming thoughtful, educated citizens and workers. But since thoughtfulness and citizenship couldn't readily be measured, he hadn't given these very much attention. Maybe he should. It struck him that the education leaders he most admired valued test scores as indicators of who schools were and were not reaching, but they also placed academic achievement alongside a more expansive view of how schools serve a democracy. It was this larger view he would need to figure out and learn to articulate. Becoming superintendent of a small but challenging school district might be just the opportunity he needed.

Mitchell's proposal had a rank smell to it. Ben would stay away from him. If he owed nothing else to the people who had perished, at least he could uphold integrity. Mitchell might have handed him an opportunity, but the man had no hold over him, and Ben intended to keep it that way.

CHAPTER 5

PLAYING CHESS

If anyone other than June Washington were running a meeting in San Jose this morning, Roxane would have sent a member of her leadership team, or skipped the meeting altogether. She disliked bay area traffic even more than she disliked being away from her building. But here she was, crawling down Interstate 880 like one more ant in the swarm.

Actually, she could afford to be away from Taylor High today. Things were slowing down in anticipation of Spring Break next week, which would provide a welcome lull before testing season. When they returned from break, the juniors would be hit with state mandated English and math tests. They would complain, but the test results didn't actually affect them. Instead, results would affect the school, since the school district, news media, and realtors used them to compare schools.

She sighed. A lot of time, effort and money poured into a system politicians thought would improve education, but teachers saw only as hoops with consequences that usually did schools like Taylor no favors.

Roxane looked forward to seeing June. Although the two had become friends while working on their administrative credentials, their subsequent employment in different school districts afforded them scarce opportunity to connect in person. Long discussions over lunch or dinner had dwindled to short texts now and then, and sometimes imaginary dialogues.

> Me: Terry's eyes shot daggers when I voiced support for the counselors' position. What would you have done?
>
> June: His eyes shot daggers? Girl, did any of them hit you?

Me: Only metaphorically.

June: Then I'd metaphorically kick his behind!

Pure therapy! So when June had called to invite her to tackle racial bias in special education across the state, Roxane accepted.

As a high school principal, Roxane tried to trim the pervasive overrepresentation of Black and Latino students in special education, but realized the problem was bigger than what happened in any one school. Kids from families in poverty, and especially Black and Latino families, simply had too little access to preschool, so by the time they hit kindergarten and first grade, the most vulnerable were already behind. Many were referred for special ed, which might not be a problem except that special ed routinely suffered teacher shortages, leaving many kids taught by inadequately prepared, emergency credentialed teachers. So, by the time she saw them in high school, most were too far behind to survive in regular academic classes.

But as she drove to San Jose, Roxane's thoughts didn't dwell on special education. Instead, she relived yesterday's filming with Jayne Brown. Jayne, along with a TV cameraman and Roxane's former student Hugo, had trailed her through the halls, filming her in short conversations with teachers and a couple of parents. Had she sounded lucid in those conversations? She hoped so. Then Jayne briefly interviewed her about how she brought her philosophy and success as a teacher into her work as a principal, and by the way, could Roxane supply her with data on how well her former English students performed on the state's tests?

The whole thing took less than an hour. Jayne wasn't sure when the segment would air, perhaps in a week or two. They filmed Hugo telling Roxane how she had influenced him; interviews with a couple more former students were scheduled.

When she arrived at the meeting shortly after 9:00, Roxane found participants settling in with coffee and scones. She greeted June with a warm hug, then turned toward the coffee urn, where people were buzzing about Ben Harris's accident.

Since the report she had seen on TV a few days earlier, she had learned he survived with non-life-threatening injuries. Now she overheard that Ben was badly banged up and wouldn't return to work right away, at least not until he could get around. Someone had visited him in Good Samaritan Hospital the previous day, finding him on the mend. No one mentioned the fact that he had applied for a job in Cypress View, and probably no one but Roxane knew about it. Comments dwelt mainly on the accident itself and Ben's injuries.

Did his colleagues like him? Respect him? Value him? What kind of person was he? Roxane couldn't tell. It was as though the accident caused a sensation, a discussion topic that invited opinions about the condition of roads and bridges, stories of friends and relatives who had survived car accidents or injury to the spleen, predictions about when a more severe earthquake might strike, and concerns about the dangers of driving in general. But Ben himself, the center of these tangential stories, never quite came into view.

As Roxane anticipated, June skillfully facilitated the meeting, which concluded with a catered lunch. June had to run off to another meeting, but as she was saying goodbye to Roxane, she had a small favor to ask.

"Ben Harris had planned to be at this meeting. I wouldn't have thought to invite him, but when he asked about it, I figured there would be no harm. As I'm sure you heard, he's laid up in the hospital. Since you'll be driving right past Good Samaritan on your way out of the city, would you mind running in with this packet for him?" June held up an envelope with his name on it, apparently stuffed with material from the meeting. "You can just leave it at the information desk. I'd do it myself, but I'm heading in the opposite direction."

"Sure," Roxane said after hesitating. *How awkward*, she thought. But obviously June didn't know she was competing against him for a job.

"Thank you. He wanted to be kept in the loop. Now this will be one less thing I'll need to think about."

They parted with hugs and the promise of getting together before summer, perhaps lunch followed by a trip to Nordstrom.

When Roxane arrived at the hospital a few minutes later, a crazy idea hit her. Why not drop in on Ben Harris herself? She had never met him, and was curious about the kind of person he was. She could certainly poke her head into his room to hand him June's envelope and extend her sympathies, then leave. A quick phone call to her office at Taylor confirmed that nothing of note had happened to hurry back for.

When she arrived at his room, she saw a man who appeared a bit older than she was, dressed in loose pants and a sweatshirt, brown hair hanging lankly. He was seated in a chair next to the bed, reading the newspaper. One leg was elevated on a stool, the other foot was in a boot, and a forearm rested on a pillow. She knocked on the doorframe.

He looked up, startled.

"Excuse me," she said. "We haven't met, but I just left a meeting I gather you'd have been at if you weren't here. I'm Roxane Bedford, I'm principal at –."

"Yes, I know who you are," he said. "Please come in. This is indeed a surprise." The smile that curved his lips didn't quite reach his eyes. Based on how quickly he reacted, she figured he knew she was a contender for the superintendent position. At the very least, he must have seen her photo.

"June Washington asked me to drop this off for you, since I'd be driving right past the hospital anyway." Roxane handed him the packet.

He set down the newspaper, took the packet and set it on the tray next to the bed. "Thank you, I appreciate you going out of your way."

"Oh, it was no bother,"Roxane said. "Since I'm here, I want to say how sorry I was to hear what happened to you. You're looking reasonably well, considering." As she got a closer look at him, she noticed a cast bulging out from under the pants of his elevated leg. Drawings of what appeared to be spiders and skulls peeked out from below his pants leg. Unconsciously, she bent for a closer look. He noticed her grin.

"My kids," he chuckled, his expression warming. "There are daggers on here somewhere. I'm being discharged this afternoon, whenever my doctor can give me the green light."

"That's good, I'm glad to hear it. I guess you were lucky. I saw the accident on the news. It looked ghastly," she said.

"I don't remember it very well," he said. "My mind was off somewhere else, and suddenly the ramp gave way and I was thrown forward. Next thing I knew, I was here. Between the impact from the car behind me and the airbag, I hit the door pretty hard." He raised his left splinted arm. "But it looks like I survived the Sultana."

The Sultana? Puzzled, she asked, "Wasn't that some boat explosion back in the 1800s?"

His eyebrows lifted, revealing hazel eyes. "You've heard of it. Most people haven't."

"My brain collects trivia," Roxane replied as she tried to work out where she had heard of it.

"The Sultana was a riverboat that exploded on the Mississippi while transporting Union soldiers from Southern prison camps back to the North toward the end of the Civil War. I had an ancestor from Tennessee who survived. Most passengers didn't." As he said this, he seemed to study her. Although neither mentioned the job, it hovered in the air between them. He added, "I'll survive this."

"I had an ancestor from Tennessee as well, although of course being Black, he wouldn't have been a Union soldier on the Sultana. He lived in Chattanooga. My mother's people are from there," Roxane said.

This should have felt like a friendly chat, but it didn't. They were both sizing each other up. When Roxane was a teenager, a neighbor had taught her to play chess. She never became very good and hadn't played for years. But this conversation was beginning to feel like a series of chess moves. Neither side was close yet to taking an opponent's piece, but it seemed as though he was setting up the board for a win.

"Well, I should probably head back," Roxane said. "I'm pleased to see for myself that you're on the mend." She took a deep breath. "You're probably aware that we both seem to have applied for the same job in Cypress View. A friend of mine who works there mentioned that you're an impressive candidate."

"I've heard you're an impressive candidate, too, Ms. Bedford. Despite how things look for me at the moment, I intend to push forward with my application."

"Good for you, I'm glad to hear it," she said. "If I were in your position, I'm not sure that I would."

"I don't let setbacks get in my way," he said. "In fact, that was how I wound up as math curriculum coordinator for San Jose before I got my present position. I turned a setback into an opportunity."

"I'm sure you'll do well," she said, unclear where the conversation was going.

"I intend to. And I believe my administrative experience outweighs yours. Perhaps you might consider the position of Assistant Superintendent of Curriculum if I'm hired?"

She was floored. *Why on earth did he say that?* Yes, his experience did outweigh hers, but could he be mocking her?

"A very unlikely scenario, Mr. Harris," she replied, pointedly ignoring his doctorate just as he had ignored hers. "I intend to be Cypress View's next superintendent."

With that, she turned and marched out.

***

As she drove back to Taylor, Roxane's anger exploded like a bonfire. How dare Ben assume he would be the victor, and then suggest she come to work for him, as though she belonged under someone else's authority rather than being in charge, herself.

Ben reminded her of another white man – John Firestone, her former principal at Sunnywood High School. She had needed his recommendation for her application to an administrative credential program, but when she approached him about it, his response was chilly.

"I wouldn't have thought this was a job you'd want, Roxane," he said after slowly removing his glasses and setting them down on his desk. "Administrators are expected to enforce policies, not buck them." She knew he was referring to her tendency to confront her department chair about policies she thought were unfair to students.

She struggled to push down her anger.

"Are you sure you'd be able to handle the demands of this program while you're working full time?" he continued, glancing at the form she had given him. "This is an intense program, two courses on weekends every semester."

"I'm aware of that. I can handle it," she replied curtly. "You won't notice even a hiccup in my work here. But I will need your recommendation and support."

Grudgingly, he prepared a tepid letter of recommendation and completed the required paperwork. But she didn't forget his hesitancy about whether she could become a school leader, and his assumption that the work involved might exceed her capability. What would he think if he knew she had completed her doctorate since then – and while working fulltime?

Yes, Ben Harris seemed a lot like Firestone – arrogant, sure of his own ideas and abilities, and unable to imagine someone like her in his place. Maybe that was the problem in a nutshell. Such people – such white people, really – were so afraid of being displaced by someone like her, that they refused to take her seriously. They shut out the possibility that she might be a serious contender, seeking instead someplace to put her, someplace to contain her.

Although many people had always thwarted Black people's attempts to advance, the Obamas' eight years in the White House had triggered a level of virulence Roxane had not anticipated. His election seemed to confirm many white peoples' fear of being shoved aside, as if it were impossible to imagine sharing power in a way that didn't leave anyone out.

The election had magnified a shift that was already in progress. During Obama's second term, Latinos surpassed whites as the largest racial-ethnic group in California; California was now one of five "majority-minority" states. The Census Bureau had projected that by 2045 nationally, white people would be in the minority. For someone who had always been in the minority, this didn't feel like an impending crisis, but for a lot of white people, it was downright terrifying.

How might Ben see his prospects on this shifting landscape? He probably wasn't part of the crowd that chanted, *build the wall, voter fraud, lock her up,* and *not a citizen.* But you never knew exactly where individual white people stood, at least not those you didn't know well.

Now she was stuck in traffic that she would have missed had she left the envelope for Ben at the information desk as June suggested, rather than going to his room for a chat. Annoyed, she picked up her phone and called Esteban to vent, hoping her call didn't go into voicemail.

"Roxane, I was just thinking about you," Esteban said. "Listen, I've been working on a proposal with one of the colleges here. We're putting together a program to prepare adults who live around here to become teachers. You know, people who can't just go back to school, or who wanted to teach but were turned off by all the young white ladies who populated education courses. You'll want to get involved in this …"

"Esteban. I love your enthusiasm, and I'd probably love this initiative. But be quiet for a minute and listen to me. I'm driving back to school from a meeting in San Jose. Yeah, I know, long drive. But anyway. While I was there, I stopped by the hospital and met Ben Harris."

"I thought you said you don't know him," Esteban responded.

"I don't, or rather, I didn't. Apparently he was supposed to be at the meeting, too. June asked me to drop off a packet for him at the hospital, but I made the mistake of deciding to hand it to him personally."

"And?"

"What a piece of work he is. He had the nerve to suggest that when he gets the job, because he's certain he will get it, that I come and be his assistant!" She slammed her brake to avoid hitting the stopped car in front of her.

Esteban burst out laughing.

"What?" she demanded as traffic began to crawl forward again.

"I shouldn't laugh," he said, "but the thought of you submissively taking orders from this Harris guy, it's so not you, I couldn't help myself. You'd be more like a mountain lion waiting to pounce." He laughed again.

"Well, I felt like he was trying to intimidate me," she replied. "But if anything, his reaction made me even more determined. I don't know if I can out-compete him, but I have to try. Of course at this point, it's all in the hands of the search committee until the interview stage, if I make it that far. So there's nothing I can do except complain."

"You'll get that far," he said. "The search committee's recommendation has gone to the full board. I know the board members, some better than others. A couple of them are bean-counters. They'll make their decision based on how many years of administrative experience each finalist has. A couple more are deeply interested in changing the status quo, and have been very supportive of my work with Raza Studies. They'll say, to hell with years of experience, where do we want to go with our kids and who's the best to take us there? Two more are new, and I'm not sure yet how they think. The board president, Darin Armstrong, I can't always predict where he'll land on an issue, but he's fair. He's less likely to take an ideological position than he is to make sure the group comes to a defensible decision that will serve the district. He also listens extremely well. Amazing guy, actually. But I don't anticipate anything happening until sometime after Spring Break."

"Okay, I can live with that. And thanks for listening," she said, feeling better.

"You'd do the same for me," he said. "Correction – you *have* done the same for me."

She chuckled, recalling the time years ago when she found herself giving him advice about how to handle a fifth grade teaching colleague who had developed a crush on him. He had been slow to take her advice – which was that he should just be honest with the young woman – but later reported that it worked. Not long after that, he married his college sweetheart. Roxane did not consider herself an authority on matters of the heart, so she was relieved when their confidences shifted from his love life back to how they would transform schools.

She pulled into Taylor's parking lot and entered the building just as the last students were straggling out. Outside the main office, three teachers were discussing plans for the coming weekend.

"Any Easter Sunday plans, Dr. Bedford?" Darlene, a young math teacher asked.

"Ah, that's when my church goes all out," she replied. "My mother and I love the pageantry, and my daughter puts up with it. I only regret that since becoming an administrator, I haven't had time for choir practice. Our choir raises the roof on Easter, and singing as part of the congregation isn't the same."

"I didn't know you sang," another teacher said. "When are you going to perform for us?"

She cocked her head. "If you all like Gospel, maybe I will. I hadn't thought about it. But Gospel is my first language."

"Seriously, what about the end of year concert? You should talk to Jack," Darlene said, referring to the choir director.

"Maybe I will, we'll see," Roxane chuckled as she headed into her office. Until that moment, she hadn't given any thought to bringing her singing self into the school. It seemed like a part of her that was extraneous to her role as principal, something she assumed her colleagues wouldn't find interesting. But ironically, she encouraged teachers to allow students to bring their home lives into the classroom, and how was this any different?

She decided to make a quick detour to her office by way of the choir room.

***

Roxane arrived home to the aroma of her mother's cooking. What she and Imani would eat if they weren't living with Mama, she didn't know.

As she threw her bag on her desk upstairs, she wondered about Ben. He must have been discharged and sent home by now. Why wasn't his wife at the hospital waiting to take him home? Maybe she wasn't in a hurry to get him back. Was Ben the kind of man who belittled women or bossed them around? If so, she wanted nothing to do with him.

She crossed the hall to Imani's closed door and knocked. Silence. She knocked again, this time hearing a mumbled response from within.

When she opened the door, she expected to see her daughter hunched over a textbook at her desk, but she was lying on her bed, wearing earbuds and staring at the ceiling. She glanced at her mother, then back up at the ceiling.

"Hi, Sweetie," Roxane said. When Imani didn't respond, Roxane gently pulled one earbud out. Imani turned to look at Roxane. "Is it time to eat?" she asked in a dull voice.

"Almost," Roxane replied. Imani's gaze returned to the ceiling.

Roxane sat on the edge of the bed. "What is it, Baby?"

"Nothing."

Roxane studied her daughter, wondering how she had grown so tall. It wasn't that many years ago that her legs, now long as fence posts, had been round and pudgy. She must have inherited her height from Richard, certainly not from Roxane's gene pool. Roxane took in Imani's sullen expression and flat eyes.

"You remind me of myself about three hours ago," she said.

Imani looked at her. "Why? What happened?"

"Someone said something to me that felt like an insult, and it reminded me of other times when I've been insulted. I can't always tell when an insult is intended, but that doesn't make it sting any less."

"You don't look hurt now," Imani observed.

"No. I called a friend and dumped out all my anger over the phone. By the time we finished talking, I felt better, and the anger had dissipated like smoke. The sting is still there, but it isn't sitting in my stomach any more."

Imani sighed. "Does that mean I should tell you what happened, and then I'll feel better?"

Roxane shrugged. "I don't know. That depends on what happened. Want to try?"

Imani pulled herself up into a sitting position. "It's Mr. Miller," she said, referring to her history teacher. "I'm going to get a bad grade in there and I don't care."

This wasn't the first time she had complained about him. Mr. Miller had been teaching middle school history for about twenty years. Roxane, who had met him a couple of times, had the impression he had grown bored with teaching eons ago. But he loved coaching boys' soccer, so that was where he put his energy. Imani, who played girls' soccer, told Roxane that he favored the boys in class. He called on them and chit chatted with them far more than he did with girls. Apparently once, she even snapped at him on her way out of class: "Us girls are here too, you know."

"What did Mr. Miller do today?" Roxane asked.

"He got mad at me and Sondra for talking," Imani said. "See, we're supposed to do this little research project during Spring Break about a famous person who did something important during the Industrial Revolution. He gave us a list of people we could choose from. Well, there weren't any Black women on the list. There were hardly any women at all, and that's what Sondra and I were talking about. He told us to be quiet. So we were, but after he stopped paying attention to us, I looked up Ida B. Wells on my phone 'cause I thought she lived around then, and she did. So I showed what I found to Sondra. We thought she'd be a great person to research, you know, her work to try to end lynching?"

Imani's story took Roxane right back into an African American history course she took as an undergraduate. The class had grappled with what it meant to industrialize an agrarian economy that was built on slave labor, after slavery officially ended and some former slaves were beginning to establish their own businesses. Lynching became a horrific tool many whites used to try to force a return to a pre-Civil War social and economic order. In fact, it had been the brutal murder of a Black friend that got Wells started. With a couple of business partners, her friend had established a grocery store that was competing successfully against a white grocery store. So he was lynched. Wells, horrified at what happened to him just for daring to create a successful business, wanted to bring the inhumanity of lynching to public attention. So, as a gifted journalist, she began documenting and writing about it.

"She'd be a great person to study," Roxane said.

"That's what I tried to tell Mr. Miller, but he said we needed to stick with people on his boring list. He said some of them would be on the test at the end of the quarter. I said I was going to write about her anyway. He said, fine, but it wouldn't count for his stupid project, and it probably wouldn't help me on the test." Imani's shoulders slumped.

"Do you have a description of the assignment?" Roxane asked. "Did he give you a handout or something?"

Imani reached onto the floor for her backpack, unzipped it, and rooted around. She pulled out a sheaf of papers. "It's in here somewhere," she said as she riffled through them.

"Here it is." She handed her mother a one-page description. As Roxane anticipated, the curriculum standards it addressed were listed at the top, although judging from the brevity of the description, Roxane figured Mr. Miller probably put them there because he was supposed to, not because he actually used them. She agreed with Imani that the list of historical figures was boring – or, at least, top-heavy with white men, mainly industrialists and political figures.

Roxane read out loud: "*History-social science 8.12, Students analyze the transformation of the American economy and the changing social and political conditions in the United States in response to the Industrial Revolution.* Ida B. Wells's work would certainly fit. Let's see what else we have. *Research Skill 1, Students frame questions that can be answered by historical study and research.* That seems reasonable."

"Yeah," Imani said, "we're supposed to ask a question about the person we research, then focus on answering that question."

"What might be your main question about Wells?" Roxane asked.

Imani thought for a minute. "How could she force herself to watch and write about lynchings? That seems too traumatic to imagine."

"Can I suggest a slight reframing?" Roxane asked. "If you ask how she got started writing about lynchings and what made her persist, you'll be able to tie her work to economic development after the Civil War. You'll be able to show Mr. Miller that your research does address the history standard for the project."

Imani nodded dubiously. "And what if he doesn't buy it?"

"Well, you have a couple of choices. Do what he wants, or write the paper you want, making clear how it addresses the expectations for the assignment, and hope he accepts it. There's always a possibility he might not. But if I were you, I'd stand up for myself." Imani's grades were usually good, so Roxane figured she could afford to take a chance in this case.

59

Imani threw her arms around Roxane's neck, murmuring, "Thank you, Mama."

As Roxane headed to the kitchen to see if she could help her mother, she thought about the way textbooks downplay the significance of lynching and the efforts of African Americans and white allies to end it. She wondered how anyone could understand Black people's reactions to shootings of unarmed young Black men today without connecting this contemporary form of violence to a long history of violence against Black people. You don't heal from trauma by ignoring its existence; you heal by dealing directly with its causes and its impact. If Imani made it clear how her version of the assignment met the curriculum standards, Roxane figured there was a reasonable chance that Mr. Miller would accept Imani's work.

There were a lot of Mr. Millers in the schools. They weren't inherently bad people, but she hated to see them stick with bad decisions that thwarted students' learning.

"Mama," Roxane asked as she set the table, "do you know anything about what our ancestors did right after Emancipation?"

Ada looked at her. "And where did that question come from? Your meeting in San Jose?"

"No. I just got to thinking. Imani's studying industrialization after the Civil War. We were talking about efforts many Southerners made to keep Black people in a position of servitude. I know we have a legend in our family about the Dwyer activist from Chattanooga, but other than that, I really don't know what our people were doing back then."

Her mother handed her a casserole. "Here, put this on the table. Watch, now, it's hot." She moved to the sink. "I haven't looked that far back. Records get a little sketchy."

"Well, do we know there actually was a Dwyer activist in Chattanooga? Do we know anything about him? His name, to begin with?"

"Aren't you the inquisitive one this evening. I may have his name somewhere. I'd have to look. Is this something Imani needs for school?" her mother asked.

"No. Imani's starting a research project on Ida B. Wells. Talking with her about it just got me to thinking, that's all. I'll go call her to dinner."

"Good for her. Wells was a fine woman. I'm glad to know the schools these days are teaching about her."

Roxane's eyes rolled as she turned toward the stairs to call Imani. It would be best not to correct her mother if she didn't want the dinner table conversation to be dominated by her mother's views about history textbooks.

CHAPTER 6

RESOLVE

New York Times, April 3, 2018

Trump Plans to Send National Guard to the Mexican Border

WASHINGTON – The White House said Tuesday night that President Trump planned to deploy the National Guard to the southern border to confront what it called a growing threat of illegal immigrants, drugs and crime from Central America after the president for the third consecutive day warned about the looming dangers of unchecked immigration. Mr. Trump's advisers said Monday that he was readying new legislation to block migrants and asylum seekers, including young unaccompanied children, from entering the United States, opening a new front in the immigration crackdown that he has pressed since taking office. But in remarks on Tuesday that caught some of his top advisers by surprise, he suggested the more drastic approach of sending in the military to do what immigration authorities could not.

Speaking to reporters during a news conference with the presidents of three Baltic nations, Mr. Trump described existing immigration laws as lax and ineffective, and called for militarizing the border with Mexico to prevent an influx of Central American migrants he said were ready to stream across it. "We have horrible, horrible and very unsafe laws in the United States," Mr. Trump said. "We are preparing for the military to secure our border between Mexico and the United States."

While the president couched his idea as an urgent response to an onslaught at the nation's southern border, the numbers do not point to a crisis. Last year, the number of illegal immigrants caught at the border was the lowest since 1971, said the United States Border Patrol. Still, Mr. Trump seized on what has become an annual seasonal uptick in Central American migrants making their way north to make his case.

***

"Dad, I can't find my bike."

Ben opened his eyes. He'd been dozing again in his recliner. Did Jason imagine he could just get up and help him find it? His energy should have returned by now, but it seemed to have forgotten where he lived.

"Where did you leave it last?" he asked. He was grateful the kids would be back in school soon.

"Out on the driveway, I think," Jason said. "I don't remember. I didn't use it yesterday."

"Maybe Evan knows where it is. Maybe you left it at a friend's house." Jason had a habit of forgetting where he put things. Ben squirmed to sit up. "Where's Evan?"

"He's playing soccer or something with Jimmy and them," Jason replied.

"Well, go look again. I can't help you," Ben replied. It was hard enough navigating between the recliner and the bathroom. He certainly couldn't hobble around looking for a bike.

Jason stomped out of the family room. Ben sighed. How could Jason be a good student in school, but so hopelessly absent-minded at home?

He opened the book about urban school reform that rested on his lap. All week he had been trying to read it to prep himself on the most recent thinking, should he land an interview in Cypress View. But he never got far before nodding off. He sighed. He couldn't imagine how he would return to work if he couldn't even concentrate on something as simple as reading for a half hour. Or even a few minutes. Maybe he should just forget about Cypress View. Returning to work might well be as much as he could handle. The naysayers who had assumed he was dropping out of the job search might be right; what had initially felt like determination was starting to feel unrealistic.

Roxane Bedford would rejoice. She wasn't even ready for that kind of higher-level leadership position, yet here they were, presumably tied neck and neck. How odd that the search committee would have landed on two people who had nothing in common except having been urban teachers and now high school principals. His brief meeting with her had convinced him that they were as different as oranges and orangutans. Chalk and cheese. Not only was their level of experience different, but he was a planner, while she seemed impulsive. Why else would she have shown up in his hospital room, uninvited? Maybe the school board was split into two factions, each valuing very different things. Now, that would make a challenging board to work with. Not an unusual one, though, just a difficult one.

Well, nothing he could do about it for the moment except concentrate on recovery. He looked down at the opened book. The paragraph at the top of the page looked familiar, so he moved on to the next one.

He awoke to find Lisa standing in front of him, the book having slid to the floor. It must have been noon. With the boys home this week and his limited mobility, she had been showing up to fix lunch every day.

"How are you?" she asked.

"Sleeping too much," he replied. "I guess my body needs it, but I'm not used to being a slug."

"Enjoy it while you can. By the way," she said as she turned toward the kitchen, "it seems Jason's bike was stolen last night."

Ben sat up, lowered the footrest, and cautiously slid his feet to the floor. "He hasn't found it yet?"

"We keep harping on the boys about locking up their bikes in the garage when they aren't using them, but you know how careless Jason can be."

Evan appeared in the doorway. "I bet it was those kids from the apartments across the highway, the ones with tats down their arms who don't speak English."

Ben regarded tall, sandy-haired, athletic Evan. He was the kind of boy who seemed to have everything. Since childhood, he had always been among the first chosen for a team. Girls gave him sidelong glances he hadn't noticed. Teachers probably let him get away with too much. Gradually Ben had recognized that Evan assumed a natural order of things with himself at the top. That was probably why he avoided associating with kids from homes below his family's income level, even kids who were good soccer players.

"Did you see any of them take it?" Ben asked.

"No, but I've seen them snooping around on our block," Evan replied. "With their old rusted out bikes, why wouldn't they steal a good one that's just sitting there, invitation written all over it?"

"Evan, you can't accuse people," Ben said, annoyed. "If you didn't see them take it, then you don't know one way or the other."

"C'mon, Dad, don't be a bleeding heart," Evan said. "Those kids steal stuff. Everyone knows that."

Bleeding heart? Everyone knows those kids steal? Where did he get that? "That's enough," Ben snapped. "Until I see evidence of someone stealing something, I will not accuse them and you won't either."

"Evan has a point," Lisa piped up from the kitchen. "This neighborhood is changing. It started with those new apartments that just opened the door for people to flood in. When the city okayed building them, I was concerned about what they would do to our property value."

Ben ran a hand over his face in exasperation. *The neighborhood is changing, so we have to move.* This was getting to be an old argument. To Ben, who was perfectly happy right where they were, the only crisis was Lisa's determination to move. "And? And what's happened to our property value? Lisa, it's gone up, not down."

Wiping her hands on a towel, she came into the family room. "It isn't going up as much as it should. I just don't feel as safe as I did when we first moved here. That's why I've been considering other neighborhoods. Rather than questioning Evan's judgment, I think you need to pay more attention to the facts."

"The fact is, no one saw anyone stealing Jason's bike. And nothing is wrong with this neighborhood," Ben argued back.

"You think my concerns are all in my head, don't you?" Lisa said as she returned to the kitchen. "I know you like to give people the benefit of the doubt, but I'm just more of a realist than you are. Now, come sit down, lunch is almost on the table."

"Jesus!" Ben exclaimed, "I work with Black, brown, and immigrant kids everyday. I'm as realistic as you are. Maybe more so. You're seeing problems where as far as I can see, there are none." Turning to Evan, he said, "Help me up, will you?"

Evan helped him hobble to the kitchen and settle into a chair at the table, where Jason was already diving into a bag of chips. Ben's arguments with Lisa about her desire to live in a more affluent and homogeneous neighborhood were hardly a secret. One would think she didn't value their warm relationships with neighbors such as Marg Wilson next door, who had looked after the boys immediately following Ben's accident. Or the Lee family down the street, whose kids were close in age to Evan and Jason. The fact that this was one of the more affluent neighborhoods in the city didn't address Lisa's incessant worry about personal safety. Her ideal, Ben supposed, would be an upscale gated community, and it didn't seem to matter how often he pointed out that they were perfectly safe where they were. Now the damn bike seemed to confirm her suspicions about rising crime rates.

Ben grimaced. Although Lisa hadn't voiced support for Trump's wall, she would probably vote for it if asked. She didn't refer to bike-stealers who didn't speak English, she referred more obliquely to the neighborhood changing, to renters, to property values plunging, to people flooding in. Ben had learned to tune much of it out, so hearing Evan's unvarnished version was jarring.

Why hadn't it occurred to him that the boys might absorb her worries and her attitudes toward strangers? Evan seemed so quick to jump on Asian immigrants, then accuse his own father of being a bleeding heart liberal just because he pointed out that people are innocent until proven guilty. But of course Lisa wasn't Evan's only influence. Over the past couple of years, it was as though distrust of immigrants permeated the water non-immigrants drank.

"Hell," Ben said to himself, "you go back a handful of generations and most of us descend from immigrants." He would need to figure out how to teach his sons a more generous view toward other people.

And yet – hadn't he viewed inner city kids in much the same way when he was their age? He didn't begin to change until he actually got to know kids whose lives were different from his. Over computers, in San Diego's Boys and Girls Club. Could he figure out something comparable for his own kids here?

"Do you want to take my bike to taekwondo this afternoon?" Evan was asking Jason. "I can take the bus to baseball practice. Or Mom can drop me off and I can take the bus home."

Jason shook his head. "I'm gonna look around the neighborhood one more time. If I can't find it, I'll take the bus. Hey, Dad, do you think you can come watch me at taekwondo tomorrow?"

"Sure thing, as long as Mom drives us both," Ben replied, relieved that the conversation had shifted. Hovering in the background, though, was Lisa's expectation that he view her dream house as soon as possible. She would probably conclude that if he was able to sit and watch taekwondo for an hour, he was able to tour a house.

If they were going to move – which was not something he wanted to do unless it was both affordable and necessary – at the very least they could wait until he knew whether they would be relocating to Cypress View or not. He hoped someone else was already making an offer.

***

By mid-morning on Monday, Ben's resilience was creeping back. He had been on the phone for an hour, and rather than feeling exhausted, he felt energized. He was relieved to find his two vice principals with things in hand. With any luck, he might be able to return to Richford part time as early as next week, pending clearance from his doctor. He would need to work out transportation, Uber perhaps, and he'd need to make sure a wheelchair was available. The possibility of going to Cypress View for an interview – well, that still felt overwhelming, but Ben cast the thought aside. It was enough that he had survived the crash and was on the mend.

As the call wound down, talk shifted to the recent Oklahoma teachers' strike and speculation as to whether California's teachers might follow suit.

Ben had just hung up when the doorbell rang. He hollered, "Just a minute" as he worked his way into a standing position, then grabbed the walker. Opening the door, he found Ann Mulholland, the mother of one of Jason's friends, standing next to Jason's bike.

"I found this behind our tool shed," she said. "I'm running errands, so rather than call to tell you about it – here it is."

"We've been looking all over – come on in," Ben said, opening the door wider. He had figured the bike would turn up, and was glad to see it.

"Another time. I remember Jason being at the house last week. The boys played video games, then I took them for ice cream. I assumed Jason had walked over, so I gave him a ride home. I think everyone forgot about the bike, your son included." She peered at Ben. "How are you doing since the accident?"

"Aside from mobility issues, things are moving in the right direction. I can't thank you enough for bringing this back."

"No problem," she said as she turned and walked back to her car.

Ben shut the door. The bike would be safe enough on the front porch until Jason could put it in the garage. He hoped after learning it had not been stolen, Evan would rethink his assumptions about the families down the street. And he hoped it would allay Lisa's fear that the family's personal security was under siege. He would have a talk with them when they got home.

He didn't feel like napping yet. Maybe he could track down more information about his ancestor Daniel Harris. What had been his experience when the Sultana exploded? When he survived, did he feel as though he had been given a second chance at life? If so, what did he do with it?

Two hours later, drawing on scant records about Daniel that he could find on the Internet, and voluminous records about the Civil War in general and the Sultana in particular, Ben had worked out a considerably more vivid image of his ancestor's experience than he had expected. He jotted down notes; it was only much later that his notes were turned into this story.

***

Confederate soldiers had clamped down on east Tennessee. Around Sweetwater, which was close to the Harris farm, they guarded the railroad, knocked on doors, and generally made their presence known. Actual fighting was far more pronounced to the north, where bands of Union loyalists periodically robbed, whipped, and even shot Confederates, who robbed and killed in return.

By late 1862, the Confederacy had stepped up efforts to conscript east Tennessee men into its army. One heard all too frequently of those who had either been hauled off in the night or fled to Kentucky to escape conscription. Daniel and three of his brothers-in-law avoided it by enlisting in the Union army, reporting for duty as members of the Third Cavalry in January of 1863. By September, Daniel was sergeant of the newly formed Company F, which, over the next year, scouted for rebel troops mainly in east Tennessee.

In September of the following year, while Company F was stationed near the Tennessee border with Alabama, in a surprise attack the Confederates captured them, then marched them and about 2000 additional Union soldiers to Cahaba Prison in Alabama. This was, in no uncertain terms, a hellhole. Built as a large storage shed for cotton and corn, it had not been intended to house human beings. When even more Union soldier prisoners arrived in December, the men found themselves packed in like cigars in a box. Only part of the shed was covered, so when it rained captives shared shelter by rotating, but during heavy rains the entire prison flooded. Food (mainly cornmeal) and water were scarce. The prisoners became as gaunt as broom handles.

After several months, the men learned of a prisoner exchange being negotiated between the Union and the Confederacy. The prospect of returning north energized them just enough to complete a thirty-mile march to the railroad, where they were transported like cattle to Camp Fisk near Vicksburg. There they languished for a month while Generals Grant and Lee hammered out the terms of the South's surrender.

Rumors circulated. Confederate bands had taken over the county where the Harris family lived, harassing families of Union loyalists and forcing some to flee their homes and farms. Was it true? President Lincoln was assassinated! Was this true? They weren't sure, since spreading rumors was a Confederate tactic to crush Unionists' spirits.

Finally they were taken to Vicksburg's wharf, where two steamboats were docked: the Sultana and the larger, newer-looking Pauline Carroll. The Sultana's two levels were already crowded and the Pauline Carroll appeared empty, so the soldiers were shocked when they were marched up the gangplank and packed onto the Sultana. The captain ignored their complaints.

The steamboat pushed off, heading north. Initially disoriented, Daniel began to look around, mentally taking roll of his company. While in prison, he had found keeping track of his men a strategy to maintain sanity. Here, he could make out only those who were right around him, jammed together as they were. As the boat churned up the Mississippi, a group began to sing "Yankee Doodle." Soon singing spread through the boat as the men temporarily forgot their hunger and discomfort. After a while, singing subsided, the few available blankets were passed around, and the men tried to lie down to sleep.

Daniel woke up as dawn broke. He and his brothers-in-law talked softly about their families as the sky lightened. In mid-morning, pieces of hard bread and uncooked salt pork were passed around, along with a bucket of water to drink. As the riverboat chugged northward, the men swapped stories, sang, and napped.

The next day, the boat pulled up to the wharf in Helena, Arkansas. As it was landing, a photographer who happened by gestured his desire to photograph the jam-packed steamboat, so the men rushed to the port side. The boat tipped dangerously. (Ben studied the photo, wondering which man might be Daniel.) After briefly unloading cargo, the Sultana continued to the Memphis wharf to unload more cargo, then across the river to load up on coal, then onward. The men did their best to ignore the light drizzle and get some sleep.

A thundering explosion startled Daniel awake, hurling him through the air and into the cold river. Shocked, he grabbed about as he tried to keep from sinking. His hand landed on a wooden plank; he gripped it. The drizzling sky rained fire, and flames shot up where the riverboat had been. Screaming men were jumping into the river, now littered with them, some alive and hanging onto what they could find, many flailing in the water and yelling for help, and others not moving at all. A couple of terrified horses thrashed nearby. Overwhelmed with fear, Daniel clung to the plank as tightly as he could.

Sometime later, Daniel heard a boat approach. A man yelled, then someone tossed a line in his direction. He grabbed it with hands numbed by the cold. As he was pulled toward the boat, someone grabbed his arm and hauled him up. Exhausted and deeply chilled, Daniel passed out.

When he opened his eyes, the sky was turning light and the drizzle had stopped. He was lying on the ground, covered with a dry blanket. Beside him were other survivors, also covered with blankets. Some groaned with pain, others were silent. Although Daniel's body ached all over and he had some cuts, he was otherwise uninjured.

"Here, soldier, take a drink." Someone passed him a canteen. He looked up into the face of a ruddy young man who was handing out water to the survivors. "You're one of the lucky ones," the man commented.

Daniel struggled to pull himself up into a sitting position, and drank in huge gulps. Then he looked around, trying to identify where he was.

"You're in Memphis," said the ruddy young man. "We pulled folks in from the river most of the night. We even found a few men hanging onto trees that were sticking up out of the water. Lot of dead bodies, too."

Sometime later, men with stretchers began hauling off the most badly hurt soldiers to a local hospital. Daniel saw several with ugly burns, a man with a crushed foot, and another with a badly broken arm. Meanwhile, survivors continued to be brought to the river shoreline, placed wherever possible. Local Memphis residents, horrified at what had happened, showed up with food and more blankets. Daniel tried in vain to locate his brothers-in-law.

Late in the afternoon, two men loaded him and some other mildly injured survivors onto a wagon, which took them to the Memphis Soldiers' Home. There they recuperated before being sent onward. Daniel was reunited with one of his brothers-in-law; the other two had perished.

Much later he learned the steamboat's boilers had exploded. They had not been repaired properly because the boat's owner, keen to earn money the government paid to transport prisoners north, rushed to claim as many prisoners as possible before anyone else could. Two thirds of the people on board the Sultana had died.

***

The process of making notes that traced Daniel's experience provoked a visceral reaction in Ben. Daniel had almost starved to death in the prison camp, then almost drowned after the explosion – how deeply traumatizing both experiences must have been! The horror welling up in Ben was not just for Daniel, however, but also for himself. Since the car accident, he had shoved fear for his life into a corner of his heart, concentrating on logistics of recovery rather than on the enormity of having almost died.

Now, for the first time since the accident, in the solitude of this Monday afternoon, Ben allowed himself to cry. He cried for Daniel, for himself, and for his family. They had suffered, too, after all. The boys had almost lost their dad, Lisa had almost lost her husband. Could that near loss have intensified Lisa's sense of insecurity? Could it have taught his sons that life was tenuous, even cheap?

Funny how kids so often dismissed the value of other people's lives. When he was small, Ben was the target of bullies who valued him only for the reaction they could get. The pain he had endured!

He remembered an incident from when he was about ten, walking home from school.

"Buck, buck buck." He heard, but couldn't actually see Curt hiding behind the bushes. Curt had latched onto Ben's overbite, calling him "Bucky," which morphed into a chicken-like cluck.

"Here comes chicken-legs." That was Matt. Ben had grown used to being teased for his broad forehead, overbite, lisp, and scrawny frame. He had learned to ignore the pain of ostracism, to shrug off the name-calling. But he couldn't shrug off the occasional beatings.

Curt, large for his age, sought targets he could dominate. He attracted accomplices who admired his tough behavior, mistaking it for maturity. Mitchell had been one of Curt's followers. Their favorite victims were African American kids bussed to Ballard from the inner city – especially the smaller kids. But small white kids like Ben were targets as well.

"Buck, buck buck." Curt waddled out from behind the bushes, flapping his arms like chicken wings. Then he pointed toward Ben's crotch. "Hey chicken legs, show us your rooster. If you've got one, that is. Show us, then we'll leave you alone." With loud guffaws, Matt and three other kids appeared behind Curt, including Mitchell, who lived just three streets over from Ben. Mitchell, apparently not completely on board with Curt, looked down at the sidewalk while Curt sauntered toward Ben. Ben felt himself turn crimson with embarrassment. If he could help it, they were not going to yank down his pants.

Curt's attention shifted to Ben's braces. "Lookie what we have here. Open up, railroad, show us your rubber bands."

Ben clamped his mouth shut.

"You ain't gonna show us nothing? Not even the rubber bands in your mouth? What color you got in there, anyway?" Curt brushed a fist lightly against Ben's jaw. "C'mon, weenie, show us what you got."

Anger welled up. Ben felt his heartbeat pulsate behind his eyes. Despite knowing what would come next, he grabbed Curt's wrist. "Knock it off, airhead."

Curt laughed as he jerked his arm out of Ben's grasp. "Airhead, is it? Hey, guys, are we gonna take crap from this piece of shit?" Before anyone could react, Curt landed his fist hard on Ben's nose. Ben tried to hit back, but Curt had grabbed him by the neck and held him at arm's length, laughing. Matt, meanwhile, yanked Ben's backpack off, threw it to the ground, and kicked Ben behind one knee. His leg buckled, and he would have fallen but for Curt's grasp on his neck. He felt blood ooze from his nose and his windpipe close under Curt's thumb. Obviously to Curt and Matt, Ben's life had no particular value.

Abruptly, Curt withdrew his hand. "That's just a warning. Next time …" Curt flipped around. "C'mon, guys, this piece of dog shit ain't worth our time."

When Ben got home, he washed off the blood, but it continued to trickle from his nose, now the size of a golf ball. He didn't want his dad or younger brother Steve to know what happened because he felt like he should be able to handle bullying on his own. They would be disappointed in him if they thought he let the bullies get away with harming him. He put ice on his nose, then joined his brother on the floor of their shared bedroom for video games.

By the time their parents arrived home, Ben's nose, no longer bleeding, was swollen and purple, despite the ice. Their mother fretted that it might be broken. Their father, quickly surmising what had happened, hauled Ben off to a jujitsu studio down the block, enrolling him on the spot.

Within a couple of months, Ben acquired enough martial arts skill to defend himself against unskilled fighters like Curt. The first time he leveraged his weight to throw Curt flat on his back, he began to earn respect. Mitchell had been the first to switch sides.

Ben learned to swallow pain, but he also learned to survive. And here he was now, a survivor with a second chance at life. What had Daniel done with his second chance? As nearly as Ben could determine from the census data, he had gone home to his wife, established a small farm, and raised several children. That alone would have been a solid, satisfying, decent sort of life.

Ben couldn't allow his injuries to keep him from moving forward. Daniel had been tough; so was Ben. He had learned to take on the Curts of the world. He couldn't allow his banged-up body to derail him from his destiny. Injuries notwithstanding, he was well equipped to lead and to tackle the difficult and seemingly intractable challenges of urban education in California. He had the tools he needed under his belt, so to speak. He just needed practice on a district-wide scale.

Like Cypress View. In truth, deep down inside he waffled about relocating to Cypress View. It lacked the intensity of San Jose. It was on the edge of Silicon Valley, not in the center. It seemed quiet, almost backwater. Cypress View reminded him of Ballard where he had grown up, but with a more ethnically diverse population.

Should he be looking for similar positions in other communities, even in other states? This opportunity had been dropped into his lap, but it was the kind of opportunity he would have sought down the road anyway. Was he limiting himself by concentrating on Cypress View?

But then again, Cypress View provided the stepping-stone he needed. He wanted to stay in close proximity to Silicon Valley, and even though Cypress View was some distance, it was still located within a workable radius. Ben would be able to leverage the contacts he already had. Yes, Cypress View should be his for the taking.

He would throw all he had into obtaining the job. The only things standing in his way were two women.

Lisa, he thought he could handle. She was nursing her disappointment about yesterday's sale of the house she had her eye on, but another one would come along. Ben's task was to make sure it was in Cypress View. No reason they couldn't relocate there. They would be no farther away from Lisa's family in Sacramento than they were already, and they wouldn't be so far from friends that they could never connect with them again.

Ben wondered when Lisa would start sleeping in their bedroom again rather than in the guest room. When he came home from the hospital, he discovered that she had moved in there. She said she wanted to give him some healing space, but that didn't seem necessary. He would have to talk with her about it.

Roxane was a different matter, mainly because he didn't know her. Could it be that she was his chief competitor because she was Black, and this majority-minority district needed a person of color in the pool?

Ben realized he had dozed off when his cell phone rang. Not recognizing the number, he almost didn't answer it. He was immediately glad he did.

"Dr. Harris?" a female voice asked. "This is Stacey Ocampo with Cypress View Unified School District." After exchanging pleasantries she told him the purpose of the call. "The Board would like to invite you to interview for the superintendent position, that is, if you're still interested. We know you've been in a very serious car accident, and have been hopeful for your strong recovery."

Ben was immediately awake. "Thank you. Yes, I'm very interested."

"That's good to know," Stacey said. "We were hoping to schedule your interview during the week of April 17."

"Yes, of course, let me get my calendar," Ben replied as he grabbed his laptop from the floor next to the recliner. He and Stacey quickly agreed on a date.

He hoped he would be able to navigate using crutches by then. He didn't want to do the interview from a wheelchair. He had to appear strong, in charge.

Lisa had not yet taken the prospect of moving to Cypress View very seriously. Now she would have to. Maybe he could get her to take the day off to drive him there and explore the neighborhood.

He had just opened a Cypress View real estate webpage when he heard the door open from the garage into the house.

"Ben?" Lisa's voice rang out. "Ben, I'm so excited, I've found an even better house for us."

CHAPTER 7

AGITATORS

Imani usually didn't call her mother at work. So, as Roxane was meeting with Margaret Jeffries, the director of Taylor High School's school-community resource room, a FaceTime call surprised her. Had something happened?

"It's my daughter, I need to take this," Roxane said. "I hope it isn't an emergency of some kind."

"Not a problem, go ahead. We were wrapping up anyway," Margaret said as she gathered the documents scattered across the table. "I'll be at my desk if you need anything."

"What is it, Baby?" Roxane asked Imani. She was unable to read her daughter's expression.

"I had to tell you that you were right," Imani announced. "I gave Mr. Miller my paper about Ida B. Wells. I was so nervous! I told him it fit the standards on the sheet explaining the assignment, just like you said."

"And?" Had he failed Imani on this assignment? Or had he listened to what she had to say about it?

"Well, at first he just frowned, and said he told me to stick to someone on his list. But then I explained that the person I really wanted to learn more about was Ida B. Wells, and she fit the assignment. I said I thought the standards were important, I wasn't trying to mess with his assignment, I just wanted it to be meaningful to me. He glanced at the paper, and then he actually started reading it. Like, I was standing right there and he was reading the first page. Then he said it looked interesting, he'd read the whole thing later, and he'd think about whether to add Wells to his list." Eyes now sparkling and a big grin on her face, Imani looked positively triumphant.

Roxane broke out in full-throated a laugh, proud of her daughter's gumption and relieved that it had gone so well. Miller could just as easily have scrawled a zero at the top of the paper. But he didn't. She had shown her daughter how to craft an effective argument, and it had worked.

"What about Sondra?" Roxane asked. "Did she do her paper on Wells, too?"

"No. She didn't want to chance getting a zero, so she picked Elizabeth Arden. She said the research on the cosmetics industry was kind of interesting, but she'd have preferred Wells."

"Or Madam C. J. Walker," Roxane mused.

"Who?"

Roxane chuckled. "She created hair products for Black women back in the early nineteen hundreds. Both she and Arden started out around the same time. Madam C. J. Walker became the first Black woman millionaire in the U.S., if I remember correctly."

"I'm writing that down," Imani said, as the video display suddenly flipped to the ceiling. "Okay, I'm back. I know you've gotta get back to work, Mama, but can I just ask a quick question?"

"Certainly," said Roxane as she headed for the door, anticipating the bell, which would bring a rush of students into the hall.

"Are we in something like the end of another Reconstruction, or what comes after it? I mean, it seems like when Obama was president, that was kind of like a modern-day Reconstruction period because some doors opened up for Black people. Now, it's like the opposite, you know, doors slamming shut, like in voting rights and stuff. I was just wondering what you thought."

Roxane almost walked into the doorframe. It was such a perceptive question, and where had it come from? Had Imani heard it from someone? Or had reading about Wells enabled her to connect some dots between past and present? As Roxane thought about her answer, the bell rang. Classroom doors flew open and students rushed into the halls.

"You've gotta go, huh?" Imani asked.

"Yes, but you've just asked the most profound question I've heard all day. I'm not sure I'd say we just went through a third Reconstruction, but the question is still intriguing. Let's talk about it when I get home."

During passing time, as she interacted automatically with students and teachers, she pondered Imani's question. The Civil Rights movement was often referred to as the nation's second Reconstruction due to the grassroots organizing that produced profound legal, institutional, and cultural shifts. Roxane doubted Imani had encountered that idea in school, however. Her history texts seemed pretty traditional. The thought that Obama's eight years in office might represent a third Reconstruction, and that the current backlash under Trump might be compared with the slashing of rights in the first half of the twentieth century – well, that struck Roxane as a bold hypothesis Imani's teachers were probably wholly unprepared to engage with.

After passing time, she circled back to the school-community resource room, where she found Margaret finishing a call.

"I have to tell you what my daughter just asked me," Roxane said when Margaret hung up. As she described Mr. Miller's assignment, Imani's response, Mr. Miller's reaction to Imani's paper, and then Imani's question about a third Reconstruction period, Margaret's eyes widened until Roxane thought they would fall out.

"What are you feeding that girl?" she asked. "My kids never asked questions like that."

"What concerns me," Roxane said, "is that I don't think most of her teachers are equipped to help her dig into the issue. I can help her, but from what I've seen of her teachers, even those who wouldn't find the question threatening don't seem to have the background to know where to go with it."

"I'm not sure how many teachers here at Taylor would know where to go with it, either," Margaret observed. "I wouldn't, but then I'm not a teacher. Howard, he would know." Howard, a white history teacher, was well-steeped in African American and Mexican America history. "Who else? Maybe those two new ladies in English?"

Roxane considered this. Central to questions like Imani's, questions that ran through the histories and experiences of people of color, was racism, and that was one issue few teachers were willing to touch. Most white teachers didn't know where to start and found the whole thing threatening. Teachers of color were generally much more accustomed to discussing racism, but didn't necessarily know how to frame it in the context of classroom instruction. In a racially mixed classroom, for instance, how do you draw everyone in, including the white students? How do you provide background information about racism that students lack without inadvertently suggesting that students' views are not welcome?

Then there was the matter of being willing to take students' questions seriously. Getting through five class periods of content per day usually overwhelmed attention to any individual student's question. But Roxane also knew that teachers varied widely in their willingness to elicit questions from students. And grappling with questions like the one Imani raised required background knowledge about racism during different historical periods.

"There are maybe a handful," she said. "Maybe. This issue is causing me do some self-reflection. When I was an English teacher, questions like Imani's were the stuff of my curriculum. Now here I am in a leadership role, and I'm wondering if I've been so caught up in the everyday logistics of running a school that I haven't given as much attention as I could to creating an intellectual environment that nurtures students of color."

Margaret's eyebrows jumped in surprise. "Dr. Bedford, how can you say that? Parents I see every day love your work here."

"But things aren't where they could be," Roxane replied. "Yes, over the past three years, we've got more kids graduating and more going on to college. And we've got a few more teachers who understand where the kids here are coming from and how to make academics relevant to them." She sighed. "I guess it's just slow progress and maybe that's how things are."

Roxane returned to her office. The last bell of the day almost drowned out the ring of her cell phone. She didn't recognize the number and hesitated answering as she moved toward the school's main entrance. But the call could be important, so she took it.

"Dr. Bedford?" a female voice said. "This is Stacey Ocampo with Cypress View Unified School District." On behalf of the school board, Stacy wanted to schedule her for an interview.

Despite what Esteban had said, and despite having announced to Ben her intention to beat him, Roxane hadn't seriously thought she had a chance at this job. This phone call told her she did, and with it, she realized suddenly how torn she would be to leave Taylor. It was one thing to say she was ready to go to Cypress View in order to out-compete Ben Harris, or to escape those on her staff who wanted to see her gone. But it was another thing entirely to leave what she was building here at Taylor.

"Dr. Bedford, are you there?" Stacey Ocampo asked.

"Yes, I'm here. You caught me by surprise," she said.

***

Roxane anticipated hashing out the pros and cons of the Cypress View job with her mother as soon as she got home. The job interview was scheduled, but deep down, she felt conflicted, and her mother was usually her best sounding board. And, of course, Imani would expect the dinner conversation to revolve around her question about whether the nation was experiencing backlash against a third Reconstruction, a discussion Roxane looked forward to. That is, unless Imani's mind had moved on to something else.

But things did not go as Roxane anticipated. As usual, she greeted her mother in the kitchen before heading upstairs to see Imani. She was surprised to see papers spread over the kitchen table.

"What's all this?" she asked her mother.

"I've been looking into that Dwyer activist in Chattanooga," Ada replied. "His name was Spencer. Spencer Dwyer." Her mother's triumphant expression made Roxane think of the cat that swallowed the canary. "Look at this." She picked up a page of newsprint titled *The Voice*, dated 1905. "This was in an envelope stashed away in a box of my mother's things. I got to thinking about that box, wondering if it held anything about our family. Sure enough, I found this envelope."

She dumped out the remaining contents of the envelope, which consisted of three photos – albumen prints, she learned later. "This photo, this is Porter Edward Dwyer, my great granddaddy. He was Spencer Dwyer's son."

Ada beamed while Roxane studied the handsome young man in the photo for family resemblance. "Maybe you have his eyes, do you think?" Roxane asked as she held up the photo. Setting it down, she studied another photo, which showed three small children, dressed as though for church. Flipping it over, she saw it hadn't been labeled. "Who are these kids?" she asked.

"Beats me. Maybe Porter Dwyer's kids, I don't know. If so, then that little boy is my granddaddy, but I can't tell. I've never seen a picture of him as a child."

Roxane studied the photo for clues. Finding none she could interpret, she picked up the third photo, a head shot of a clean-shaven older man who appeared to be white, in front of an American flag. "Who's this?"

"I don't know," her mother replied. "There's no label. Could be a relative, but he doesn't look like any of us."

Roxane shrugged as she set the photo down and picked up the page of newsprint again. It appeared to be one of those independent Black newspapers that most Black communities had at one time or another. The typeset page featured eight short articles. The one that caught her attention was entitled: "Spencer Dwyer urges Boycott." The three-sentence article had to do with Jim Crow streetcars and Spencer's advocacy that Blacks set up their own transportation system.

"I looked into what this story might have been about. I can't wait to take this stuff to my memoir class tomorrow morning. I've got to get busy writing it up somehow. I feel like I've spent all day in early 1900 Chattanooga doing research," Ada said. "Did you know Bessie Smith grew up there? I listened to her records all during my younger years, and never knew she could have been rubbing elbows with my own ancestors. Anyway, let me tell you the story as I've been able to piece it together."

"Alright. Want me to get Imani? This sounds worth all of us hearing."

When Ada had her audience seated at the kitchen table, freshly-baked cookies in front of them to tide them over until dinner, she launched into her reconstruction of Spencer Dwyer's activism in Chattanooga in 1905. Telling the story to Roxane and Imani helped her figure out how to begin writing it up.

***

Spencer hunched his shoulders against the icy wind whooshing off the river as he walked home. At least the rain had stopped and this week's worksite – a hotel saloon – wasn't far from home. He smiled. This would be a fine saloon indeed, in no small part because of his labor. Sturdy shelves along the back wall framed by dark wood molding set off the long, smooth oak bar he had polished until it shone.

Spencer had become one of Chattanooga's most skilled Black carpenters. Rufus Hadley, his employer – also Black – liked to joke that he feared the loss of his best carpenter one of these days if Spencer were to decide to start his own business. That was unlikely, however. Mr. Hadley had a knack for finding building projects that needed carpenters, and Spencer didn't want to have to run all over town like Mr. Hadley did. With a good employer, Spencer could put his own work aside at the end of the day.

Plus, he liked Mr. Hadley. The man was fair, he always treated his employees well. Not like Mr. Hiram Thomas, whom Spencer had worked for earlier. That man treated his Black employees almost like they were still slaves. Although he paid them, he barked orders at them, picked at their work as though they didn't know what they were doing, and occasionally smacked them across the shoulders. The minute Hadley considered starting his own carpentry business, Spencer volunteered to be his first employee.

Spencer chuckled as he recalled how Robert Martin reacted. Martin ran a newspaper, The Voice, he used to cajole Black folks to do business with each other rather than continuing to help white people get rich. When Martin learned about Spencer's shift from Thomas to Hadley, he opined: "More colored men should follow the example of Mr. Spencer Dwyer, who stopped selling his carpentry skills to the highest white bidder and now works for the best colored carpentry business in town." Martin had a point. Chattanooga's pool of Black businesses was expanding, due partly to Black people supporting each other. Why, the city even had its own Black-owned bank. When it came to uplifting the community, white people wouldn't be much help, a point Martin drove home every week.

Spencer had left his parents' home outside Madisonville, Tennessee fourteen years earlier. He had joined a large, diverse wave of migrants – whites from the North and the South, Southern Black freedmen, and immigrants from all over Europe. Given the South's post-war economic turmoil, migrants sought opportunity in Chattanooga's rapidly expanding industries. When he arrived, Spencer found thriving establishments like machine shops, boiler shops, plow makers, and pipe manufacturers. Freedmen and their offspring, like Spencer, could find work here, and some, like Rufus Hadley, had even started their own businesses.

Spencer found a room in a boarding house tucked into a Black neighborhood in the heart of the city. He became a day laborer, and within a few months, was able to use skills he had learned working on his parents' farm to hire himself out as a carpenter. He found he had a good eye for design and wood quality, and a steady hand with tools. Mr. Thomas snapped him up as soon as he saw what Spencer could do. Spencer might have stayed with Mr. Thomas if the man knew how to treat his Black employees.

Spencer also began attending a neighborhood Baptist church. The church back home had been tiny by comparison, since relatively few Black folks lived near Madisonville. This church, although small by Chattanooga standards, was bustling by Spencer's standards. People crowded into the small sanctuary every Sunday and on evenings for community suppers, committee meetings, and Bible study that doubled as literacy development. Lively Sunday services involved congregants in singing, testifying, praising the Almighty, and generally releasing the week's pent-up emotions.

It wasn't long before Spencer's eye was drawn to a young lady in the choir who sang with the clearest voice he had ever heard. Jesus must have been smiling down every time she opened her mouth. And she was pretty, too, small of stature with dark sparkling eyes, her round face framed by a high-neck lace collar, and her full hair neatly pulled back into a knot at the nape of her neck. Spencer missed most of what the preacher had to say as he studied every detail of her.

He learned her name was Carrie Jackson. Born and bred right here in Chattanooga, she wasn't yet married, although he was told that half the church's single men were trying to woo her.

Having no idea how to woo a lady, Spencer simply approached her at a community supper one evening. "Ma'am, I wasn't sure whether I believed in angels 'til I saw you and heard you sing. My name is Spencer Dwyer. I'm new here, but I'd be honored if you would go walking with me one evening this week."

To his surprise, she consented.

Within three weeks, Carrie had determined that he was honorable (he had barely touched her yet), had a sense of humor, and was gainfully employed. So when he fumbled through a marriage proposal, she accepted.

Now, thirteen years later, Spencer knew that marrying Carrie was the best thing he had done. As he opened the door to their small shotgun house, he was greeted with a delectable smell of fried chicken, collard greens, and cornpone. He heard running footsteps. Lulu, age ten, threw her arms around him as Porter, age four, crashed into Lulu. Sharon, the eldest at twelve, stuck her head out from the kitchen where she was helping her mother prepare supper. Spencer kissed the top of Lulu's head as he hoisted Porter like a sack of flour.

Because it was too blustery outdoors to use the clothesline, damp sheets draped the furniture. Carrie worked as a laundress for a hotel on the next street over. Monday was washday, and Friday – tomorrow – was when she ironed the linens, folded them, and returned them to the hotel.

After supper, the family walked to church. On arrival, the children scurried off to their friends.

Spencer had no sooner hung his coat on peg than his friend Ellis waved a copy of The Voice. "You seen this?"

"Seen what?" Spencer asked.

Ellis grinned. "Mr. Dwyer, you're becoming a true agitator. Milton, Cora, come listen to this." The three of them, along with Spencer, served on a committee that helped needy church families.

Ellis made a show of squinting as he located the passage, then reading: "Mr. Spencer Dwyer, one of the colored men trying to board the streetcar, told the crowd that colored people should not pay a white company that won't allow colored riders on any but the shabbiest of Jim Crow streetcars. Instead, we should set up our own transportation system. We will give that idea some thought."

"Huh," Cora grunted. "I almos' fell off the streetcar las' week." Pushing fifty, Cora's shape reminded Spencer of a potato, and while he could picture her falling off and rolling down the sidewalk, she was actually a valued elder who merited the best seat rather than having to fight for space on the running board.

"I couldn't get on it," Spencer said. "Damn thing was bustin' at the seams with people. Then along came a white streetcar, not crowded at all. Wasn't that long ago we coulda hopped on if there was standing room. Now it's 'Wait for the colored car!'"

"I like your idea," said Ellis, stroking his chin.

"What idea? You mean setting up our own transportation system? I was just talkin'. But I suppose we could round up folks when they ain't working and have them drive a cart or something."

It actually wasn't a bad idea. Spencer had spent his whole life learning to put up with indignities because of his color. Some things he just flat out ignored, like the European immigrants who seemed to be arriving in droves. Rumor had it that whites thought the city would look nicer, less run down, if its Black population were replaced with these white immigrants. As though Black folks actually liked living in rundown shacks. It didn't seem to occur to them that squalor resulted directly from Blacks' lack of access to resources and sanitation.

But there were many other things he couldn't ignore without endangering himself and the family. He learned not to look at white women at all, to always address white men with more respect than most of them deserved, and to stay away from certain neighborhoods after dark. The recent prohibition against riding on white streetcars was part of a broad net of restrictions that seemed to be tightening. Sometimes his self-control snapped.

That day last week at the streetcar stop was one of those times. If a white person had heard him, he could have gotten a beating or worse. Instead, Robert Martin heard him, and in Spencer's complaint, a rallying cry for action.

"It's an idea worth thinking about," Cora said. "These families we're helping, like Miz Richards whose husband passed and now she *can't feed her children with what she earns, if she was paid like a white person, she'd be able to manage."*

"What does that have to do with the streetcar?" Ellis asked.

"It has to do with segregation," Cora said firmly. "Everything's segregated now. Some of it's silly, like drinking fountains. But some of it comes down to life and death. White folks say havin' separate facilities guarantees us things we wouldn't get otherwise, but that's just a sugar-coated way of saying they don't want us around except to do their work. Lot of folks don't talk about jobs as being segregated, but they are. White folks give us the jobs they don't want, then pay us as little as they can get away with."

"So you saying we should boycott those jobs? And then do what?" Spencer asked, thinking about Carrie's work as a laundress for a white hotel owner.

Ellis looked at him. "That's what you did, when you said goodbye to Mr. Thomas."

"The hard truth," Cora continued, "it that our parents' and our grandparents' hard work made their masters rich, but most of our people didn't get a penny to pass on to the next generation. We all know that, even if white folks won't admit it. Most of us didn't even get that forty acres and a mule I heard talk about back when I was a young'un. Now those masters' chillens are grown, and some of them are rich because their parents kept all the money we made for them, right in their own family. And they the ones that have a hard time opening their pocketbooks to pay us decently."

A laundress like Carrie, Cora was on intimate terms with hard work that paid little. She, Carrie, and a couple other laundresses did their wash together. Early every Monday morning they brought laundry from their employers to a shared iron pot hung over a fire where they boiled, hand scrubbed, rinsed, blued, and wrung the laundry out to hang for drying. Only a handful of laundresses in Chattanooga were white; the vast majority were Black.

"If our men was white," she added, "they'd get paid enough that the women could spend their days looking after their own house and children instead of taking care of white folks."

"Now, you know they's some white folks as poor as us," said Ellis.

"And some Black folks a lot richer than us," Milton added.

"But she's right," Spencer said. "You remember back about ten years ago, when the Democrats took over the government of this city, and the first thing they did was fire all the Black city employees? Milton, you weren't here yet."

"Nah, but I heard about it. And now you can't even run for city council unless you put up thousands of dollars."

Spencer said, "Each of us could make a list as long as your arm of things that are wrong about segregation. But we'd be wasting our time swapping stories about what we already know when we need to figure out what to do."

"Ellis, read the last line of that paragraph from The Voice again," Cora said.

Puzzled, Ellis opened the paper and read: "We will give that idea some thought."

Cora nodded. "So Mr. Martin's thinking about Spencer's idea of boycotting the white streetcars and creating our own transportation system. Let's go have a talk with him. He uses that paper to tell us what we should be doing anyway. Maybe he'll want to use it to organize folks." She looked at Spencer, who was grinning. "You wanted to say something?"

"It's just – you know, when I walked in here this evening, I looked forward to us getting something important done, like helping out Miz Richards. But I had no idea we'd be thinking about a streetcar boycott, and I wouldn't have brought it up myself, except for what Mr. Martin wrote. At the time, I was just spouting off, you understand. I didn't have a plan and all, but here we are now, with a plan." He gave his shoulders a shrug.

"It was a good idea, man," Ellis said excitedly.

"It's as good as any idea I can think of," Spencer said. "I just can't take credit for it, that's what I'm saying. Milton, you been sitting there all quiet, what do you think?"

Milton said, "I'm all in. I been waiting for something like this."

***

"Wow," Imani breathed almost reverently as her grandmother's story concluded. "And that's all true, Grandma?"

"As true as I can get it, what with the census data I have and all. I've ordered this book about Bessie Smith. You can read it when the print copy comes. I read some of it on Kindle. It's loaded with information about life in Chattanooga back then." Ida pointed to the digital version on her laptop. "Plus, it's so interesting to read about the life of someone I've always admired."

"I'll read this one," Imani said as she slid her grandmother's laptop onto her own lap.

"Did the strike succeed?" Roxane asked. "What happened?"

Ada ran a hand over her hair. "As near as I can tell, it fizzled out. The strikers were able to transport each other for a while, but after a month or so the whole thing bogged down, partly because it didn't have the support of Black ministers and political leaders, Heaven knows why. I suppose they figured they'd lose the toehold they had in the white power structure if they threw their weight behind agitators. But boycotts like this became an important tactic in Black struggles against Jim Crow." She turned to Imani. "You know about Jim Crow, don't you, child?"

"Yes, Grandma. Mama's been telling me about it for years."

Roxane's mind raced as she took in her mother's story. Stories like this should be everyday fare in the school curriculum, but they were not. The person she knew who best understood how curriculum could lay the foundation for understanding historical roots of racism was Esteban. Now principal of the only high school in Cypress View, he had spent years reworking his school district's curriculum through Mexican American knowledge. Although he did not have Roxane's background in Black Studies, he recognized its value. Yes, to make the changes she wanted to make in schooling, Cypress View, small as it was, might just be the best place to work.

She wondered what Cypress View's middle schools were like. Would they nurture Imani intellectually better than her current middle school was doing?

"Mom?" Imani was waving a hand in front of Roxane's face. "Are you there?"

"Sorry, I spaced out a minute," Roxane said. "I got called this afternoon for an interview for that job in Cypress View. What would you think about maybe all three of us moving there?"

Her mother simply nodded while opening the oven door, but from Imani's shocked expression, Roxane realized she hadn't mentioned her job application to her daughter. Discussing the ramifications of that opportunity eclipsed consideration of a possible third Reconstruction.

***

An email from Jayne Brown the next morning alerted Roxane that the segment profiling her would air on KTOP's local news that evening at 6:00 and 10:00. Roxane considered how to spread the word. She didn't want to come across as boastful, but many colleagues would feel insulted if she didn't mention it to them. She settled on a short email to her superiors within the district, the leadership team in her school, teachers who appeared in the segment (however briefly), and a few others, like Chandra and Margaret, who would enjoy viewing it.

Then she got on about her day.

That evening, 6:00 in the Bedford household found Roxane, Ada, and Imani in front of the television with dinner on TV trays. Normally Roxane forbade watching TV at mealtime since it cut into meaningful family conversation. But not tonight. The three impatiently watched the evening's late-breaking local news, weather, and sports segments.

With just five minutes to go before local news switched to national, Jayne Brown suddenly appeared at the KTOP news desk. She chirpily asked what teachers can do to educate students more successfully, given the rapid demographic changes sweeping through the state and nation, and the persistence of an "achievement gap" between white students and students of color. Then she asked whether school leaders should be drawn from the ranks of the teachers who had developed the most skill in closing the achievement gap.

The scene cut to a hall in Taylor High School, where Roxane was talking with a teacher. In a voiceover, Jayne introduced Roxane in her current role as a high school principal. Then the camera cut to Jayne interviewing Roxane's former student Hugo Lattimer about what made Dr. Bedford an extraordinary teacher. This was followed by brief clips of testimonials from three more of her former students.

Seeing Hugo, now a poised young man, took Roxane momentarily back to when he was a kid in her English 9 class during her second year at Sunnywood High School. One afternoon, the class had been writing what they might see in their neighborhoods if they, like Chuy in Gary Soto's YA novel, *The Afterlife*, could watch from heaven, or wherever the spirits of dead people went.

When she had called on Hugo to read his story, Hugo burrowed nervously into the page. His story concluded, "And then when they weren't looking, I took all their fireworks to an empty garbage can and I lit them and it made a big noise when they went off and everyone got scared." Some of the boys snickered.

"You took the fireworks?" Roxane asked, making a mental note to work with him on run-on sentences. "You were a ghost, you couldn't take anything. Your story was clever, but I think you changed some of the rules. What might have happened if you just watched?"

"My little brother might have lit the fireworks and gotten hurt," Hugo replied. "That's why I took them away."

"Ah. So you saw someone trying to put your little brother in harm's way, and you intervened so he wouldn't be hurt."

"Yeah."

"Okay, I can accept your rule change. Thank you, Hugo, your little brother's lucky to have you."

The TV screen showed test score data from Roxane's teaching at Sunnywood. Then Jayne was interviewing Roxane in her office about how she brought her teaching success into her work as principal. "I always place the students first," her image was saying on TV. "As adults, our job is to support them intellectually and personally. I try to make everything I do as a leader flow from that."

"Thank you, Dr. Bedford, most inspiring. And there you have it. Good teachers can make good leaders." A crescendo of upbeat music, Jayne beaming at the camera, and it was over.

"Mama, you were awesome!" Imani proclaimed.

Roxane was relieved to see Imani smiling. The previous evening, things had been tense as Imani tried to process the prospect of leaving her friends in San Jose should her mother be offered a job in Cypress View.

"Well, it was alright but I think they made me look too much like a superhero," Roxane replied.

"Honey, to a lot of people you *are* a superhero. And we're very proud of you," her mother emphasized.

"So you're in demand and that's why this other place, Cypress View, that's why they want to interview you for a job," Imani declared. "Awesome."

"Well, they wouldn't have already seen this news show, obviously," Roxane said, realizing that she should have alerted Esteban. "But in essence, the things Jayne focused on are things they're looking for. Some of them, anyway."

Imani grabbed her phone. "I'm finding the link so I can send it to my friends."

Roxane's phone rang. It was Chandra, ecstatic to see her principal featured so beautifully on the news. As she accepted praise from a few other friends and colleagues she inwardly acknowledged that her work as a teacher hadn't been all that much different from what many other outstanding teachers did. She wasn't a magician, and she didn't teach through the force of an amazing personality. She used principles she knew and understood well about the relationship between young people, their realities and identities, academic knowledge, and the adults entrusted to teach them.

For example, the English Department had always taught Steinbeck's *Of Mice and Men*. Roxane's first year, she followed suit, using the class set she found in her classroom. But despite its characters being migrant workers like members of some of her students' families, and despite the book's setting in California, her students couldn't place themselves in a 1930s Great Depression context, nor a context where the migrant workers were white. It wasn't that they couldn't learn to appreciate the book. But these students – mainly Mexican American, Black, and Filipino – first needed to connect with literature by seeing people like themselves in it and writing it. That was a huge draw of Soto's *The Afterlife*. The characters reminded many students – especially those who were Mexican American – of home. Learning to connect academics with students' lives wasn't magic, it wasn't something Roxane invented. It was a principle of teaching and learning that excellent teachers used, and probably all teachers could learn to use.

This would be the heart of what she could bring to Cypress View, should they decide to offer her the position.

She got the link from Imani and texted it to Esteban.

CHAPTER 8

COMPETING VISIONS

The job interview was just days away. Ideas somersaulted through Ben's head. He wished his body could do the same. The boot was off his foot, but his left calf was still encased in plaster, his forearm in a splint. He hoped walking laps with crutches around the house and driveway would restore strength and mobility. After the Sultana exploded, his ancestor Daniel had survived and went on to thrive as county clerk for several years. If Daniel could succeed, so could Ben.

To prepare for the interview, Ben studied Cypress View's schools. Academic achievement wasn't where it should be. Lots of immigrant students, mostly from Mexico, with parents who didn't speak much English. The district's budget was lean. Cypress View had wealthy families, but most sent their kids to private schools. Occasionally white parents agitated to carve out their own school district, but that effort hadn't come to much. The teaching staff was aging; a wave of retirements was on the horizon. Replacing veterans at the top of the salary scale with new teachers would free up a chunk of money.

He had mixed feelings about popular trends in urban school reform. Partnerships between education and technology – there was one trend that was clearly Ben's strength. Charter schools, however, another major trend, were overblown. They drained resources from regular public schools and produced a decidedly uneven track record of academic success. Besides, when they worked, they worked for specific schools but didn't improve the whole school district. Ben hoped the Cypress View school board wasn't wedded to the idea of expanding charter schools. The district did have a large proportion of English learners. Perhaps he could find a good online English language development program to adopt.

Most importantly, good leaders leveraged teachers' ideas, good leaders built a culture of trust. Ben's teacher self understood the classroom in considerable detail. He was good in the classroom. He was known for getting results with even some of the most challenging kids. He recalled an afternoon years ago when a student he didn't know appeared in the doorway.

"Mr. Harris?" the student asked tentatively.

"Yes, come in. How can I help you?" The tall, thin boy wore a Golden State Warrior's shirt with the number 30. "You're a Curry fan, I take it?" he asked. The boy even looked a little like Curry.

He grinned. "Yeah."

"Take a seat. What's your name?" Ben asked.

"Curtis. I don't want to keep you, it looks like you 'bout to leave."

"Right now, you're my first priority," Ben replied. "What can I do for you?"

Curtis twisted the hem of his shirt as he studied the floor. Ben waited. Curtis looked up and said, "I want to see if I can get in your algebra class."

Ben blinked. "My algebra class? Whose class are you in right now?" Two other teachers also taught algebra.

"Miss Jacobson's," Curtis replied. Mary Jacobson was a second-year special ed teacher. Curtis must be in special ed.

"I ain't learning nothing in that class. All we do is easy problems, like multiplying and dividing little numbers. I know how to do that already. I heard you're a good teacher, you teach kids how to solve number puzzles. My friend Robert, he's in your second period, he said I should ask you if I can get in, too."

Number puzzles? Ben thought for a minute. Yes, he did weave puzzles into his math instruction. But he couldn't simply move a student from one class to another even if he wanted to. He would need to work with a counselor. But a special education student?

"Let me see what I can do," he said, feeling dubious. When a smile broke over Curtis's face, he added, "I'm not saying yes, just that I'll look into it. Write down your name for me. Who's your counselor?"

Ben was able to convince Curtis's counselor that Mary Jacobson, being new, was probably under-challenging some of her students. The counselor agreed to let Curtis try algebra. The next day, to find out what Curtis could do, Ben handed him some problems. As Curtis worked, Ben noticed him occasionally using his fingers to count. By the end of the class period, Curtis had completed about half the problems, all correctly. The youngster worked slowly, but could obviously think.

Curtis stayed in Ben's classroom the remainder of the year. While he never performed to the level (or speed) of the rest of the class, Ben was certain he learned far more in his classroom than he would have otherwise. To Ben, it all came down to believing in students and giving them a chance, forming relationships with them, and keeping their attention with humor. That's where his carefully honed skill in entertaining an audience came in. And of course, he knew math well enough to figure out multiple ways of explaining almost any concept to anyone. This was the formula he tried to instill in the teachers at Richford, and one he would take with him to Cypress View.

Cypress View. An opportunity for the whole family to reboot. His current house, his current neighborhood had become linked, irrationally and inadvertently perhaps, but linked nonetheless with the trauma of Ben's near-death experience. The house hadn't caused it, but the event seemed to have put everyone on edge, almost as though everyday life were fraught with danger.

He had thought the return of Jason's bike would have made Evan and Lisa reevaluate how they'd leaped to conclusions. But no. When he confronted them with the contradiction between their assumptions and the bike itself, each had simply shrugged as if to say, "If not this bike, then something else."

Yes, the family needed a fresh start. Earlier that afternoon he had identified two Cypress View neighborhoods he thought Lisa would like, one of them with a house just listed for sale. He would make an appointment with the realtor to view it with Lisa immediately after his interview. Then they could top off the day with an early dinner in a cozy restaurant in downtown Cypress View. He smiled as he pictured her nodding in agreement that this was a place where she would feel safe, this was where they could start their lives together anew.

The noise level suddenly rose tenfold. Lisa and the boys were home.

"Rotisserie chicken for dinner okay?" she hollered into the family room.

"Sounds delicious," he replied.

"It'll be a few minutes. We seem to be running late here." He heard her unloading bags in the kitchen.

"Can I help?" he called in to her.

"Got it handled," she replied

"I keep biting my cheek," Evan complained as he joined his father. The boys had just been to the dentist, who apparently filled a cavity in Evan's mouth.

"I'm surprised Dr. Mellish took care of you right then and there rather than setting up another appointment. That's what she usually does," Ben said.

"It was just a little one," Evan said.

"I didn't have any cavities," Jason announced proudly, displaying his open mouth.

"The Novocain will wear off soon," Ben said as he reached for the remote. "Let's catch a little local news while Mom gets dinner on the table."

"Aw, Dad, that's boring." Jason scampered up the stairs to his room.

As Ben clicked on the TV, the newscaster was reporting on an incident in a Philadelphia Starbucks where two Black men, who had arrived for a meeting but didn't order anything, had been arrested for trespassing. They were released shortly afterward because they hadn't committed a crime. It was becoming apparent that the cops had been called only because they were Black. The image shifted to a reporter in a local Starbucks as she interviewed employees about any racial awareness training that might be in the offing.

With all the recent attention to the harassment of Black people, Ben was surprised that the Starbucks employee's first instinct was to call the cops. He thought about the considerable time he had spent in coffee shops as a student. Had he ever felt threatened there? If someone entered but didn't order anything, would he think to call the cops? He wondered what would happen if he walked into a Starbucks and just sat down without buying anything. Probably nothing. He might give it a try.

His mind was wandering. He missed most of the meteorologist's weather report; he gave sports some attention.

Ben was about to limp into the kitchen when Jayne Brown appeared in the last local news segment, asking viewers what teachers today can do to educate students more successfully, given the rapid demographic changes in the area.

"Dinner's ready," Lisa announced.

"Coming," Jason hollered from his room.

Ben sat dumbfounded. Roxane Bedford was talking with a teacher in the hall of what was apparently her school. In a voiceover, Jayne was introducing her.

"Ben, do you need help?" Lisa asked from the kitchen.

Ben shushed her without taking his eyes off the TV screen, where Roxane's former students sang her praises. Then her test score data flashed across the screen. It was impressive, better than that of any English teachers at Richford. The whole segment was moving too fast for him to piece together exactly what Roxane did to get those results, but the overall impression was remarkable. She was now explaining how her teaching informed her work as a school leader. Jayne thanked her, and the image moved back to the KTOP newsroom where the anchor invited listeners to return at ten for more local news updates. Ben felt the blood drain from his face.

"What was that all about?" Lisa was standing behind him in the family room.

"My main competitor for the job in Cypress View," he said. "How on earth did she arrange that kind of publicity, right before the interviews?"

Lisa shrugged. "She looks kind of young to be a superintendent."

"That's not the point, Lisa. They made her look good. She spoke exactly to the kinds of outcomes school boards look at. She gets test scores up, kids like her, teachers seem to like her, she uses resources well, she's very articulate – and here I'll come, lumbering in with half my body plastered up ..."

"Mom? Are we eating now?" Jason yelled from the kitchen.

"Yes, and don't shout." Lisa returned to the kitchen. "Come on, Ben."

As Ben struggled to stand, his phone rang. Mitchell. He picked it up.

"You saw the news segment, I take it," he said to Mitchell.

"Did you know this was coming?" Mitchell asked.

"I had no idea. I'm trying to process what it means," Ben replied.

"It means Jayne Brown made Bedford look like God's gift to education," Mitchell said. "Wonder why they didn't pick a white person to feature. White people get passed over a lot these days, ever notice that?"

"Mitchell, cut the crap," Ben said. Mitchell could be right, but Ben didn't want to get pulled off into one of Mitchell's rants.

"If you say so. But there is another side to Ms. Bedford. Want to hear it?"

Mitchell's question took Ben right back to his office at Richford almost a month earlier when Mitch had said something about Bedford's daughter and earlier life. His curiosity had led Ben to a collapsing exit ramp where he almost died. If he hadn't given in to that curiosity, he wouldn't be all banged up now. Not that his curiosity had caused the accident, but still. How curious was he to learn what Mitchell had?

On the other hand, what could it hurt to at least hear Mitchell out?

"Can you just tell me without making me meet you somewhere? That's what got me into trouble earlier," Ben replied.

"Sure. I found an article in the *San Francisco Chronicle* about a former Oakland community activist named Richard Sellers. He's in a federal prison in Minnesota for murder. The word is, he and Bedford were entangled with each other for about a year, and right around when he disappeared, she turned up pregnant. She kept the kid, a daughter named Imani."

"That sounds like unsubstantiated gossip," Ben said.

"It does," Mitchell agreed. "But it's a little more substantiated when you put a photo of Sellers next to a photo of this daughter. She's his spitting image."

"Ben, are you joining us?" Lisa hollered from the kitchen.

"In a minute," he yelled back.

"We can finish this later, if you'd like" Mitchell said.

"No, let's finish it now. Just what are you suggesting I do with this information?"

"I'm not suggesting you do anything with it," Mitchell said. "But it feeds right into the stereotypes some of these white parents have, the ones who have been trying for years to secede from Cypress View and create their own district. I'm thinking of passing it on to a reporter friend of mine who can link the prospect of hiring a lady who climbs into the sack with thugs and outlaws with the problem of keeping the district together. That kind of thing."

Everything inside of Ben screamed, *No!* Mitchell's proposal was flatly unethical. But then Mitchell had never demonstrated a strong moral compass his whole life. This was one more shady deal he wanted to use to promote – well, himself, really. Mitchell probably figured if Ben became superintendent, he could simply attach himself to Ben's star, gaining status and influence by association. After all, that had been his whole modus operandi during his youth.

On the other hand, there was no way Ben could make himself appear as attractive as Roxane. She seemed to have a track record of success with students that he could not emulate. She also sparkled in a way Ben could not do on crutches. But if anyone on the Cypress View Unified School Board caught wind of a serious backlash that hiring her could provoke, that could tip the balance in his favor.

And yet, Ben just couldn't bring himself to agree to Mitchell's idea. Upset as he was with KTOP's segment, he couldn't climb down into the gutter with Mitchell.

But he did want the job. It felt as though his whole future depended on it. The professional regard he craved – becoming the authority whose voice about urban education was sought, being that man everyone looked up to, seeing himself interviewed on CNN, MSNBC, and the PBS Newshour – this was the future he wanted for himself.

He just couldn't support Mitchell, he wasn't that kind of person. Ben had integrity even if Mitchell didn't. But a little voice deep inside didn't want to stop Mitch, either.

"You do whatever you want," he finally said. "To me, spreading unsubstantiated slime is never a good idea."

"It won't get back to you. I guarantee that."

"Well, I don't approve of it. But it's a free country," Ben said, and hung up.

Ben was the better candidate. As a teacher he could match Ms. Bedford, more or less, and as an administrator, he had her beat. He had worked hard to become excellent as a teacher, then as a leader in an urban setting. He had worked damned hard, in fact. Too hard to have it all taken away.

Now just as he was ready to move up to the next level, along comes a younger woman with less experience, muscling her way to the front of the line and getting rock star attention. Yes, she was smart, she was pretty, and she got results from the kids she taught. He could give her credit where it was due.

But Ben had a deeper pool of experience to marshal than Ms. Bedford. And he also had a wider network of connections outside education that he could draw on. With his contacts in business and technology, he could solve a broader range of problems than she could. What would she do about the high cost of housing for teachers, for example? Did she have the connections to work out a solution to a problem like that? Probably not. Did she have experience negotiating teacher working conditions arrangements in a way that prevented talk of a strike? Probably not.

It simply wasn't fair that she was suddenly catapulted to the front of the line. He didn't like to admit it, but it felt like the tables were turning against white people, even those who, like him, weren't racist. No wonder Evan didn't like the immigrant kids across the highway. He probably sensed that one day they'd try to elbow him out of the way rather than waiting for their turn.

But that didn't make dirty fighting right. If Mitchell wanted to wade in the sewer, let him. Whatever Mitchell was planning, Ben couldn't stoop that low.

***

Three days later, candidate Ben was studying his reflection in the bedroom's full-length mirror. Did this tie give the right image? His hair seemed thinner than he had noticed before. Maybe some of Lisa's hairspray would help. Was he standing up straight? Did a cane look more dignified than a crutch? Yes, but when walking he leaned on it too heavily. And he limped. Extra-strength Excedrin might take care of that. He needed to project confidence and decisiveness, not weakness or imbalance.

He was glad he'd seen the Bedford woman on TV because it gave him a better idea of the main competition. Visualizing who he was up against psyched him, the same way nervousness used to psyche him right before a martial arts match when he was a teenager. It made him focus, concentrate, feel a little edge.

He had probably overreacted to her news segment. In the moment, it had seemed his head would explode with anger. But after cooling off, he realized that his interview would be much more potent than her rushed feature on television. He figured Mitchell had cooled off as well, since nothing had apparently resulted from his threat to make Bedford's past into a news story. When you thought about it, what self-respecting newsperson would pick up a lame tip like that, a base attempt to discredit a successful professional? No, Ben was the better qualified, and could win this match fair and square.

As he mentally ticked through his attributes, he gradually relaxed. He downed a quick breakfast, then, with Lisa driving, headed to Cypress View for his 10:00 interview. Lisa would have the day to look around, maybe do a bit of shopping, then pick him up at 3:00.

Ben felt he aced the formal interview. He quickly warmed to board president Darin Armstrong, who reminded him of his cooperating teacher in San Diego – encouraging, comfortable, and portly. Two board members asked questions that struck Ben as coming out of left field, such as what he would do to strengthen the district's Mexican American Studies program. He knew he didn't field their questions well, but figured he could afford to lose two votes. Three asked detailed questions about things like budget management, handling personnel issues, and school safety policies – things he could speak to easily – and they seemed interested in his ideas. One board member honed in on recruiting and retaining the best teachers. Like San Jose, Cypress View lost teachers to the high cost of living, she explained.

She seemed receptive to Ben's idea of working with local businesses and real estate developers to build housing specifically for teachers and other city employees. By the end of the formal interview, Ben calculated he had five of the seven board members with him.

This was followed by a tour of the central administration office building (Ben was relieved Mitchell was not part of the tour), lunch, and short visits to three of the district's schools. He had looked forward to meeting the high school principal, Esteban Ayala, but met with one of his vice principals instead. Apparently Ayala wasn't available that day.

At any rate, Ben appreciated the fact that Armstrong organized these visits in a way that minimized the amount of walking Ben had to do.

"I still remember how hard it was when I broke my pelvis skiing," Armstrong explained on their way to the first school visit after lunch. "That was at least twenty years ago, but some memories don't fade with time. I still walk with a limp, although most people don't notice it."

They arrived back at the central office a little after 3:00, where they found Lisa seated in the lobby, chatting with the receptionist. Ben introduced her to Armstrong. A bit more chatting, and it was over.

"We'll finish the interviews next week," Armstrong said. "You'll hear from us sometime after that, one way or the other."

Ben liked Armstrong, and felt as though he would enjoy working with him. But like a skilled poker player, Armstrong didn't give anything away. Ben couldn't quite read his reaction, which was unsettling.

Nonetheless, Ben felt optimistic about the job. The people he met didn't seem much different from school administrators and board members he had worked with over the years. They weren't what drew him. No, what drew him even more strongly than before the interview was the opportunity he would have to stretch his wings. In Cypress View, he would be able to develop innovations between the business community and not just one high school, but the whole district. He would be able to take on problems facing individual schools, such as budget challenges, testing, and student discipline codes, and address them at the district level. In short, Ben would learn on a small scale to work out solutions to vexing and pervasive challenges educators face, and this would prepare him to address the same kinds of problems on a large scale. This job was just the ticket he needed to move forward.

Back in the car, he bubbled over with enthusiasm for how the interview had unfolded. When Lisa didn't say much in response, he asked how she had spent the day. Since they had an hour until their meeting with the realtor, Lisa suggested they head downtown. "You have to see this, it's so quaint and cute."

The town dated back to the 1800s, and while most of the buildings were relatively new, some proudly displayed Gold Rush facades. Old brick buildings now housed boutiques, restaurants, and ice cream shops. "Looks like a tourist destination," Ben said.

"It is. I talked with a couple of shopkeepers. See that store over there on the corner? I almost bought a new outfit, but restrained myself. I gather things get crowded around here during summer."

"There's where we have a dinner reservation." He pointed as they drove past a tiny bistro.

"Nice," she said.

"So what did you see by way of housing?" he asked.

"Well, we can look," she said evasively. She turned the car down a street lined with oak trees. "We're heading to Eastside Knolls, one of neighborhoods you mentioned. I only zipped through it quickly while you were interviewing."

Within five minutes, they were driving through a neighborhood that resembled the one where they currently lived. Midsized homes, most built in the 1990s, were tucked onto small lots dotted by mature trees and bushes. While a few people maintained lawns, most had replaced grass with drought-resistant plants.

"Looks nice," Ben said.

"It's not bad," Lisa shrugged. "Now we're heading to Pine Haven, the neighborhood where we're meeting the realtor."

As they drove, he hoped she would show more enthusiasm for door number two. Presently they pulled up behind a car with Sotheby's signs stacked in the back seat.

"This is it," she said.

The house appeared somewhat newer and larger than their current house. Kids on the sidewalks, obviously arriving home from school, gave some indication of who lived nearby. To Ben, the residents appeared to be the typical California mix of white and Latino, with a few Asians. He didn't notice any African Americans.

A blond woman approached them. "Hi, I'm Samantha. You must be the Harrises?"

Samantha escorted them into the house, which was still full of the current owners' possessions. She explained that it had just gone on the market and would be vacated in a couple of weeks. She walked them from room to room, stopping along the way to point out this feature or that.

Ben could easily picture the family living there. It was spacious without being ostentatious. Comfortable. A place where you could kick off your shoes and relax. The greatest challenge for the boys wouldn't be the house itself, but rather leaving their friends in San Jose. He would need to find activities to enroll them in over the summer so they could begin to make friends here.

He couldn't quite read Lisa. Did she like the house? The neighborhood? She chatted easily with Samantha, but communicated very little of what she was feeling. When the tour finished, she asked about additional houses Samantha might be able to show them at an unspecified later date. She took Samantha's card, they both thanked her, and everyone headed to their respective cars.

On the way to dinner, Lisa asked Ben more about his interview – what the school board was like, what they asked him, and what he thought of the schools he had visited. What she didn't do was give any indication of liking – or disliking – anything she had seen except the cute downtown area. He wanted to ask her directly, but didn't want to push her. Maybe she didn't like that particular house, but could warm to another one.

By the time they were seated, he knew he had to prompt her. "I sense the house we just saw isn't quite what you'd want. It would work for me, but there's no rush, we'll have all summer to find something we all like. If I get offered the job, that is."

"Well, I guess that's the elephant in the room, isn't it?" she responded. "I mean, the house we just saw isn't that much different from the one we live in right now. Bigger, maybe. It has some nice features, like the patio out in back. But to me, it feels like a lateral move. And have you thought seriously about what moving to Cypress View would mean to the boys? And to me? I'd have to relocate job-wise, hopefully staying with the same insurance company, but there's no guarantee. Evan and Jason would have to start all over making friends, which as you know is harder for Jason than for Evan. Jason doesn't have all that much self confidence. And I wouldn't be able to see my friend Sara as easily as I can right now."

"The boys young and adaptable," Ben replied, defensively. "Kids adapt to a new location all the time. We can sign them up for sports activities through the park department over the summer so they can meet other kids."

Lisa took a sip of water. Ben watched her while his thoughts flew, scattered. "Look, Lisa, I suppose an alternative could be that you and the boys stay put, and I could get an apartment here. I'd be home on weekends, but spend the work week here."

"Now tell me again why you want this job so much?" Lisa asked. "I know you don't want to be a high school principal for the rest of your life. Other openings come up in San Jose all the time, so I'm not quite sure what the appeal of coming here would be."

"It's a stepping stone," Ben replied. "I've told you that. I don't see staying here forever. What I want is to become San Jose's next superintendent – or maybe superintendent of Los Angeles Unified or San Diego Unified. But I don't think I'd get there directly from my current position, at least not anytime soon. If a deputy position were to open up in San Jose, that would work. But I don't see one on the near horizon. This opening in Cypress View more or less fell into my lap. I establish myself here as a successful superintendent, and I'm ready when the position in San Jose opens up."

"And you're hot on being superintendent in San Jose, why again?" she pressed him.

"Or another major urban district." As he said this, he realized he wasn't answering her question, or addressing her reluctance. He decided to try again.

"Look, Lisa. I'm meant to work on a larger stage. It's in my bones. I know that when you met me, I was kind of shy around people, but I've always been an idea person. You know that. I love solving big, important problems, and I just plain relish my work being recognized. But I've been at Richford for a few years, and my learning curve is slowing down the longer I'm there. At some point, the job I have now would become boring, routine. I need to move up to the next level in order to stretch myself."

Lisa picked at the salad that arrived. Ben could tell she remained dubious.

"And face it, I know a lot more about fixing education than some of the pundits who write their op eds in the newspaper, or financial wizards that buy their way into school reform with their millions. I can make a difference for the nation's schools, or at least for California's schools, but I need a bigger platform to work from. I need to be at the helm. This isn't the only stepping stone that would get me there, but it's the one I have access to right now. And I'm trying to stay local so I don't disrupt life for you and the boys any more than necessary. I mean, I'm not looking, say, in Chicago."

He sensed he was still avoiding her main concern: why he was allowing his career to drive fundamental concerns of the rest of the family. He studied her. Or rather, he studied the top of her head as she continued toying with her salad.

"Well, this could all be fantasy," he added. "I haven't been offered a job here, and maybe that won't happen."

He picked up his fork, although his appetite had left him.

Lisa shrugged without replying. For the first time, it hit Ben that she might not want to come with him on the journey he had charted out for himself. She had latched herself onto his star back before they married, and he had always assumed she would continue to be content to follow him. But maybe he hadn't really been listening to her. Maybe her house fantasy symbolized her desire to stay in San Jose, but with a more elegant and exclusive lifestyle than they currently had. Maybe it symbolized her desire to be independent of him. Or maybe she wished he were something other than a high school principal – an executive in a tech company, perhaps. And just maybe, while he envisioned the boys following in his footsteps, she wanted to groom them to become part of California's elite.

CHAPTER 9

THIRD RECONSTRUCTION

Roxane hung up her desk phone, puzzled. She had just arrived at school when Esteban had called. Could she meet with him later in the day? He would make the trek to Taylor, at least an hour's drive each way. He didn't say what he wanted.

"It's nothing to do with your interview here on Thursday," he assured her. "I'm completely disconnected from the search. The Board knows I'm friends with one of the candidates, so I don't even meet them when they come to interview. You won't see me when you're here."

Could it have to do with his sister? She was a middle school teacher in Colorado where the teachers were planning to strike if the state continued to refuse to put more money into schools. Roxane hoped his sister was okay. Well, she would find out soon enough. In the meantime, she had a classroom to visit, a conference call about special education, a group of students to congratulate on an award they won – and on it went.

Not long before Esteban was due to arrive, Roxane was seated at her conference table with two of Taylor's nine history teachers: Brian Sandoval and department chair Frank Roberts. In front of them sat a large chocolate cake. The two teachers had prep periods after lunch, so Roxane used dessert to lure them in for a chat.

She couldn't stop thinking about the provocative question Imani had raised about a contemporary backlash to a possible third Reconstruction. She was familiar with the statistics showing that, although since the Civil Rights movement African Americans had made gains in many areas of life, gaps with whites remained fairly constant in things like rates of unemployment, homeownership, and poverty. But the Obama administration had tackled disparities more effectively than most other administrations. Under his watch, access to

111

health care expanded greatly, the Black unemployment rate declined significantly, Black household income rose and poverty declined, Black enrollment in college increased, racial disparities in sentencing for drug-related crimes were reduced – life for Black people had improved.

In many areas, but not all. On Roxane's desk lay a *U.S. News and World Report* opened to an article entitled *Segregation's Legacy*. It provided an exposé of ongoing racial segregation, particularly in housing. The article began, *Fifty years after the Fair Housing Act was signed, America is nearly as segregated as it was when President Lyndon Johnson signed the law.*

She would call those eight years under Obama an improvement, not a reconstruction. Still, she could understand why Imani would see it that way, given the backlash her daughter was growing up with. Black high school graduates were finding it increasingly difficult to get into selective universities because of challenges to affirmative action. Several states were actively suppressing voters of color prior to the November mid-term elections, using tactics such as enhanced voter ID requirements, purging the rolls of voters who had not voted in previous elections, gerrymandering, and closing polling places located in communities of color. White supremacist hate groups were on the rise; the Southern Poverty Law Center counted over a thousand of them in the U.S. And an ABC News poll the previous summer found almost one tenth of respondents to consider neo-Nazi views acceptable. Yes, she could see how Imani might make a case that the U.S. had slid into a third post-Reconstruction era.

Roxane wanted to find out how prepared Taylor High School's history teachers were to address student questions like Imani's, and how their preparation might be strengthened. She decided to start with the history department chair and another history teacher who shared his prep period. After slicing a generous piece of cake for each, she got to the point of the meeting.

"You both history, I don't," she said after describing her conversation with Imani. "I want to find out how you would handle my daughter's question if she were in your class, and how well prepared your colleagues are for kids like her."

Frank had been teaching for years. Tall, blond and single, he was often trailed by a small entourage of hopeful women. Roxane suspected he was gay but reluctant to come out, probably fearing parents who might want to remove their kids from his classroom. She would defend him if that happened, but he probably didn't know that.

He seemed stumped by the idea of a third Reconstruction. "Obviously, the current era isn't anything like the late 1800s. In my experience, kids don't have much grasp on what the past was like. I mean, we're talking almost a hundred and fifty years ago. So to make that kind of comparison – was this something she read on Facebook?"

Roxane felt her stomach clench.

"I don't exactly agree with you, Frank," Brian responded. Roxane had hired Brian two years previously. Having visited his classroom several times, she figured he would find a question like Imani's intriguing. "You're right that kids can't picture what happened before they were born. But her question's interesting, and I can see a kid asking something like that. It's not a parallel I would have drawn, but I don't see it as off the wall. By the way, Roxane, where'd you get this cake?"

Both were cleaning their plates as if they hadn't just eaten lunch. "Jen's Bakery. It's my favorite. My intent wasn't to discuss what you think of the parallel my daughter was drawing, but rather how well prepared you believe our history teachers are to work with kids around questions like this, questions they might have that we adults wouldn't necessarily think to ask. Are there things we can do to help our teachers do that better?"

Frank looked dubious. "I encourage discussion in my classroom, I think all of us do. But our job is to teach as much history as we can, without getting sidetracked by random ideas that occur to kids. If your daughter were in my class, she could certainly bring up something like that, and I might invite other kids to jump in. But then we'd have to move along. As I said, kids know so little history as it is that we wouldn't be doing them a service by going off on tangents all the time."

Tangents? Roxane asked herself. Questioning the state of race relations in the country today is a tangent? She glanced at the wall where the words of Frederick Douglass on the fifth of July in 1882 were displayed:

> *It is not light that is needed, but fire; it is not the gentle shower, but thunder. We need the storm, the whirlwind, and the earthquake. The feeling of the nation must be quickened; the conscience of the nation must be roused; the propriety of the nation must be startled; the hypocrisy of the nation must be exposed; and its crimes against God and man must be denounced.*

Imani's question burned with fire, thunder, and earthquake. It was a question that needed to be taken seriously.

Brian studied his plate. "I don't agree, Frank. The things kids will remember come from pursuing their own questions. We can shovel them full of information, but that doesn't mean they'll absorb it."

"I don't think any of us *shovels*," Frank said frostily.

Roxane raised her hands, catching herself before "now boys" slipped from her lips. "Here's where I'm trying to go with this conversation. My daughter's question rests on her recognition that race relations in this country right now are fraught and seem to be deteriorating. I'm wondering how well prepared we are as a school to help our kids delve into issues involving race that they might be thinking about."

Frank's eyes cast about as though searching for a response.

Brian replied, "Not as well as we should be," just as Frank sputtered, "Everything isn't about race."

"Go ahead, Frank." Roxane nodded toward him.

"I wouldn't say we avoid these issues," he said as he struggled to regain composure. "We don't. Look, Roxane. We welcome kids' questions, but we also have a well-structured curriculum to take them through. Race has a place there. If kids pay attention and do their assigned readings, they'll learn."

"We tiptoe around issues involving race," Brian countered. "I do, too. I haven't learned to work with these ideas very well. Think about it Frank, even the slavery unit whitewashes things. And if kids believe what the curriculum tells them, well, Martin Luther King solved everything before they were even born."

"I know you and I see things differently, Brian," Frank retorted. "But we do have a curriculum that was written by history experts." Turning toward Roxane, he said, "I would think the ethnic studies class we added this year would take care of the matter. I suppose we could add another section or two."

Roxane found it fascinating how neatly Frank sidestepped the conversation she was trying to have, taking up a related but different issue. She supposed his inability to delve into his department's readiness to address sticky issues involving race in the classroom was, in itself, an answer to her question.

So she let the conversation shift to ethnic studies. Previously Frank had resisted the idea of offering more than one section. Experience had taught her that anything she suggested to some of the academic departments – history being at the top of the list – would be dismissed, so she learned to trick teachers into thinking her ideas were theirs. Now Frank had apparently forgotten that she was the one who had initially prompted his department to add more sections of ethnic studies. Oh well, whatever worked.

Brian shrugged. "Of course we should offer more sections. We started to talk about that a couple months ago, then it got tabled. But I don't think adding more ethnic studies sections will change the way the rest of the department approaches history, which I think was your original question, Roxane."

"It was my original question. And to your point, Frank, while everything may not be directly about race, race permeates every aspect of this country's history. I know it's a hard issue to address, but kids are hungry for discussions that will help them understand the racial dynamics of life they see everyday. More sections of ethnic studies are welcome. Adding more sections, though, doesn't address my original concern about how well-prepared the history department is to take up issues of race," she replied. "But as to ethnic studies, we could make it a graduation requirement. The school board has been discussing that for the district, and the state Assembly is debating it even as we speak."

"We'll consider it at the next department meeting," Frank said.

"Good, then, we have a plan," Roxane said, fully aware that the plan's focus had shifted from her original intent. "Let me know how I can help."

"Thanks for the cake, ma'am," Frank said, and shot out of the office.

Brian shook his head. "He'll stonewall at the department level."

"Maybe on the graduation requirement idea, but hopefully not on expanding sections. After all, that was his idea," Roxane said with a wink.

"Yes, but it pulled the conversation away from where I think you were trying to take it. Do you have a minute? Mind if I close the door?"

"What's up?" she asked.

The door closed, Brian said, "You might already be aware of this, but your VP Terry would stab you in the back if he could."

"Why do you think so?" This wasn't news to Roxane, but she wondered what Brian knew. Although she didn't condone teachers tattling on each other, she sensed that Brian was concerned about something he wanted to bring to her attention.

"The other day in the men's room," he said, "I happened to be in a stall with the door closed. I overheard Frank and Terry, they didn't know I was there. They resent you because they think people let you jump ahead in line because you're Black. They probably thought the same thing about Obama. Terry's upset that you're principal and he's vice principal, when he thinks it should be the other way around. Frank thinks all you can see are the Black and brown kids and staff, and no one else. Both of them resented that news spot about you on TV the other day. It's like, they don't think you earned your position and recognition. Maybe I shouldn't be telling you these things, but I worry about what they will do." As he talked, Brian's brow wrinkled deeply and he twisted the hem of his shirt. He was obviously uncomfortable reporting on his colleagues.

Roxane sighed. "My radar picked up on Terry the day I met him. I don't allow him to become anything more than annoying.

I'm not around Frank every day, but I'm not surprised. I would have thought he'd have more sensitivity ..."

"Because he's gay?"

"If he is," Roxane replied. "I've wondered. He hides it."

"He doesn't know who to trust," replied Brian.

"He'd have my full backing, if he'd allow it." Roxane was exasperated, but appreciated Brian's honesty. She had never had this kind of conversation with him before. She was surprised he initiated it, but gratified to know he was an ally who would stand up for her.

"Thank you for alerting me," she said. "You've confirmed what I suspected, which is helpful. I'll keep my eyes open."

Brian looked relieved by her reaction.

There was a knock at the door. When Roxane opened it, her secretary said she had a visitor. Esteban was seated in a plastic chair next to the office entrance.

She had nearly forgotten he was coming. She said goodbye to Brian and ushered Esteban into the office, glad to have a meeting in which she wouldn't need to keep her guard up – even if she had no idea about the meeting's purpose. After cutting him a generous slice of cake, then taking him on a quick tour of the school, she brought him back to her office.

"So now tell me, what brings you to my neighborhood?"

Esteban's eyes danced. "I have something personal to ask of you."

"Fire away."

"I think I told you Brenda and I are expecting a daughter in a couple of months."

"You did," she said, surprised that he came all this way to talk about his family life, and during a workday at that. Esteban and Brenda had married after an on-again, off-again relationship that began when they met in college. After graduating, Brenda left Los Angeles to earn her law degree on the east coast. When she returned to California, Esteban was afraid to trust her again He alternated between reaching for her and rebuffing her. During that time, he had latched onto Roxane as his reluctant love life confidant, a role that fit her about as well as one of her father's suits. She rejoiced when Brenda agreed to marry him. What could be the matter now?

"Brenda and I would like you to consider being our daughter's godmother," he said.

Roxane's jaw dropped. As she gathered her wits, she stammered, "Of all the things I thought you might want to talk to me about, this never entered my mind. I'd be truly honored. Yes, of course I will. But why me?"

He leaned back in his chair, grinning broadly.

"And don't you need a godfather?" she continued. "Aren't these things usually done by couples?" Godparents were not a tradition in Roxane's church.

"Usually, but not always," he replied. "You're who we want."

"But I don't even live near Cypress View," Roxane said. "I can't be there for your daughter on a regular basis."

"That could change," Esteban replied with a grin. "But whether it does or not, you have the same values as us, you're grounded in our same reality. You treat young people of color as brilliant, beautiful, and loveable. You don't try to make them think and act like brown-colored white people. I could see that from how you approached issues when we were in the admin program together. I see that in how you work with your daughter, I saw it in the TV spot last week, and I can even see it in how you run this school."

Roxane felt speechless.

"It's a deal then?" he asked.

"Deal," she managed to say, voice choked with emotion.

***

Thursday night, Roxane tossed and turned. She knew the next day would be a big one for students who planned to participate in the national protest against gun violence in schools.

But what really held sleep at bay was a stream of replays from her interview at Cypress View earlier that day. Had her response to the board member with the long blonde hair been too short? Had she babbled too much over lunch? Did her new suit look too flashy? She thrashed about, critiquing everything that had happened from the moment she arrived until she left. Gradually she drifted into a montage of images involving problem solving with the Cypress View school board, working with the principals, holding meetings with community organizations, greeting heads of local businesses.

Darin Armstrong, school board president, had seemed genuinely pleased to meet her, and served as a gracious host throughout the day. He had been impressed by the news segment that featured her, as had others she met. During the formal interview, she was able to connect some board members' interest in the district's Mexican American Studies program with her own background in Black Studies and her work to transform curriculum and pedagogy for racially and ethnically diverse students. Since a bill making ethnic studies a statewide graduation requirement had recently been introduced in the California Assembly, several board members were keen to probe her perspective. Roxane was also able to link her approach to improving education for students of color with her penchant for collaborating with community organizations.

Three board members grilled her with questions she was able to field reasonably well regarding the nuts and bolts of running a school district – budget planning, federal and state requirements for special education, math curriculum packages that were popular in the state, and so forth. By the end of the day, she felt wrung out, but satisfied that she had presented herself as well as she could.

Her family was solidly behind her, despite what it might cost them to uproot and move. Before the interview, when Roxane had asked her mother and daughter what they really thought about the prospect of moving, they looked surprised by the question.

"Grandma, you'll come with us, right?" Imani asked.

"Yes, of course, Baby," Ada replied. "As long as there's God's work to do wherever we land, I can always make myself useful. If you wanted to go to the moon, Roxane, we'd be right there with you."

Mama knew how to adapt. Back when Daddy was still alive, gentrification had forced the family out of Oakland. A condo complex her family clearly could not afford now occupied the block of her childhood. Why was displacement of people called "development"? What did that word say about the people who had called that block home before it was "developed"?

But Mama had a gift for making a home wherever she was. As long as she had her church, and as long as there was volunteer work to be done, Mama settled right in. That's what she did when the family relocated from Oakland, and that's what she would do again.

For Imani, a move would be less straightforward. She would miss her friends, especially Sondra, although they would text each other, talk on FaceTime, and generally remain connected. And she would certainly miss her favorite shops where she studied fashion trends. Imani plucked her budding sense of style from magazines, websites, and a few favorite small boutiques.

Imani wouldn't miss her school, however. In three years of middle school, she had never said anything positive about the place. She liked individual people and she enjoyed a few classes. But the school itself didn't feel like home to her. Next year she'd start high school. Might as well do that in Esteban's building.

The alarm jerked Roxane awake. She wished it were Saturday rather than Friday morning. She dragged herself out of bed and got ready to face the day.

***

Monday morning, Roxane was in the kitchen, pouring a second cup of coffee as she glanced through email, when she heard her name coming from the TV. She almost dropped the cup.

A news reporter was interviewing a woman Roxane hadn't seen before. Apparently the woman had children in Cypress View's schools.

"... a former Black Panther and I don't know what all, but she had a child with this thug who is in prison for murder." Roxane's smiling photo was followed by a photo of Richard. "You can check it out for yourself in the *San Francisco Chronicle*." The screen returned to the woman being interviewed. "And now she's being considered for school superintendent here. If she gets hired, a bunch of us concerned parents are pulling our kids out of this district's schools and reopening our petition to create a new school district."

The reporter shifted to another interview, this time with a well-known proponent of creating the new district. But Roxane was so upset that she could barely process what he was saying. She heard him conclude, "We've had concerns about this district for a long time, and now we learn that we may be in for a superintendent who chummed around with Black radicals when she lived in Oakland. Cypress View used to be a nice, quiet school district. Our new district will maintain that sense of stability."

The reporter concluded the interview, and the station moved on to a segment about baby seals in Monterey Bay.

Trembling, Roxane set down her coffee cup and gripped the counter.

"You're up early," Ada said as she entered the kitchen, then stopped as she took in Roxane's ashen face. "What's wrong, Baby?"

"Mama, they – they – just now on TV ..."

"Grandma, will you fix me a couple of eggs for breakfast?" Imani called as she came down the stairs.

Ada put her arms around Roxane, feeling her whole body quivering. Imani entered, her eyes widening as she saw her mother and grandmother clinging to each other. "What happened?"

Roxane took a ragged breath. "Someone is trying to keep me out of Cypress View. Some group of parents who think I'm some radical who will tear the schools apart, and who want to create their own separate school district. Someone fed them stories from a long time ago. They tracked down Dad's history with the Black Panthers and they think I was a Panther. I'm proud of Dad, but the Panthers were gone by the time I was born."

"That sucks," Imani exclaimed. "They can't just create their own school district, can they?"

"They can petition to the state to do that," Roxane replied. "It's been done before, many times, in fact. What am I going to do?" Roxane felt as though he floor had dropped out from under her.

"You just keep your head held high, Baby," Ada said as she stroked Roxane's cheek. "It sounds to me like someone's either jealous of you or just plain outright racist."

Roxane's shock shifted into anger. "Mama, this is 2018, not 1890. Who would do a thing like that, and why would the news station take it seriously?" *Terry* floated through her head, but he didn't know she was interviewing for another job. Besides, he wasn't clever enough to plan something like this.

"This is like a modern day lynching," she continued. She wondered who all at Taylor had seen the morning news? What would her staff think of her? How would she be able to carry on her normal day's work? She said to Imani, "Maybe you were onto something when you asked about this being the aftermath of a third Reconstruction."

She took a step back and studied her daughter. "Sweetheart, you'll get cold today if that's all you're wearing. Run upstairs and get a jacket."

Looking surprised, Imani started to protest, but Roxane shooed her toward the stairs. When she was out of earshot, Roxane whispered to her mother, "I don't want her hunting for that news clip. The lady talked about Richard."

Ada shook her head. "Maybe we need to tell her the truth about her daddy, Baby." She sighed. "Well, you just keep standing, this will pass."

"How did they even know I was interviewing?" Roxane said. "Names weren't released until a few days ago. How did this lady dig up this stuff my past so quickly, then turn that into a news story?"

"I suspect someone's behind it," Ada said. "Someone who already had information and enough clout to be listened to."

"Like that white guy who got in the car accident? Maybe he set the whole thing up." Imani had returned with a fuzzy pink jacket over her short-sleeved shirt.

"That's much better," Roxane said. "I doubt Mr. Harris had anything to do with it. He didn't strike me as someone who would stoop that low. Although, it could be, perhaps ..." She remembered their conversation a few weeks ago, Ben smugly assuming he would best her. Did he play fairly, or would he do whatever it took to win?

Ada said, "You just keep standing up straight and looking the world in the eye, Baby. They slung dirt at Obama and it didn't stick. Anyone who knows you can put these kinds of things in perspective."

"It's the ones who don't know me I worry about. This will cost me that job, I just know it will."

"Then it's not the job that's meant to be," Ada said. "You can only control the things within your reach. You can't be worrying about things you can't control."

Roxane knew she would need to watch her back. Someone was trying to bring her down. And she would need to hope Imani didn't track down the interview on the internet. Imani would start asking questions about her biological father. She would be furious that some stranger in Cypress View knew more about her paternity than she did.

But her mother was right about where she should keep her focus. She gave her mother and daughter a fierce hug and left for work, back straight and chin held high. After all, if any of her staff mentioned the news segment, she could simply reply that it was gratifying that some other school district had recruited her to apply to become superintendent there – a position she may or may not actually be interested in.

CHAPTER 10

QUALIFICATIONS MEET TREACHERY

The Uber driver waited at the curb while Ben slung himself on crutches up the walkway to the house. After he unlocked the front door, the driver waved and left.

It was Monday morning, his first day back at work part-time. Lisa dropped him off at Richford on her way to work, a wheelchair got him around the building when he wasn't sitting in his office, and Uber brought him home at noon.

Despite having tried to keep up with work over the phone, he had missed a good deal. You had to be present in a school building to follow its streams of activity. For example, last Friday was National School Walkout, when students across the country held a thirteen-minute protest against gun violence. About two hundred students from various schools in San Jose had marched to city hall, carrying protest signs. Ben watched the event on the evening news, recognizing several Richford students. He admired them for their courage, and wished he had been there to witness responses from teachers when they walked out, to overhear whispers and glances of students who opposed the march, and to congratulate them on their return.

Ben was back on the job now, at least during mornings. As he shut the front door behind him, he felt an odd combination of energy and exhaustion. While his brain hummed, his legs and torso ached, and his body craved a nap.

He had finished eating a turkey sandwich and was about to throw himself onto the couch, when his cell phone rang.

"Hello there, Ben, this is Darin Armstrong from Cypress View," a rich voice boomed through the phone.

"Darin, it's good to hear from you." Ben's heart raced. Would this be a good call? Or would it be the polite but regretful we-have-selected-someone-else call?

"Ben, I have the happy task of offering you the job as our next superintendent. We finished the interview process last week. The board conferred over the weekend and again this morning. We're prepared to offer you a starting salary of one hundred seventy thousand, with the benefits we discussed when you were here. We hope you accept our offer. There's paperwork I need to begin moving, but with your verbal agreement, I can start that process right away."

Ben felt a mix of emotions. On the one hand, he felt relief that this process was over and euphoria at having been recognized and selected, having achieved what he set out to do. The prospect of bringing home thirty thousand more per year was like whipped cream on top. But these emotions competed with his fear about how Lisa would respond, and his anxiety about Evan's and Jason's reactions, now that the prospect of moving was no longer hypothetical. Surprisingly, nostalgia for Richford elbowed its way in for attention.

Ben's voice bubbled. "Darin, I'm thrilled. I'm excited and honored by the board's faith in me. Would it be possible to think about it for a few days? I need to make sure my family is completely onboard before signing my name on the dotted line, so to speak."

"Certainly, I understand. How much time do you think you'll need?" Darin responded.

"Shouldn't need more than a week, I would think, maybe less. My wife is a little skittish about relocating, and my sons haven't given the prospect any serious thought."

"Well, if there's any information I can provide about the district, our compensation package, or the town itself, let me know. My wife might be someone your wife – Lisa, is it? – would like to talk with."

"Yes, of course, I'll tell her that. Thank you. I'll get back to you just as soon as I can give you a firm answer."

Ben's exhaustion vanished. He imagined himself sitting at his desk in the Cypress View superintendent's office. Which items from his current office would he want to take? What look did he want to give his new office? The student artwork he had collected over the years, alongside his framed degrees and certificates, would make a good start.

He should begin a list of people to spend some time with in Cypress View, particularly the outgoing superintendent Al Cordero, as well as heads of businesses and civic organizations. In the interview, he had said something about tackling affordable housing for teachers. His idea had sounded good at the time, but he couldn't quite recall specifics. Another thing to get going on.

Whatever misgivings he harbored earlier about shrinking opportunities for white people in this new multicultural reality – well, here was a clear affirmation that strong qualifications still counted, regardless of race. The Cypress View students were mainly students of color, but the board recognized that a white superintendent could be just as effective as a Black, Latino or Asian superintendent. Race didn't matter. No one was jumping places in line. Qualifications won out.

Should he call Lisa? Or wait for her to get home? How would she react? Well, he knew she wouldn't be happy. To her, Cypress View was a just cute town to visit on a weekend, not a place she wanted to live. There must be an area close to Cypress View she would like. They had plenty of time to look. And what about her job? Would she even need to work? With Ben's salary increase, he didn't think so. She could take as much time as she wanted fixing up their new home, maybe become involved in civic work.

What about the boys? Ben jumped into the Cypress View Parks and Recreation website to identify summer activities they might enjoy.

By the time the family came home, he had figured out options for everyone to consider. They were just options, of course, conversation starters. But the move felt right to him, it excited him. He felt like the universe was looking after him.

The door burst open. "Dad?" yelled Jason. "Can I show you something?"

"I'm in the family room," Ben replied. "And don't shout."

Jason dashed into the family room, tossed his backpack on the floor, and began rummaging through it. "I got an A on a poem I wrote. You know, that one I was working on last weekend."

Jason's poem was about being bullied. His teacher used creative writing to engage students in grappling with personal issues. She believed it was good for kids to learn to name problems they experienced and think of strategies to confront those problems. Jason, like his dad, had been bullied since he was young. Lisa dealt with it by requesting frequent meetings with Jason's school principal. Ben's approach, much like his own father's, was to teach Jason how to defend himself.

The page Jason handed Ben was crumpled from having been stuffed in his backpack – Jason rarely remembered to place paper in a folder or notebook. Across the top was scrawled "A. Beautiful work, Jason!"

Ben read the poem. It was filled with verbs and adjectives, which Mrs. Wong must be teaching as a way of spicing up writing. In the poem, Jason characterized himself as a superhero wiping out bullying from the face of the earth.

Ben smiled. If you didn't know Jason had been the frequent target of bullying, you might think his superhero was a bully himself.

"What does F4G mean?" Ben asked.

"Force for Good. It's my name in the poem."

Ben laughed and ruffled Jason's hair. "I'm proud of you, son."

Grinning, Jason blushed as he picked up his backpack and ran to his room.

Lisa appeared, having changed into leggings and a sweatshirt. "How was it back at the salt mine?"

"Good. Sit down, I need to tell you something," he said.

As she sank onto a stool, her face registered concern. "What happened?"

"Cypress View called to offer me the job. To the tune of one hundred seventy thousand dollars."

"Oh." She drew out the syllable as her eyes widened. "What did you say?"

"I said I need time to talk it over with my family."

She nodded slowly.

"Think what we can do with the salary increase," he said. He knew money wasn't Lisa's main issue, but he thought it would help. "It would give us a cushion to work with."

She stood, folded her arms, and looked at him. She was especially beautiful when she was angry. But she shouldn't be angry, he thought, she should be pleased that he won.

"By talking it over with family, do you mean pushing us into something we don't want? You can move there if you like, but I don't plan to. I thought you understood that." Her voice quavered.

"I understood you had reservations," he replied, his mind whirring through arguments he might try using to convince her.

"Reservations. That's what you thought I was expressing?"

They stared at each other. Lisa continued, "You can go but I won't be joining you. You haven't talked with the boys yet, have you?" With that, she turned on her heel.

"Wait, Lisa," Ben said. "I need to know whether it's Cypress View you don't like, or me as a school superintendent."

She turned looked at him coolly. "You can take your pick. But I certainly have no interest in moving to Cypress View. As I told you when we were there, it's a cute little town, but it plays no part in my future."

As she left the kitchen, Ben felt the warm wind he had been riding since talking with Darin suddenly vanish. How could this be happening? How could he have so clearly misread her hesitation about moving to Cypress View? At least, he had seen it as hesitation, not as complete refusal. Or had her determination not to follow him there hardened over the last few days? Was she thinking about leaving him?

That question felt like a kick in the gut. A couple can have problems, but one spouse shouldn't just walk out on the other one. Ben's parents had been the kind who married for life. Not necessarily because they were happy, but because they believed that's what you did. As a child he grew used to hearing them quarrel – not constantly, never loudly, never violently, but decisively enough to leave cracks in the domestic atmosphere. But the idea of breaking the family apart, of going their separate ways – that never seemed to occur to them. Family was the bedrock of life. You didn't take a sledgehammer to it. At least, that was what Ben grew up believing.

What now? He couldn't simply turn down the position he had dreamt of for months. And it wasn't just the position itself, it was the whole trajectory he had staked out for his future. But on the other hand, family meant commitment. Was there a way to hold onto both?

Commuting every day during heavy traffic seemed like a bad idea, but he would be able to afford a small apartment in Cypress View. Maybe that would work. He would come home as often as possible. He would miss some of Jason's taekwondo matches and Evan's weeknight ball games. But he would be home every weekend. Everyone would have what they wanted, more or less.

As he heard Lisa rattle pans in the kitchen, he flicked on the evening news. Images and sounds from the TV buzzed by him, until he heard a woman's voice saying, "I understand Ms. Bedford is a former Black Panther and I don't know what all, but she had a child with this man who is in prison for murder." An image of Roxane filled the screen. In shock, he watched as this Cypress View parent, then the leader of a school district secession effort, discredited Roxane using exactly the information Mitchell had tracked down.

Mitchell! Ben had told him not to publicize this information. Hadn't he? Didn't he make it clear that smearing someone like this is completely unethical? Or – no, he didn't make that clear. What had he actually said? *I don't approve but do whatever you want.* If that was what he said, tacitly Ben had given Mitchell license to go ahead.

Ben punched in Mitchell's number. The phone rang until it went into voicemail.

"Damn you!" Ben yelled into the phone, then hung up.

Where did Mitchell find that woman? He supposed that if there had been rumblings about some parents wanting to create their own school district, all he had to do was tap into one of them. This spot must have been on the morning news as well as the evening news. Did anyone on the Cypress View school board see it? Armstrong mentioned a phone conference this morning. Might this spot have triggered it? Was Roxane their first choice, were they ready to offer her the job until this aired?

No, that couldn't be. He was best qualified, after all.

But might Roxane think he was behind it? Would Armstrong think so? Would Mitchell sing?

CHAPTER 11

FALLOUT

Roxane felt exhausted. It was only Tuesday afternoon, and she couldn't wait for the week to end, worried as she was about possible fallout from that terrible news clip about parents wanting to secede from Cypress View Unified School District because the board was considering hiring Bedford the Black Panther. Would it somehow fuel those on her staff who already distrusted her? And what would happen if Imani discovered it, and realized that her mother and grandmother had not leveled with her about her biological father?

But so far, only a few members of Roxane's staff had mentioned it. Like Tiffany, a new art teacher who caught her in the hall. "I heard you're looking for a job in Cypress View. Is that true?" Tiffany wrinkled her brow over her worried blue eyes.

"I was recruited to apply to become superintendent there," Roxane replied. "I made it to the interview stage, so we'll see what happens."

"Well, I saw that stupid interview on TV. You'd have your hands full with some racist parents, it looks like."

"Racist parents are everywhere," Roxane replied. "Holding a school district together when some of them want to form their own club would be the challenge."

"Well, I'd really hate to see you leave, and I hope you don't. But you'd make an awesome superintendent," Tiffany said.

Maybe it would all blow over. She'd still like to get her hands on whoever was behind that interview. If the station wanted to do a segment about parents wanting to secede from the school district, they could have done so without dragging Roxane into it, without the sloppy journalism and racist innuendos. The news director could have at least had the decency to call her and check on the story's accuracy before airing it. She considered calling the station's news director, but was afraid the news team might turn her call into more of the story. Best to let it die.

Roxane arrived home in late afternoon. Home, the one place where she could relax. But when she opened the door, the air felt tense. Everything looked normal, but something felt off.

She stuck her head in the kitchen to greet her mother, but Mama wasn't there. So she headed upstairs to her bedroom to dump her coat and bag, then see Imani.

Imani's door was closed. Roxane knocked, and her mother opened it. Imani was sitting on her bed, her face streaked with tears.

"What –?" What was going on?

"Don't come in," Imani said. "You lied to me, I don't want you in here."

Roxane was dumbfounded. Lied about – oh Lord, had she somehow seen the TV interview? Imani, the girl who never watched TV news?

Ada stepped out into the hall, closing the door behind her. "Some kids at school apparently saw that news segment, and began calling her a murderer's daughter, but *daughter* wasn't the term they were using."

"Oh my god," Roxane gasped.

"She didn't even say hello to me when she got here, she just tore up the stairs and slammed her door. Apparently she found the video of the segment on the internet. She didn't want to watch it with anyone else around. Then she tracked down that article about Richard. Once she saw the photo of his face and recognized its resemblance to hers, she knew everything. She screamed, and I came running. I've been trying to talk with her. I think what upsets her most isn't that he's in prison for murder, but the fact that the story we gave her about her father being a good man who died before she was born – that we weren't truthful with her."

Roxane clearly remembered the conversation that had led to that decision. She had been breast-feeding baby Imani in the kitchen of their former home in Oakland while her mother fussed over something on the stove. Roxane's father wasn't due home for another hour or so.

"Someday she's going to want to know who her daddy is, and I don't know what to say," she said to her mother. "He got arrested for killing someone, I don't know if he was actually guilty or not. He could be locked up somewhere. He sure hasn't been anywhere around here since then."

"You could tell her about Richard, the kinds of things you loved about him," Ada suggested.

"But what would I say about why he isn't in her life? He knows I was pregnant with her. By now he has to know he's a father. What do I say about a father who runs away from his own child?" As Roxane said this, she became angry all over again. "Back when our people were enslaved, white slave masters snatched children from their parents to sell all the time. Why would a Black man today abandon his own child when he doesn't have to?"

Roxane knew many young people who had been abandoned by a parent, usually the father. You couldn't work in an urban school and fail to notice children with missing parents. Imprisonment was a big factor, joblessness was another. But to her, it was no excuse. She didn't think she could ever forgive Richard for walking out on his own daughter.

"You could just say you don't know where he is," Ada had said. "He disappeared. That would be the honest truth."

"It's the truth, but how will Imani feel when she learns her own father chose to disappear? That he never cared enough to even come find her?" At that moment, baby Imani began to cry.

"Shhhh," Roxane had soothed her daughter as she rocked her gently. "Maybe I should just say her daddy died. For all intents and purposes, he did die."

Later, when Imani was old enough to ask about her daddy, the story they gave was that he had died. As Roxane concluded, it was better for Imani to think of him as dead than to think of herself as unlovable.

And now, here Richard was, not in person, but still alive and in the penitentiary, in the form of a newspaper article unearthed by a news reporter and a woman in Cypress View who only wanted to keep a Black woman away from her children's schools. In choosing to craft the news story as he did, did that reporter have any idea the pain he caused?

"I have to try to talk to her," Roxane said. She slowly opened Imani's door. Her daughter was curled in a ball on her bed, her back to the door.

"Baby? Baby, I never, ever meant to hurt you. I thought he was dead," Roxane said softly. Now she wondered if fabricating a claim that he had died had amounted to taking the easy way out. As Imani got older, perhaps Roxane should have explained that she didn't know where Imani's father was. That would have been more truthful.

Imani didn't move, so Roxane stepped toward the bed. "I was so angry at him for disappearing, I figured he must be dead. Why else would he have not come back?"

Imani rolled over, her angry face streaked in tears. "You could have told me you didn't know. You didn't have to tell me what a good person he was, when that was a lie. What other lies have you and Grandma told me?"

"In some ways, he was a good person, or I never would have loved him. He organized food for hungry families in Oakland. Without him, a lot of people would have gone without. And he spoke the truth about Oakland's political problems." Of course, these things had nothing to do with Imani. He might have fed other families, but he hadn't helped to feed his own flesh and blood.

Roxane tried again. "Mama and I didn't ..." But they did lie to Imani. This may be the only lie they had knowingly told her, but it was gigantic. It went to the core of who Imani understood herself to be, and how much trust she believed she could place in the two people she loved most.

"Baby, it seemed better to tell you he died, than to tell you that maybe he didn't love us enough to stay. Truly, I thought he must have died. I couldn't imagine him choosing to abandon us. Maybe it was wrong of us not to tell you the whole truth, but we did it out of love."

"When were you planning to tell me that you didn't know where he was, and that maybe he was in jail somewhere?" Imani demanded. "Never? Did you know about that newspaper article before it was on TV?"

Roxane sighed. "Yes, your grandmother found it a couple weeks ago. We were trying to shield you from being hurt."

Imani flipped over and curled back up into a ball. "I never counted on my father," she said raggedly between sobs. "I counted on you and Grandma. Now I can't even do that."

Roxane gently rubbed her hand across Imani's back. At least her daughter didn't move away or tell her mother to quit touching her.

Roxane had momentarily forgotten about her own mother. She glanced over her shoulder. Ada was standing in the door, arms wrapped around herself as though trying to hold herself together. Roxane reached out and enfolded her mother into her free arm.

When Imani had stopped sobbing, Roxane and her mother quietly left her room. As she was leaving, her mother said softly to Imani, "I'll finish getting dinner on the table. You come down whenever you're ready, Baby. Whatever mistakes we might have made, know that we're imperfect people who love you more than anything."

**

Imani didn't come downstairs for dinner, and she said very little to her mother and grandmother at breakfast the next morning. Roxane felt as though she was tip-toeing around hot coals, trying to avoid putting her foot in a wrong place but not entirely sure where those wrong places were.

She arrived at Taylor exhausted. The only thing she could do was to compartmentalize, to tuck her concern about Imani into a safe cupboard in her heart where it would rest as unobtrusively as possible for a few hours. She donned a mask of normalcy, and got on about the day.

Second period was getting underway when Jacob Martin, one of the math teachers, tracked her down.

"Someone defaced the boys' bathroom in the east wing of second floor. Let me show you," he said.

As they walked to the bathroom, he explained that he rarely went into the boys' bathroom, but was glad he happened to do so today.

"What is it?" Roxane asked. "Defaced how?"

"You'll see."

When they arrived and Jacob made sure the bathroom was empty, he led Roxane inside. Roxane gasped. There on the wall in marking pen was a rough cartoon of someone who could be Roxane, judging from the hairstyle and heels, under a swastika. Oddly, the swastika was drawn backward.

"I don't know who did this," Jacob said. "I'm not sure we have any way of finding out, although I can do some asking."

"I should …" Roxane struggled to think what to do.

"If you don't mind, I can ask some of the boys. I have a good relationship with a lot of them, and I see them coming and going in this part of the hall since my classroom is just right over there." He nodded toward his door.

Her mind spun. Did a student hate her, despite her efforts to treat all of them with respect? Would this drawing qualify as hate speech? If so, the student might be looking at suspension. But why was the swastika drawn backward? Did the cartoon figure represent her or someone else? Perhaps the perpetrator drew it rapidly in anger or to get attention, but without understanding much about the symbol itself. He could even be a special education student.

"Hate speech?" Jacob suggested.

"I was just wondering the same thing. If it is, if this were a noose, say, I'd need to call in the police and we'd need to close down the bathroom while they investigate. But the way it's drawn …" She waved a hand. "Backward. And the whole thing wasn't drawn with a very steady hand."

"I was wondering the same thing. The kid who drew it may not have had a very clear idea what he was drawing. And that kid may not have great motor skills," Jacob said.

"Is there a neo-Nazi or some other white power group in the school that I don't know about?" she asked.

"Nothing I'm aware of. I think this was done by an individual kid who may need help more than punishment."

"That's what I'm thinking. I need to report this to the campus supervisor, but let's leave the cops out of it for the time being. I want to identify the perpetrator, but I don't want to blow things out of proportion. This drawing needs to be removed before anyone else comes in here." She pulled her phone from her pocket. She snapped some pictures, then called the custodian.

"Ma'am, for what it's worth, this drawing doesn't represent anything I've heard kids say about you. To most of them, you're just the principal, for better or for worse," Jacob said.

Roxane tried not have favorite teachers, but if she did, Jacob would be near the top of the list. He was one of those people who radiated positive energy. A soft-spoken white man with curly brown hair flecked with gray, he had been teaching for years, and was one of the best teachers in the building. Roxane trusted his judgment.

Marshall Lewis, the custodian, arrived. He let out a long whistle. "First time I've seen somethin' like that in this building. Any idea who drew it?"

"None," Roxane said. "I took some pictures of it. For the moment, we're treating it as a young person needing help rather than as hate speech. Can you scrub it off and close the bathroom until it's gone?"

Marshall rubbed his finger over the drawing. "Permanent marker. Well, I've got a cleaner that'll dissolve it. Should have it completely gone by the end of this period."

Roxane thanked both men, then walked back to her office. This was turning out to be a nerve-jangling day.

Roxane figured it was about to become even more nerve-jangling when she saw Terry Schmidt walking toward her wearing a sour expression on his face.

"Ma'am, is it true you were a Black Panther?" he asked without preliminaries. "This school being the Taylor Cougars, that would fit. You know, cougar, panther, same animal?"

Roxane sighed. "No, Terry, the party fizzled out a year before I was born. Why?" His question showcased his ignorance.

"I thought that's what I heard on the news the other night," he replied.

"Well, the woman who was interviewed didn't have her facts straight. My dad was a member. But now that you ask, I'm curious what you know about the Black Panthers."

Terry's startled look told Roxane that he actually didn't know much. "They were cop killers. I think. They tried to get power by using violence."

Roxane gave him a withering look. "Sounds like you don't know anything except the stereotype. Any Panther violence was far outweighed by policy violence against Black people. How much of the stereotype you heard do you think applies to me?"

"I didn't mean to suggest it did," he tried backpedaling. Roxane didn't believe him. He continued, "Sometimes I think you try to change things too much, too fast. We both know there are things we don't agree on. You're the boss, but I don't agree with everything you try to do. And then when I heard about that news report ..."

"So you didn't actually see it?" Roxane asked.

"No, I just heard about it."

She sighed again. "I don't imagine all that many people around here know much about the Black Panthers. I'll need to do something about that. See, when all you know is ..."

"Wakanda!" A couple of boys, apparently having overheard Roxane mention Black Panthers, passed on their way to the library. "You saw the movie, Ms. Bedford?" one of them asked.

"Best movie of the year," she said, giving them a high five.

As she watched them go, she said, "Associating Black Panthers with the movie isn't a bad thing, I suppose, but there's a whole piece of history missing." She looked back at Terry. "If you hear anyone else either say I was a Black Panther, or that the Panthers were mainly a bunch of cop killers, can you at least tell them they don't have their facts right? Let me figure out a way to do a little educating."

Terry looked at her. "I hear you're leaving, so what does it matter?" With that, he turned and continued down the hall.

Roxane stared after him. What would her possible departure have to do with whether people's ignorance of local history should be addressed?

After lunch, Roxane decided to pop into Frank's classroom to find out whether any attention was given to the Black Panther Party in the history classes.

"Howard might teach about it. I really don't know," he said. "Why? Something to do with that news feature? You'd rather be in Cypress View than here?"

"A friend there encouraged me to apply, otherwise I wouldn't have thought of it. I would like to become a superintendent some day, but I hadn't imagined it might be this soon," she replied. "I may or may not get the job, but the opportunity to move up interests me. Now, about that interview in the news. It was my father, not me, who was a

Black Panther. But the issue is bringing to my attention how woefully little folks here seem to know about that part of history that took place not all that far away from here. As far as the kids are concerned, Black Panther means Wakanda, not Oakland, and I imagine some of the more zoology-oriented people around here see panthers as another name for our school mascot."

"Well, we can't cover everything, you know," he grumbled.

"Let me show you something. Mind if I jump onto your computer?" she asked. Frank gave her his chair. Roxane went into YouTube and found the video, *5 Things to Know about the Black Panthers*. "Watch this, it's short."

When they finished, she said, "There's a lot of misinformation floating around here, misinformation that downplays violence perpetrated against Black folks, disparages collective efforts to challenge racism, and gets pinned on people like me at the drop of a hat. That news segment the other day that probably none of the kids watched, but some of their parents did, has triggered some ugliness. Do you see any way you and your colleagues might be able to use this video, or something like it, to replace stereotypes with historical information?"

Frank was still staring at the computer screen. "I'll admit that's a different view of the Panthers than I had. I had no idea they fixed meals for kids and provided a health clinic."

"My dad was one of the breakfast organizers," Roxane said.

"How did you find this video?" Frank asked.

"Just do a Google search," she said. "The point is, we can't just sit here while some people in our school think the Panthers were mainly out to kill cops, and if they believe I was one, I must be a wannabe cop killer, too."

"Oh." Frank looked as though he suddenly connected some dots. "Uh, let me see if I can come up with something."

As school was letting out, Jacob tracked her down. "I haven't identified the perpetrator yet, but it seems only a handful of kids saw the drawing," he said. "One of them actually began describing it to me before I could ask him about it."

"Thank you for trying, Jacob," she said. "I told the campus supervisor that we're looking into it."

"I'm not done yet. I'll let you know as soon as I find out anything."

Driving home that afternoon, she thought about her ancestor Spencer Dwyer, and what he must have confronted in the early 1900s. Her mother hadn't been able to find more information about him, but Roxane had learned more about what life was like in Chattanooga when Spencer lived there.

Shortly after the streetcar uprising, a mob of white Chattanoogans had lynched a Black man who was in jail for purportedly raping a white woman. The lynching sparked mass protests by the Black community, just like those following police shootings of young Black men today. But organized Black protests scared white people, who responded by placing more restrictions on the lives of Black Chattanoogans, and cutting them out of political participation. Previously, Chattanooga's Black community had wielded some political power. But by making ballots more complicated and by shifting from ward to city-wide representation, whites managed to regain exclusive control of the city government. Spencer had faced voter suppression and the beginnings of gerrymandering. Black business owners who didn't want to lose white customers kept their mouths shut; Black progressive activists were silenced through threats of violence.

Spencer would have learned to navigate threats of violence in order to fight for racial justice. Roxane knew he lived on for several decades, but there were no records of what he did during that time. Her mother had found records showing where he had lived, when and where the children were born, and when he had died. But what did he do during his life? From her own experience, Roxane was certain that he didn't give up the struggle he started with the bus boycott. When you get a feel for making things right, you don't just stop.

Well, she would probably never know. Most historical records were written by white people, and most white people weren't going to document the work of Black agitators.

But now her first concern was facing her angry daughter. Emotionally draining as the workday had been, Imani's pain and the rifts it caused in their relationship dragged her heart down and twisted knots in her stomach. Was it wrong of her to have lied, even when the lie came from a place of love? Would it have been better to have told Imani the truth about her father, or at least as much truth as she knew, even if that truth might have left Imani feeling rejected by someone who should have loved her?

She was just pulling into the driveway when her cell phone rang. Esteban. She debated letting it go to voicemail and calling him back, but wasn't in a hurry to confront the iceberg that Imani had become.

"Hi there," she said.

"Hi back." His voice sounded flat.

"What's up? You sound as down as I feel right now," she said.

"I really hate to dump more cold water on your day, but I just found out they've offered the job to Harris."

"Oh." Roxane's brain seemed to freeze. Should she yell and scream? Cry? Brush it off?

"Are you still there?"

"Yeah, I'm here. Thank you for telling me," she said.

"I gather Harris is thinking about it. He hasn't accepted yet. But I'll have to say I'm surprised. I really expected them to offer you the job. I stayed out of the decision-making process, but I hear things, you know, and what I heard about you was glowing. I'd be willing to bet they did a quick re-think after that disaster news item the other day, which probably made some of the board members start to worry about how many parents might actually pull their kids out."

"Ahhh, I don't know what to say, Esteban. I've spent all day combatting an image floating around Taylor that I'm some gun-wielding Black radical out to destroy public education. Okay, I'm exaggerating, but that's what it's felt like. The station could have done their story about white parents wanting to secede without dragging me into it. Maybe I should sue them for defamation of character. Do you know who was behind it?"

"No," he replied. "I don't know where they came up with that information about you. The whole thing smells and tastes like someone orchestrated it. I don't know that parent who was interviewed, but there's no way any parent would have that jumbled information at her fingertips so soon after names of finalists for the position were released. Someone was behind it, I just don't know who."

"Well, if they've already offered someone the job, then I guess this one just wasn't meant for me." Roxane closed her eyes and pictured herself curling up in her car, going to sleep, and just staying there. Permanently.

"I'll see what I can find out," he said.

CHAPTER 12

TRUTH-TELLING

It had been three days since Ben left Mitchell his initial voice mail, and he still couldn't reach the man. His messages – text, email, and voice – went unanswered. Obviously, Mitch was avoiding him. Ben feared he might have to travel to Cypress View to confront him in person, except he couldn't drive yet. And he certainly couldn't ask Lisa to take him because he didn't want her to know about his connection with Mitchell's treachery. He felt frustrated and stuck.

That damned TV interview had really torpedoed Ben's excitement about Cypress View. He should have been dancing on his crutches. All he had to do was say "yes" to Armstrong and he was in, he was on his way. But now he couldn't trust the school board's decision.

What if the board initially planned to offer the position to that Bedford woman because she was Black, then did a quick re-think when that news segment blindsided them? The interview might have served as a wake-up call to the possibility that they were about to use race to discriminate against a well-qualified candidate who could keep the school district together, who happened to be white.

How could he find out what the story actually was? He could contact Darin Armstrong and just ask him. But that could be risky. He didn't want to start things out by making the board own up to having engaged in reverse discrimination. No, he needed to talk with Mitchell. But would Mitch level with him?

Assuming he agreed to the job offer – which he wasn't sure about now – the next problem was how to get the family on board. Lisa had already made her views clear: she would not move to Cypress View. But what if the boys wanted to go? If he could persuade them, might she acquiesce?

Jason would be easy. He was still young enough that he didn't see himself as separate from his parents. If they planned to go somewhere, of course he would follow. But Evan was a different animal, and Ben was still perplexed about what angle to take with him.

***

Friday at noon, Ben was in his office loading up his backpack before going home, when he heard a familiar voice behind him. "Thankfully we won't be facing a teacher strike this year."

Patricia Knowles, assistant principal of instruction, sat down in the only chair not stacked with books or file folders. "After the LA strike a few months ago, then the waves of strikes following West Virginia, you couldn't predict where it would happen next. Personally, I support the teachers, but I've kept my fingers crossed that we don't end up in that boat."

"Our teachers have a good contract," Ben pointed out. "I haven't heard rumblings from the union. By the way, have you heard Gerald's leaving?"

"Yes, I'm so sorry we're losing him! I know he'd love to stay here if he could afford it."

"I think a long-range solution is to work with some of the larger corporations to build affordable housing for city workers, teachers included," said Ben. "I'm starting to run my thinking by a few business people." Or, at any rate, he was planning to do so.

"I'm so glad to see you back at work, even if it's only part-time. When do you anticipate being with us full-time?"

A wave of guilt passed over Ben. He hadn't mentioned Cypress View to anyone on his staff. Should he tell Patricia? After all, she was one of the Richford staff members he worked with most closely. No, better to wait until he actually made a final decision. No sense telling people he would be leaving, then not leave, should it come to that.

"Certainly by the time school starts in August, maybe even mid-way through summer," he said. "The doc wants me to stay off this leg as much as possible until it's fully healed. My energy isn't back yet either, but it's better every week."

Patricia paused. "By the way, did you happen to see that interview on the news a couple days ago, with a parent in Cypress View talking about some Black radical trying to become superintendent there?"

Ben's heart dropped to his ankles. "Uh, I heard the tail end of it. Why?"

"Oh, it just struck a nerve," she said. "My aunt used to live there. Nice little town. I've wondered how someone like that got as far in the search process as she apparently did."

With that, Patricia left. More guilt pangs stabbed Ben. He might be better qualified than the Bedford woman. But still, trashing the reputation of a fellow professional was wrong.

But then again, maybe Dr. Bedford was a radical who would try to push things too far. She could be one of those people who couldn't see beyond her own race. Had Mitchell done Cypress View a favor? Ben didn't know. In actual fact, Dr. Bedford could well be a skilled and hard-working administrator who had learned to produce remarkable results, and who he had allowed to be sullied with mud.

And if Ben accepted the benefits of Mitchell's mud-slinging, despicable as it was, what kind of a person did that make him?

***

That afternoon Ben was keeping a close lookout for Evan. He needed to catch him alone to talk with him about the potential move.

The front door opened, then slammed shut. "That you, Jason?"

"It's me," Evan replied.

"Hey, Sport. Got a minute?"

"Sure, Dad. What's up?" Evan walked into the family room and plopped down into an overstuffed chair.

"I want to find out how you would feel about us moving to Cypress View if I take the job there. I know you're aware they want me to become their next superintendent, but I told them I need to talk with my family first. I want to hear from each of you individually." Should he barrel on about the sports programs in Cypress View, or give Evan a chance to react?

Evan looked down at the floor. "Are you giving me a choice?" he finally asked.

"I'm asking each of you what you think. Jason is good with it. Look, I know you don't know much about Cypress View, and you have friends here and activities you're involved in. I looked into the sports programs there, and they have a bunch of things. We could run up there this weekend to take a look. You could probably continue doing the same activities there as here, but with different kids. And that's the part that would be hardest, I imagine."

Evan looked directly at Ben. "I don't want to go. If you're asking my opinion, that's it. I don't think Mom's going either."

Ben's stomach sank. Had Lisa already discussed it with him? Evan stood as if to leave. "Can I go now?"

Ben said, "One thing you might want to consider is the big salary bump I'd get. We'd have extra cash to work with. That trip to Hawaii you've wanted us to take, we could do that over Christmas. And I know you've been admiring electric dirt bikes."

Evan stared at his father. "Yeah. But Dad, are you saying we can't afford a dirt bike if we stay here? And I thought we didn't go to Hawaii because you were too busy. You're not trying to bribe me, are you?"

Ben felt his face flush. Evan was right, of course, that was exactly what he was trying to do.

Evan continued. "Besides, my girlfriend Becky lives here. She doesn't live in Cypress View."

Girlfriend? Becky? When did that happen? Did Lisa know Evan had a girlfriend?

"Who's Becky?" was all he could think to say.

"She's a girl I hang out with. Is that all, Dad?"

"Uh, yeah, sure." A fresh problem. Who was Becky, and why didn't Ben have any idea his son had a girlfriend?

A few minutes later, Lisa arrived home. Ben went into the kitchen to see her.

"Do you know anything about someone named Becky?" he asked.

She rolled her eyes. "More than I wish I did. Is Evan home? I was just talking with the teacher in charge of the play he's supposed to be in."

"Supposed to be in? What do you mean?"

"Sit," she said. He sat and she continued. "Earlier today I phoned the school to find out exactly when the play is scheduled, you know, because we haven't received anything and Evan hasn't been very specific when I've asked him."

"And?" Ben was puzzled. "He's up in his room, he can't hear us."

"He'll hear us soon enough. He hasn't been to practice for almost two weeks. Ms. Cruz, that's who I talked with, she said she dropped him from the play after warning him about his failure to attend rehearsal. I asked if she knew what he was up do. She wasn't sure, but she said she thinks he's been spending time with a sixteen-year-old high school girl named Becky."

Ben was puzzled. "How would Ms. Cruz know about Becky?"

"Apparently she was in Ms. Cruz's class a couple of years ago, and she didn't leave a good impression. Ms. Cruz expects her to be pregnant before she graduates, unless the girl at least has the sense to use birth control. She said she saw them together last week, and then a couple evenings ago on her way home from rehearsal."

Ben felt furious. Not because his son was allowing himself to be seduced by an older girl. Lisa probably didn't realize that most boys experience that at one time or another. But Evan had not been truthful with his parents about where he was. He said, "Becky aside, Evan shouldn't have lied to us about attending rehearsal."

"What do you mean, Becky aside? Becky is *why* he wasn't attending rehearsal," Lisa shot back.

"Yeah, but I think you and I see her differently. To me, it's normal that a boy whose hormones are kicking into gear would latch onto a willing girl. That's what boys do."

"Did you?" she asked.

How could he explain to Lisa that when he was in high school, he would have done exactly what Evan did, had the opportunity presented itself? But it didn't because no girl looked twice at a guy with acne and braces.

"I didn't pay much attention to girls until I got into college," he said. "But the point we agree on is that Evan lied to us, and he shouldn't have. Right?"

"Right."

"I'll go get him," Ben volunteered.

"No, you sit here. I'll get him," Lisa replied.

She returned to the kitchen with Evan in tow. "What?" he said, looking back and forth at his parents.

Ben said, "You've been lying to us. We just learned that you haven't been attending drama practice, or whatever it is, like you told us. Can you explain what you were actually doing and why you lied?"

Evan looked like a trapped rabbit. He hung his head. "You wouldn't understand."

"Try us," said Lisa. "A long time ago, we were thirteen ourselves, you know."

Evan stumbled through a confession. Becky had encouraged him to ditch practice, and he had been sufficiently enthralled with her to agree.

Ben said, "Son, when we found out that you weren't where you said you were, we were concerned for your safety. It isn't just a matter of us trying to keep tabs on your business. We worry about you when we don't know where you are."

Evan shook his head. "I'm sorry, Dad." The boy still had enough of a little kid in him to be ashamed of lying to his parents.

Lisa added, "Ms. Cruz told us you aren't in the play anymore. You missed too many rehearsals. Because you lied to us about your whereabouts, we're grounding you until school is out."

Ben tried not to register surprise. Grounding wasn't something they had discussed.

Evan was looking at the floor, his mouth working like he was trying to figure out how to object.

Ben asked, "Evan, how important is this Becky to you? Could we meet her?"

He couldn't read Evan's expression. Evan finally muttered, "I don't know. Maybe. Can I go now?"

Both parents nodded.

As Evan fled, Lisa looked at the clock. "I'm almost late to get Jason from taekwondo. Be back in a flash."

After she left, Ben felt his body deflate. He thought about Roxane Bedford. Who was he to ground his son for lying, when all he had to do was look in the mirror to see someone who would allow a much bigger lie to destroy someone else, then take no responsibility for it, just so he could get what he wanted?

***

Saturday morning Mitchell finally answered the phone. He was surly. "You wanted that job, didn't you? And now you have it, don't you? I did what I knew would work. And you're pissed?"

"I didn't call you to argue." Ben shut his eyes and ran a hand over his face. "I just want to know if that news segment affected the board's decision."

"Of course it did," Mitchell snapped. "Armstrong was about to make an offer to that Bedford woman. How do you think they would have felt if they hired her, then found out she had a daughter by a murderer, and had been a Black radical activist back in the day? That's all it would take to split this school district in two. They hire you instead, and they're safe."

Mitchell actually believes he's done everyone a favor, Ben realized.

"They thought she was most qualified, at least before that news segment?" he asked. He wanted to believe that qualifications would ultimately prevail.

"I think they were hoping she'd come up with some ideas they hadn't thought of to improve student achievement levels," Mitchell replied.

"That material you dug up about Dr. Bedford," Ben said, "that material nearly got me killed a couple of months ago. It's poison."

"Do you know the thing about you that's bothered me since we were kids? You can be so damned sanctimonious. That material, as you call it, didn't almost get you killed, it was your desire to see it that almost got you killed. For a while there, you were going at this job as if you'd do anything to get it. Well, now you have it. You could at least show some gratitude."

And there it was. Mitchell's stunt had succeeded in changing the minds of board members at the last minute. They would have given the right of first refusal to Dr. Bedford without Mitchell's intervention. The board saw her, not him, as best qualified to lead the district.

Deep in his soul, Ben had feared that might be the case, which was why he had not stopped Mitchell. Tacitly he had given Mitchell a green light. He knew what Mitchell was capable of.

And now he had what he wanted.

A victory that tasted unbearably bitter.

Ben was much like Mitchell after all.

***

For the next twenty-four hours, little was said about Cypress View in the Harris household. It was as though everyone was tiptoeing around it, even as it loomed large in their minds.

That is, everyone except Jason.

"What middle school am I going to next year?" he asked Sunday morning at breakfast.

Lisa responded with the name of the school Evan currently attended; Ben with one of the Cypress View middle schools.

Silence followed. Jason frowned, then continued eating. Evan kept his eyes trained on his cereal bowl.

Ben didn't know what Lisa was thinking and was afraid to ask. He suspected she was figuring out how to keep herself and the boys right here in San Jose, regardless of what Ben did. Well, maybe the whole family would be staying put and she just didn't know it yet.

Ben found he could no longer visualize himself in the superintendent's office. When he tried to picture himself talking with Darin Armstrong, or meeting with Cypress View school principals, he felt like a dishonest fraud, a feeling that only grew as hours passed. He needed to give Armstrong an answer, should have done so already. But he could neither bring himself to accept a job he had been offered on the basis of his own subterfuge, nor turn down the job he had desired so ardently.

I can still climb to the top, he told himself. *My route just might not go through Cypress View.* He began making a list of other school districts that could be looking for a superintendent soon.

But if Roxane Bedford actually out-competed him for this job, how did she do that and who might beat him in the next competition? He might run into the same thing again. And what message did that send his sons, both on their way to becoming white men looking for a fair shake in an environment where white people were increasingly in the minority?

These thoughts made him angry, angry enough to want to take the job, regardless of what he did to get it. He was, after all, the best qualified candidate.

***

Ben had dozed off when he heard the slap of papers tossed onto the table next to him.

"What's this?" he asked, groggy, wishing he didn't still need a nap. Maybe returning to work fulltime, regardless of what the doctor recommended, would restore his energy.

"Take a look," Lisa said. "I'll be back in a minute."

While she ran upstairs, he shuffled through brochures, one for a house in a gated community not far away, the other for a private school in San Jose. Annoyance bubbled up inside.

A minute later, she returned and perched on the edge of a chair across from him. "We need to talk."

Ben nodded.

She picked up the brochure for the house. "I'm not moving to Cypress View. I've thought and thought about it, and it just doesn't work for me. If you want to get an apartment there, fine by me. This …" she waved the brochure. "This is where I want to move. We can go look at it tomorrow. Or not. But I've seen it. I'm ready to make an offer and put this place" – she extended an arm to indicate the room where they sat – "up for sale."

Suddenly Ben was wide-awake. Over the past six months, he had grown so used to hearing Lisa talk about this or that house, that he had gradually tuned her out. Now she no longer seemed to be asking his opinion. She simply announced her plans. When had she become so bull-headed?

They had disagreements before, of course, like all married couples. Their clashes first became serious when Jason was in second grade and other kids bullied him. Jason participated in taekwondo now because Ben believed he needed to learn to stand up for himself. Lisa's approach, on the other hand, was to blame the school for doing too little to stop the bullying. She literally harassed the principal and teachers. In retrospect, Ben's approach worked better – Jason could now defend himself. But Lisa, regardless of the wisdom of her ideas, increasingly ignored Ben and went her own way.

In addition, her life priorities seemed to have shifted. She had always been skittish about the potential for danger around her, and did what she could to protect herself from threats, real or imagined. Her parenting style took on the same aggressive style of protection. Somehow that wariness had morphed into a drive to achieve a safely gated, upwardly mobile lifestyle that surpassed what Ben could offer as a school administrator, maybe even as a superintendent. Where did that drive come from? If he were a corporate executive bringing in a huge salary, would she be happier? But then, Ben wouldn't be Ben. He wondered if she was infusing her image of the boys' future with her own unrealized dreams. She seemed to be grooming them for a much more affluent and materialistic lifestyle than Ben could provide or even wanted. Did she imagine affluence and exclusivity would be their best protection, and protection from what?

She was waving the school brochure in his direction. "I've been looking at private schools for the boys. Maybe not for Jason just yet, but Evan, certainly, because of everything that happened with Becky, I've decided this is the best place to send him." She handed the brochure to Ben. Ben was familiar with the school; he didn't need to study the brochure. It had a strong reputation for its college preparatory curriculum, particularly in the sciences.

"More Asian students than any other group, but Evan will have to get used to that. I've visited every private school in the area, and this is the one he can get into that I think would suit him best."

"Are you asking for my opinion?" Ben finally asked.

She shrugged. "Sure. Tell me what you think. But this is what's going to happen. Go ahead and take that job in Cypress View. I'm done dealing with the fallout of the boys attending the public schools. Your jump in pay should cover the cost."

"Look, Lisa," Ben said. "Evan's lying has nothing to do with which school he's in. And whatever school he attends, he needs to have access to a strong athletic program. It's not like he's going to become an engineer. He doesn't even want that."

Lisa didn't respond. Ben knew she loved their sons, but she projected her own worries too forcefully onto them. He couldn't allow her to control his life, either. He could listen to her, he could compromise with her, but he couldn't simply accede to her wishes. The boys needed to come first. Whether he rented an apartment in Cypress View or stayed put, he would need to be present with them more than he had been, and he would also need to be true to himself.

Lisa shook her head and walked out of the room. Ben took a deep breath, then picked up his phone to call Darin Armstrong.

CHAPTER 13

SECOND

There was a knock on Roxane's opened doorframe. Roxane looked up, finding Jacob Martin with Billy Watson, a small quiet ninth grader. From the guilty look on Billy's face, she surmised that he must be the one who defaced the boys' bathroom.

"Billy has something he wants to say to you," Jacob said.

"Yes, Billy? Would you like to come on in?" Roxane asked.

Billy's feet seemed glued to the floor. He mumbled, "I'm sorry, Mrs. Bedford."

She glanced at Jacob, who nodded, then said, "I'm not going to hurt you, Billy. Tell me, now, what is it you're sorry for? Come on in, please."

Billy stepped forward, looking down. "I'm sorry for making that cartoon on the bathroom wall."

"Ah. Can you tell me why you made it?" she asked.

He looked up. "DeShawn Newell always picks on me. He won't stop and no one does anything about it. My dad said – he said you wouldn't do anything to DeShawn either, because he's Black and you are too, and he didn't think Black people should be in charge of anything because they just help each other."

Roxane tried not to get sidetracked mentally enumerating all the ways white people help each other, such as in hiring workers, voting for candidates, making laws, selling houses, adopting textbooks, selecting juries – on it went.

She knew DeShawn. She would definitely have a word with him. He was tall enough that some white women teachers found him intimidating, so they let him get away with too much, and behavior that should be nipped in the bud ended up growing like weeds.

"I'll deal with DeShawn," she said. "Now, I wondered why you drew a backward swastika."

"What do you mean, backward?" Billy asked. "It's just a sign to show I'm proud of being white. That's all it means."

"To many people, it means hatred," Jacob said. During the second World War, it was a sign associated with the mass murder of Jewish people. I'm Jewish, by the way."

Billy's eyes widened. Jacob continued. "Billy, how much do you know about racial discrimination?"

"A little. My dad says there's a lot of discrimination against white people. He says Black people are making it hard for white people to get ahead. They get all these preferences, you know." While Billy's voice sounded defensive, his face crumpled as if he was about to cry. No mystery why bigger kids would pick on him. "And white people keep getting blamed for slavery, but that was a long time ago."

Roxane figured Billy must regard what he was saying as obviously factual. Otherwise, why would he openly make such claims to a Black school principal? "Do you know anything about Jim Crow?" she asked.

"Who's he?"

After a pause, Roxane thanked Jacob for bringing Billy to her. She asked Billy to follow her down the fall. She had an idea that might plant two trees with one shovel.

She found Frank Roberts at his classroom desk grading papers. She briefly explained what had happened, and Billy's apparent lack of understanding of the Holocaust, Jim Crow, and institutional racism. To Frank's blank look, she proposed that Billy do some research, either for his class or as an extra project, assembling materials Frank could use to teach about Jim Crow and institutional racism in one of his history classes.

"If you complete the work, we'll consider your fine for defacing the bathroom wall paid off," she told Billy. "Mr. Roberts here will supervise you and let me know when you've finished."

"You aren't letting me off the hook, are you?" Frank commented.

"You're a smart man with influence around here," Roxane said. "I'm just making use of your talents."

As she turned to leave, Billy caught her attention. "You're not gonna call my dad are you?"

"Do you think I should?" she asked.

"He'll beat me," Billy said.

"Then I guess I'm not," she said. "As long as you do the work Mr. Roberts expects of you, I don't see a need to call anyone. This will stay between the three of us. Okay? Now, let me go find DeShawn."

Roxane left the room and turned down the hall. Last week when Esteban had told her Ben Harris got the job, she had cried. The pain and disappointment seared. She hadn't realized how excited she had become at the prospect of working with her friend. His ideas were so in sync with hers that they would have made a formidable team, and she would have been able to figure out how to implement at a district level what she had learned to do at a school level.

That possibility had opened up a well of excitement. She knew she carried around buckets of insights and ideas for addressing district-wide issues, but her ideas often had nowhere to go. At principals' meetings, sometimes she had to bite her tongue to keep from blurting out this proposal or that. On more than one occasion, she had seen her own superintendent latch onto an idea, forgetting that initially it came from her. Yes, picturing herself as the one in charge felt energizing.

But then came the crash. That TV interview with that white parent that was designed to humiliate her did its job, she was sure of it. Ben Harris, with more experience than she had, shouldn't have needed to play dirty to win. That is, if he had anything to do with the TV news segment. She wasn't sure. But now thoughts of Cypress View left a sour taste in her mouth. Would she be able to face some other school board for a future job without wondering which of its members were ready to believe the worst about a Black woman candidate?

Well, there was nothing she could do about it. She might as well focus on the job she had, the people she worked with now, the school she led.

***

By late afternoon, Roxane's stomach began to knot as she wondered what kind of mood Imani would be in. She hadn't yet forgiven her mother and grandmother for lying about her father, but she seemed not to want to cut them out of her life, either. Would her normal warmth toward them still be hidden behind a veil of cool politeness? To Roxane, Imani's aloof demeanor felt like an arrow that needed to be directly extricated. But her mother cautioned her to give the girl time. Be there for her, but honor the space she needs to come to terms with what happened.

When Roxane arrived home, to her great surprise she found her daughter and mother in the kitchen, huddled over her mother's laptop, closer in proximity than they had been for days. Printouts covered the table.

"What are you two up to?" Roxane asked cautiously.

"Mom, Grandma's found all this interesting stuff about Spencer Dwyer's parents. Look at this." Her face glowing with excitement, Imani handed her mother a printout of a census record from 1880. She pointed to the Dwyer family name. "See, there's Edward, age 38, he was born in Tennessee, and here's his wife Maisie, age 34, and she was born in Virginia, and here's their thirteen-year-old son Spencer, our ancestor."

The old Imani was back! Roxane wanted to hug her, squeeze her, pour love all over her. But instinct told her to act normally, so she held the page as she studied it.

Ada added, "They must have been owned by a white Dwyer family, but I don't see any Dwyers here. There's one more Black family on this page. All the rest of the people are white. A lot of freed Black families pretty much stayed put after Emancipation. From things I've been reading, I can construct a Dwyer story in my head, but I have no idea what the real story was."

"Tell us the story in your head, Grandma," Imani pleaded.

Ada looked squarely at her granddaughter. "The story in my head isn't exactly what happened. It can't be 'cause I wasn't there. Seems to me you want us to tell you the complete truth about things, you don't want our stories."

Imani frowned. "I don't want stories when you know they aren't true. But you've been doing a lot of reading, so you can add stuff to what you know is true."

Roxane asked, "So are we forgiven?"

"I know you were trying your best, Mama," said Imani. "You didn't know what happened to my father, and you didn't want me to feel like he didn't want me. He didn't, but he never even knew me. So it wasn't me he ran away from, it was the idea of me. You were just trying to protect me. I get that."

Roxane smiled, relieved.

Imani continued, "But what was he like? Did you love him?"

"Yes, I loved him, Baby," Roxane said as she put an arm around Imani. "I loved him very much, at least until he abandoned us. It's funny. He was smart, kind, funny, and so supportive of me until he found out I was pregnant. He could deal with all kinds of problems other people had, but not his own. Not that I saw you as a problem. To me, having you was my life's greatest blessing."

Imani threw her arms around Roxane's neck. Roxane nuzzled her hair. "No more secrets, Baby. Do you want to find your dad? I'll help if you do."

Imani looked at her. "Maybe, some day. Right now I want to hear Grandma's story."

Ada raised her eyebrows, then shrugged. "Alright, here we go. Ready?"

"Ready," Roxane and Imani said in unison.

"It was, let's say June in 1865, right after the Civil War ended. Edward Dwyer was a young man then, living in Monroe County, Tennessee."

***

Edward stepped back to view his modest cabin through Maisie's eyes. Would she agree to live there if they married? It was certainly no rougher than the shack she grew up in. Actually, it was nicer. Edward had carefully filled all the holes and cracks, and even used scraps of wood to build a floor over the dirt. His younger sister Abby had used fabric remnants to braid a rug and fashion curtains.

But with both of them now free, shouldn't he be able to offer her more than this?

Freedom. Ever since he was small, freedom had been an intoxicating but elusive dream, a mirage that drew him but never seemed to get any closer. While walking distances to collect bills for Master, he used to fantasize what it would be like to be free. He fashioned his free self after the white people he saw. He imagined himself owning rather than sweeping the master's enormous two-story brick house. Every morning he would dress in a fine suit, then ride off on a richly saddled horse to do business with whoever he pleased. He would read and do sums, keep a ledger of his earnings and expenses. Mama would no longer cook for other people. A free woman, she would spend her evenings doing needlework by the fire, or playing the piano, or even reading. His little sister Abby would fashion clothes for her doll rather than washing other people's linens, and his older brother Sam would own a nice store. Daddy, well, he never lived long enough to see the war, much less taste freedom. Died of yellow fever ten years ago.

Then Edward would open his eyes to the world he knew. He would tuck these wisps of fantasy away in a drawer at the back of his mind, ready to haul out some other day.

That day had arrived, but it did not even tip its hat to Edward's dreams. Three months ago, freedom came when Tennessee amended its constitution to eliminate slavery. Master was so ill he seemed unaware that he no longer owned anyone. He died the following month. He didn't live to see the end of the war nor the return of his grandson who served as a Union soldier. Missus was on her own to see to the burial and figure out what to do with her three former slaves.

Despite Edward's dreams, things didn't change much after Emancipation. Mama continued to cook and care for the house, Abby continued to care for Missus, and Sam kept building a road Master got started, although the foreman now paid him.

"Where would we go?" Mama said when Edward asked her what she planned to do now that she was free. "I been livin' here mos' my life. Missus don't treat us bad, and she needs help. Only difference is now she pays us for our work, and I give it right back to her for rent and food."

Food was a problem. Before the war, everyone had enough to eat. Master grew wheat and hogs to sell, and Edward helped care for a small vegetable garden. While growing up, he had learned to tend *the hogs, butcher them, and smoke meat for bacon, and while Master sold most of the meat, he doled out bits of it, along with vegetables from the garden, to Edward's family. No one starved.*

But now, well, food was downright scarce, and it was mostly the fault of the Confederate soldiers. During the war, they swooped in, helping themselves to whatever they could find. Then they burned down Union soldiers' houses and destroyed Union farms as best they could. Confederate soldiers had raided Master's storehouse, so by the time spring came, nothing was left except whatever Missus could buy when shipments arrived by train. Everyone was thin these days.

Master's grandson sensed the situation the former slaves were now in — having been freed with nothing but their dreams. He saw former slaves with no money, no animals, no land, nothing but a few simple possessions. Some masters even claimed those. Now here was Edward, wanting to start his own family in his own cabin on his own farm. A proud young man, he wanted to offer Maisie a step up in life.

So the grandson approached Edward with an idea. "You rent these here acres from me at three dollars per acre, but no rent's due until you sell your first crop."

After turning the offer over in his head, Edward accepted.

"And, until you can buy your own tools, use whatever you can find around Grandpa's farm. Hell, keep them if you want, no one else is using them."

Corn and wheat were beginning to poke their heads up through the soil on Edward's farm. Abby's curtains fluttered through the window of his small cabin. Would Maisie say yes? It was time to find out.

***

"Oh, what a romantic story," breathed Imani. "Of course Maisie said yes, because here they are in the census, married and with a son."

Ada said, "Well, things might not have happened the way I imagined. Master's grandson might not have been so generous, for instance."

"But it makes a good story," Roxane said. "Baby, let me see that census sheet." Roxane took it and studied it. "Hmm, a Harris family lived next door to Edward and his family. The man I lost out to in Cypress View is named Harris."

"So are hundreds of other people in Tennessee, thousands in the country. You have that name on your brain," Ada said, then turned to Imani. "Anyway, Sweetheart, these are our people. I'll keep digging away to see what else I can learn about them."

Imani kissed her grandmother's cheek.

Mama was right, Roxane said to herself. She asked, "How can we help with dinner? Imani, you clear off the table and set it. Let me take my bag upstairs. I'll be right down to pitch in."

***

Later in the week Esteban called just as she was locking her office. "What's up?" she asked. "More bad news for me?"

"Hold onto your hat," he said.

"I'm not wearing one," she replied.

"Okay. Well, the drama from Cypress View only gets weirder. I just confronted the slimeball who was behind that smear job about you."

"Really?" Roxane sank into her administrative assistant's empty chair. "How did you figure out who did it?"

"I know the people around here, and had a suspicion. I wasn't sure, but when I confronted the guy, I acted like I was dead certain. He didn't realize I was still fishing, so he started spilling a lot of shit about how he thought you were the wrong person to lead this district, you had somehow hoodwinked board members into thinking they need you, yada yada yada. It turns out he and Harris grew up together. I still haven't figured out whether they're actually friends and cooked up this scheme together, or maybe this guy just anticipated favors if Harris became superintendent."

Roxane shook her head. "What will you do with this information? What kind of position does this guy have in the district?"

"He works with the math and science curriculum in Central Office. I've already told Al Cordero, our outgoing superintendent. You met him briefly when you were here. I suspect Al will fire the turd. But the other thing that just happened is that Harris turned down the job offer."

"You're kidding."

"Nope. Al told me Harris phoned Darin Armstrong Sunday night. Apparently family issues have become complicated, and Harris thinks he needs to stay where he is for the time being. So, methinks ..."

Roxane interrupted. "Esteban, I'm not going to get my hopes up again. This has been a real emotional roller coaster for me. I've made peace with having tried my best and lost, or at least I'm working on it. Your board will need to decide what to do, but I won't sit around here with my fingers crossed."

"You're right. I hear you."

"But thank you for telling me where that story came from. I guess we'll never know if Harris was involved or not," she said as she gathered her bags again and stood.

"Probably not, although my guess is that he was. If I hear anything else, I'll give you a holler."

"Thanks, Esteban. And give my best to Brenda, will you? I think about the almost three of you quite often."

In high school, Roxane had a huge crush on James, a school basketball star. For months her heart stopped every time she saw him. Every morning, she spent what felt like hours in front of the mirror, imagining him as she styled her hair. She figured out his schedule so she could pass him between classes, but if he glanced her way, shy as she was back then, she looked everywhere but at him. When she went to bed at night, she fantasized kissing him, melting in his arms.

Then one day one of her friends told her James wanted to meet her. She couldn't believe it! *He wants to meet me?* Apparently he had noticed her and wanted to check her out. So his friends and her friends arranged a time after school to hang out at the mall. When James approached, Roxane turned to jelly inside, but she managed to talk with him. For about a week, they spent time together every day.

Then he disappeared. When she heard he was seeing another girl, she felt devastated. What had she done wrong? Was she too boring? Too plain? Too smart? She felt as though she had been tossed overboard, left to fend for herself in cold, swirling water.

Until a month later, when he showed up at her front door, wanting to know if she would attend a party with him, just like nothing had happened. She turned him down. She had finally begun to heal and had no desire to go backward. Emotionally she was incapable of being someone's girlfriend only when it suited him. She never regretted turning him away.

As she walked to her car, she thought of James, and felt much as she had in high school when he had shown up at her door. She couldn't want something fiercely, feel it within her grasp, lose it, and then reach for it again when it reappeared. While being second choice for a job wasn't the same as being second choice to a fickle boyfriend, the experience still jerked her around like a leashed Rottweiler she couldn't control. This was not an experience she wanted to repeat.

Roxane arrived home to find her mother and daughter huddled over the laptop again.

"What have you found this time?" she asked.

"Hi, Mama. We found some of our Dwyer relatives on Facebook. Want to see?" Imani swiveled the laptop toward Roxane.

"Gary Dwyer," she read. "Great. Who's he? How do you know he's a relative?"

Ada shuffled through a stack of papers and produced a diagram. "I've been working on this family tree. You've seen it before. But I'm adding people now. I hadn't thought about using Facebook to track down relations until this one showed me how." She winked at Imani.

Imani pointed to the diagram. "See, we already had the names of Grandma's grandparents, Edward Porter Dwyer and Myrtle Tower Dwyer, and we knew this Samuel J. Dwyer was a cousin. I just started looking for Dwyers who were Facebook friends with other Dwyers in Chattanooga, and Grandma looked up Chattanooga Dwyers in the census, and we came up with this list of a few people we're probably related to."

Roxane scanned the list. No one she had heard of. "What do you plan to do next?" she asked.

"I've sent friend requests to all of them. If they friend me back I'm going to message them and see if any of them want to chat."

Ada said, "Tell your mother what you told me about your biological father."

"Oh. Well, yeah." Imani took a deep breath. "I never thought about him until I found out he's actually alive. Then it was like, hey, I'm connected to this person I didn't even know about. Not that I'll probably ever see him, you know. I might look for him someday, but he's way out in Minnesota in the pen. So, anyway, I thought maybe I have more Bedford and Dwyer family somewhere. It isn't that you two aren't enough family, you are. And of course there are my two aunties and my cousins in Oakland. But I wondered if I have other relatives I didn't know I had. So I started looking on Facebook."

"Now you're getting me curious," Roxane said. "Let me know if any of them friend you back."

"Yeah, they'll probably wonder who's this Bedford person from California. We'll see." Imani turned to her grandmother. "Grandma, want me to clear this stuff and set the table?"

An hour later, just as the family was sitting down to dinner, Roxane's phone rang. She didn't recognize the number, but it was from Cypress View. She slipped into the hall to answer it.

"Dr. Bedford," came a rich, familiar voice. "This is Darin Armstrong from the Cypress View Unified School District board. I'm calling to see if you are still interested in becoming our next superintendent. Actually, I'm calling to do my best to persuade you to say yes."

"Oh my," Roxane said as her heart began to pound. After talking to Esteban, she should have anticipated this call, but she didn't. She had intentionally put the whole matter as far from her mind as possible. Which, in truth, wasn't very far.

But now here it was. The call she had wished for last month, the call she didn't get, the call she now found as paralyzing as James showing up at her door.

Armstrong continued. "You may have heard about the chaos here surrounding that search. Look, I'm not sure I expect you to say yes or no over the phone. What I'd like to do is take you to lunch, say next Monday if you can get away for an hour or so. Then we can actually talk. I'll meet you at Richford. I'd meet you sooner, but we have family visiting from out of town."

To Roxane, his offer felt like reopening a wound that had scabbed over. But then again, he seemed like a good person. She could at least hear him out.

She agreed to lunch on Monday.

But she couldn't bring herself to mention the nature of the call to her mother and daughter. That would make the job offer real. Correction. It would make real the fact that she was Cypress View's second choice.

CHAPTER 14

AMBITION'S COST

"I turned down the job," Ben announced after hanging up the phone. "There were complications in Cypress View that bothered me, and the pressure the move was putting on us as a family, well, that wasn't something I wanted either."

He expected Lisa to look relieved. No more talk about relocating the family. Wasn't that what she wanted?

But she didn't look relieved at all. She was studying him coolly as though he were a specimen in a lab.

"Sure," she said. "Yeah. Okay, you changed your mind. I'm surprised but I didn't quite get why you wanted it in the first place."

"So we're not going anywhere," he added. "I thought you'd be pleased. I'll look at that house if you want, but there's no reason to rush."

She stared. "You haven't heard me, have you? The boys and I will be moving this summer."

Ben stammered, "You'd split up our family, regardless of what I think?"

Lisa glared at him. "How would me moving out be any different from you taking a job in Cypress View, then renting an apartment there?"

"But ..." But what? He couldn't refute her accusation. He _had_ considered accepting the job offer in Cypress View and renting an apartment there. But just for the workweek. He would be home on weekends. Except he turned the whole thing down, he wouldn't actually be going anywhere.

He ran his hands through his hair. "You can't intend to split up the family, can you? It feels like you're blackmailing me into going along with something you want."

"I'm not blackmailing you any more than you were about to blackmail me," she said, "and I don't expect you to join us. In fact, I hope you don't insist on it. Ben, I don't know how to put this, but

I think we need some space from each other. Just for a while. Like a time out in our marriage or something."

Ben blinked. He hadn't expected this. When had things gone so wrong? He knew he often let work consume him, but he was present more often than not. After all, he came home every night, he ate with the family as often as he could. He didn't flirt with other women, and he didn't go out drinking like some men did. He remembered her birthday in January, although she hadn't seemed enthusiastic about the workout ensemble he gave her.

And why was Lisa still sleeping in the guest room? He had asked her, invited her to return to their shared bed, but she just said he needed his own space while he was healing. He disagreed, but didn't want to turn sleeping arrangements into one more issue. Come to think of it, when was the last time she had wanted to snuggle up with him in bed? He couldn't quite remember, but knew it was long before the car accident.

He and Lisa had their disagreements, but he had always seen them as resolvable. Maybe they weren't, and hadn't been for longer than he had been aware. He asked, "What do you mean by a time out?"

"A separation. We live apart for a while. See how it goes. And I want the boys to live with me. I supervise them more actively than you do, although of course we'll work out when you have them."

"No!" Ben slammed his fist onto the table. "I don't know where this is coming from, but you are not taking the boys away."

Lisa folded her arms and regarded him coolly. "You're just too permissive," she said finally. "I give them more structure, more direct guidance than you do. I didn't intend that you wouldn't see them, though. You'd get no less time with them than you spend with them right now, anyway."

That stung. He took a deep breath, then asked, "Have you said any of this to either of them?"

"Of course not. I'm telling you first. They're probably as oblivious to my desire to get out of this neighborhood as you've been. We'll need to have a chat with them, and we should do it together," she said.

"A chat, right. But I'm still trying to wrap my head around …" Ben felt as though his brain had frozen. "You can't afford that house you just showed me."

"You're right, I can't, not if we don't sell this place," Lisa replied, gazing around the family room as though it were an old coat she was considering donating to Goodwill. "If you stay here, I'll have to rent something for the three of us. I had anticipated you'd be moving to Cypress View, but apparently you're not, so you'll need to live in San Jose somewhere, in this house or some other place. But whatever I rent will be located in a safer, and I hate to say this because you won't like it, but it will be in a better neighborhood, with more people who look like us, than this one. I suppose, I'll have to give up the idea of private school for Evan, since that's something I'm not sure we'll be able to afford."

"I don't want you to go," Ben said. "I don't want a separation."

"But I do. I'm sorry," she replied.

Ben felt like he was thrashing about, drowning, while the lifeguard looked on. "Is there anything else you haven't told me yet?" he asked. "Just so I can have the whole picture, if I don't already?"

Lisa sighed. "Yes, there's more. I've met someone else. So far it hasn't gone beyond flirtation, and with the boys around, I'm not sure it will. They come first. But becoming interested in someone else speaks volumes to where we are, or where we aren't, doesn't it?" She waved a hand as if to brush something away.

Anger roared through Ben like wildfire. Another man was trying to steal his wife? And Lisa was letting him? She was flirting with this other man, spending time with him that she could have been spending with her own husband? He wanted to claw the man until he bled, until he was as ugly as Ben felt, until he begged for mercy. Or claw Lisa, who was, after all, standing right in front of him and apparently had encouraged this guy.

"You're interested in someone else," he spat out. "You've met someone and you've already made up your mind about all this, haven't you? Will he be moving into this house that I'm supposed to help pay for?"

"No, Ben, he will not. As I said, it may never get beyond the flirtation stage. I'm a mother first and foremost. You know, you left us behind several years ago. When you started your doctorate, you were so focused on your work, it felt like you didn't have time for us. Back then, your constant absence made me depressed, but I thought when you finished your dissertation, maybe things would go back to how they were when you were a teacher, or even a middle school vice principal. Those days, you worried about the kids in your school, but you didn't bring all that home with you. But it seems like the higher up you go in the system, the more it consumes you, and the more of it you want to consume. Somewhere along the way, we got lost in the rearview mirror. I used to feel angry, hurt, rejected. But I'm moving on now."

Ben thought about their life years ago, back when the boys were small, when Ben's world was less complicated, and – yes – when he was around more. Like the Saturday he piled the family into the car without telling them where they were going, then drove to Great America for a day of rides and hot dogs. Or the Sunday when he packed a picnic lunch and drove the family to the beach at Half Moon Bay. When was the last time the four of them had spent a day laughing together? He couldn't recall.

"Why didn't you tell me?"

Her hard laugh startled him. "I did. Oh, believe me, I did. Why weren't you listening?"

It hit Ben that he had taken Lisa for granted, and had done so for far too long. The one person he used to talk with, listen to, share his feelings with had become like a fixture on the wall to him. Maybe she had tried to resolve problems with him, but he hadn't given her much more attention than he gave the refrigerator. If an issue she brought up didn't seem important to him, he simply tuned her out.

"So who – who …" he stammered.

"Who did I meet? Just one of our clients. Recently divorced, has a couple of teenage girls. We got to be friends talking about our kids. Ironically, Gary might know more about Evan's struggles with school than you do."

The arrow hit its mark. "How could you let an outsider know more about my son than I do?" he demanded.

"I'm the one who's always monitoring how they're doing. I'm here when they get home from school, I'm the one who meets their friends, I'm the one who calls their teachers. You get to them now and then, but I'm there every day. Gary, well, we just talk easily together about our kids. He tells me stuff about his daughters, I tell him stuff about our sons. Stuff I probably would have been telling you, or asking you about, if you were around. I mean, even when you're here physically, a lot of the time you aren't here mentally or emotionally."

She looked at her watch. "Let me get dinner started. The boys should be home any minute now."

"We need to figure out what to say to them," Ben muttered.

"Yes, we do. I think Evan's already figured out some of what's going on," she said, then headed for the kitchen.

How could Lisa tear Ben's world apart, then go fix dinner? And how was Ben supposed to sit at the dinner table, chatting with the family after what had just happened?

His head fell into his hands. Her words held too much pain, too much truth. How could he not have seen it? He remembered moving up from being a vice principal to principal. The work, the challenges, and yes, the status – all that had energized him. Then there was his year coordinating the district's math curriculum, a position that enabled his reach and his influence to extend to the whole school district. He was becoming somebody others noticed and looked up to.

That was when he began his doctorate. He drank in the ideas, the research, the writing with all the enthusiasm of a foodie in a Michelin 3-star restaurant. Then, as the new principal of Richford High School, still writing his dissertation, he struggled to project an image of effortless competence. When he finished his doctorate, he channeled the time it had consumed right into his work as principal. Not back into his family.

All the while, he saw now, the time he spent at home, and the time he spent thinking about home, shrank. Lisa noticed it, the boys noticed it, but he didn't. He came home every night, and he managed to find scattered chunks of time on weekends to spend with the boys, so he figured he was doing what everyone expected. Now it was clear to him that he fell far short.

The boys. Because he and Jason were cut from the same cloth, Ben understood his younger son. His elder son, however, puzzled him. He couldn't automatically put himself in Evan's shoes, anticipate what Evan might be feeling or thinking. Probably because of that, he didn't even recognize when Evan needed him.

Ben didn't even realize he was missing in action much of the time, but Lisa did. He saw that now. While she hovered over the boys far more than necessary, no one could accuse her of not being present. Ben felt mired in the detritus of everything he had worked for, now shattered around him.

Noise of the boys' arrival home shot through the door.

"Dad," Jason shouted as he ran into the family room. "Dad, can you help me with this project for school?"

Jason shoved a sheet of paper into Ben's face. As Ben took it, one side of his brain read it while the other struggled to gather his wits.

The assignment was to write a story about an ancestor. It could be any ancestor, even a grandparent. The story was to include some specific information, such as when the person was born, where the person lived, what kind of work the person did. Students could also include any family tales they had heard about that ancestor. Students were encouraged to work with a parent.

Ben briefly wondered why Jason's teacher gave out this assignment so close to the end of the school year. Teachers usually started family history projects early in the year so students had time to work on them.

"I could write about Grandpa or Nana," Jason said. "I don't know any other ancestors to write about."

"I don't suppose I ever told you about our ancestor Daniel Harris," Ben said. Somehow mentioning Daniel's name calmed him. Daniel had survived far worse than Ben was experiencing. Daniel almost died twice, but he survived. Ben was his legacy. If Daniel could survive all he had been through, Ben could survive, too.

"Daniel fought for the Union in the Civil War," Ben said. "He was captured and sent to a terrible prison camp in Alabama, where he almost starved to death. Then he was put on a boat to go home, but the boat exploded. Daniel almost died again, but he survived. He's my hero."

Jason's mouth hung open. "Dad, you're just making that up."

"I'm not. He was a real person. He's your ancestor and he's my ancestor. Tell you what. After dinner, let's see what we can find about him."

"Okay."

"Now, go wash your hands so you'll be ready for dinner."

"Okay, Dad."

As Jason headed to the bathroom, Ben leaned back, eyes closed. How could he bear losing this bond with his son, a bond so secure and taken for granted that neither gave it much thought? No, he wouldn't lose it. He would fight to stay connected with both sons.

***

After dinner, Ben retrieved the notes about Daniel he had compiled a while back. "Let's look at Ancestry.com," he suggested. "I've never used it, but I understand you can find a lot of information there."

With Jason at his side, Ben opened the website and signed up for a free trial. On the Search page, he entered Daniel's name, an estimated date of birth, and the location Monroe County, Tennessee, where Daniel and his family had lived.

Daniel and Harris were indeed popular names. Several different Daniel Harrises appeared. One of them lived in Monroe County and was born around 1840, although in Arkansas rather than Tennessee. The birthplace must have been wrong but everything else looked right, so Ben plowed ahead.

As he wallowed through pictures of gravestones, a couple of headshots that could be Daniel, Ancestry.com member stories about Harrises with family members named Daniel, and images of documents of various sorts, Ben realized he should have familiarized himself with this hodgepodge before offering to help Jason. Somehow he needed to anchor the information floating by him on the screen in a conception of who Daniel was, where he was born and to whom, where he lived, who he married – the information in front of him was too scattered.

"Hey Dad, what's this?" Jason was pointing to a JPEG document labeled "Deed of Trust."

"Don't know. It's a deed of some sort. Let's open it up and see. Let me slide over and you take the driver's seat," Ben said as he gave control of the keyboard to Jason.

Jason clicked on the document. It appeared to be a fragment of something hand-written. Enlarging it, they were able to make out:

> ... *do hereby bargain, sell, transfer and convey unto D. E. Harris two cows, one a jersey red cow about 6 years old, and the other a red muly cow same age. Said jersey cow will soon bring a calf which is included in this sale and transfer, also one sorrel horse about 8 years old to have and to hold [illegible] the said D. E. Harris, his heirs, and assign forever and [illegible] with said Harris that I am lawfully seized and possessed of said stock and have a good right to sell and convey them and that their title is good and unencumbered and that I warrant and defend the same to the said Harris, his heirs, and assign forever. But this deed of conveyance of trust for the following purposes and none other I have this day borrowed from said Harris (20) twenty dollars for which I have executed my note. Now if I shall on or before the 24th day of December, 1886, pay in full said note and interest and the cost of this proceeding, then this obligation shall be void and of no binding, otherwise to remain in full force and effect and the said Harris shall take possession of said stock. I am to hold said stock until said note is paid, or until said 24th of December, 1886. I agree and bind myself to take good care of said stock, and ...*

Jason scrunched up his face as he tried to read and make sense of the document. "What does it mean, Dad?"

"I'm trying to figure it out, myself," Ben replied. "The top and bottom seem cut off. D. E. Harris must be Daniel Harris. It looks like he bought two cows and a horse from someone. Or maybe he loaned someone twenty dollars and the animals were collateral. You know what collateral is, don't you?"

"Uhhhh ..." Jason clearly didn't.

"It's when you pledge something you own to guarantee a debt. If you don't pay the debt, the person you owe gets the thing you pledged," Ben explained. "I wonder why they wrote out this legal document for a twenty dollar loan."

"So it means if the other person doesn't pay back the twenty dollars, then our ancestor would keep the animals?" Jason asked.

"So it appears."

"Did they write everything out by hand back then?" Jason asked.

"Looks like it. Not bad handwriting. I don't think this will help you with a story about Daniel, though," Ben said.

"I could make up a story." Jason's face lit up. "You know what I like about what he did? He didn't just take the animals away from this other guy, whoever it was. He bought them, but let the guy keep the animals as long as he paid back the loan. Daniel seems like a pretty nice guy."

Ben smiled. "You're very perceptive! Well, I suppose you could turn this into a story. Sounds like you've already started doing that in your head."

"Let's see what else we can find," Jason said as he turned back to the computer.

A half hour later, Jason had downloaded various other documents about Daniel Harris, or D. E. Harris, as he was known while serving as county clerk.

As Jason worked, Ben thought about Daniel raising his family during the rise of the Ku Klux Klan. What would life have been like for a former Union soldier living in the South during the 1880s? Slavery was no longer legal but throughout the South, groups like the Klan were trying to recreate that peculiar institution, using violence to enforce their will. If you were a white Unionist, did you support the emancipation of enslaved people, or just keeping the South in the Union, without caring much about newly freed people? Did Klansmen regard you as the enemy, or as just another white person? Did you try to keep a low profile so as not to become a target yourself? Funny, even though Ben had taken U.S. history in high school and at the university, he had never thought about these questions before.

Over the next couple of days, Jason worked furiously on his story. When he had it as good as he could get it, he read it to his dad. Ben elaborated, adding some context. Between them, they crafted a father-son duet about their shared ancestor, which was later written up more formally.

***

Daniel Harris was riding his horse down the road toward home in Monroe County, Tennessee, one spring day in 1886. Finishing his last term as county clerk, he spent much of the day in the county courthouse. Now, as he breathed in the warm spring air, he felt like a bird freed from its cage. He had mixed feelings about finishing his term. On the one hand, he relished the prospect of spending more time with his family and farm. His oldest son Ben, no farmer at heart, would leave soon. So would Ellie, his teenage daughter who was approaching marriage age, lining up suitors like she lined up shoes in her closet. But the two younger boys needed their father's supervision when not in school, a point his wife never tired of making.

But he enjoyed his work as county clerk, and he would miss it. The work itself involved signing and keeping track of marriage and death certificates, and managing property transactions, birth records, census rolls, and whatnot. After eight years, he reckoned he knew more about folks all over Monroe County than anyone else. Plus, he had a flare for putting things in order.

As his horse turned toward home, the sight of his neighbor's teen-age son slugging at the ground with a hand-held hoe, sweat pouring down his face, caught Daniel's attention. Why a hoe rather than the horse hitched up to the plow?

Daniel stopped and the young man looked up. "Afternoon, sir," he said.

Daniel tipped his hat. This was a family of former slaves, now making their way as freedmen. Daniel liked them. "Good afternoon. Might I ask why you've taken to the soil with a hoe on this fine day?"

The young man looked angry. "The plow got busted up last night. Pa forgot to lock it in the barn. I reckon the Klan got to it, sir."

The Ku Klux Klan again. They were ruffians, but increasingly dangerous and violent. Since the end of the war, they patrolled roads at night, whipping any Black person who was out after dark. Recently they broke into the home of a nearby Black farmer during the night and beat him senseless simply because he had demanded full pay for his corn crop. A plow sitting outside the barn of a Black family would have caught their attention.

The Klan was becoming more violent, and had more and more white support. A lot of white folks wanted to go back to how things were before the war. Many were livid that Tennessee had four Black state legislators. Before the last election, mobs threatened so many Blacks that few showed up at the polls. While Klan members led some of the mobs, the Klan itself simply inspired others. And as white people elected more Democrats into office, fewer white lawmen tried to rein the Klan in. Daniel, a Unionist and a Republican, had seen his party shrink as Democrats appealed to white voters by working to restore their version of the "natural order."

Daniel's disapproval of the Klan showed up in the name he chose for his eldest son. Benjamin Franklin Butler, a Union general in the war, had negotiated the release of Union captives held in southern prison camps. As a survivor, Daniel felt indebted to Butler. Later, when Butler was elected to Congress, Daniel admired his bold co-sponsorship of legislation guaranteeing everyone, regardless of race, color, or previous condition of servitude, equal treatment in public accommodations. To Daniel, this was the kind of legislation that paved the Union's way forward. But the Supreme Court declared the legislation unconstitutional on the grounds that it overstepped its bounds by attempting to regulate what private individuals could do.

So Daniel was disgusted when he learned the Klan had threatened his neighbor. But he felt powerless to do anything about it, since white people who tried to intervene often became targets, and he did not want to endanger his family.

He did want to find out more about what happened, though. "Where's your Pa?" he asked.

"He rode over to see Sullivan about fixing the plow. It's all smashed up, I don't know what can be fixed, but we don't have money for a new one. Meantime, we got to get seed in the ground."

This was the worst time of year to lose a plow, since every farmer was full throttle into preparing ground for planting.

"Sullivan's a good blacksmith. If anyone can fix it, he can," Daniel said, trying to feel hopeful. He couldn't picture the family buying a new plow, especially not at this time of year. White storeowners routinely overcharged Black customers, especially when they sensed a customer's urgency. "Tell your Pa I came by."

As Daniel rode home, his mind churned. Damn those ruffians! If they put half the energy into their own farms that they put into harassing people, this county would be a good deal more prosperous.

What his neighbor probably needed most, short of a new plow, was money – either to buy a new plow or to pay for repairs on the old one. But he and his family refused to take money from anyone. They did not want handouts, as Daniel learned from having tried to bail the family out financially one particularly hard year when crops failed.

Daniel could extend a loan, however. How might that work? An idea struck him.

The following morning, he found his neighbor and neighbor's son at work with their hoes. His neighbor looked up at the sound of a horse approaching. "Good morning, Mr. Daniel sir," he said as he removed his hat.

"Morning. Can you spare a few minutes?"

"Sure. You know about the plow, I hear."

"I do, and your misfortune concerns me. What did you learn from Sullivan?"

The man wiped his brow with a large, tattered hanky. "He can make new iron handles and a plow point. I should be able to put the rest back together somehow."

"Good. How long do you reckon it would take him to do that?"

"About as long as it'll take me to come up with twenty dollars for iron."

Daniel nodded slowly. "Would you be willing to take out a loan, due in full after you've sold your fall harvest?"

The neighbor studied the ground. "I can't take nothing from you, sir. I jess can't do that."

Daniel looked off into the distance. "Those two milk cows look mighty healthy. Looks like one of them's in a family way."

"Yes, sir, we're expecting her to calf nex' month."

"The two of them together would fetch, what, about fifteen dollars?"

His neighbor looked up, startled. "I can't sell them, sir, we need them for milk."

"I'm not suggesting that they leave your farm, only that the deed of ownership be transferred. Temporarily. Until you can buy them back after harvest. And Chestnut over there, I know she's getting old, but she ought to bring around five dollars."

"You're offering to buy them for twenty dollars?" the man asked cautiously.

"Now, I don't have anyplace to keep them, so if I were to buy these animals from you, I'd need to leave them right where they are. Come harvest time, I expect you could buy them back."

A grin began to light the man's face. "I expect I could, sir, I expect so."

"If you're agreeable, I'll go draw up a deed of sale. It will specify that you, and only you, have until December of this year to buy the animals, and that they'll remain in your care in the meantime."

"Yes, sir." His neighbor was now smiling broadly.

Daniel hopped back up onto his horse. "I'll be back within the hour with the twenty dollars and the deed. If it looks okay, you should probably go see Sullivan as soon as you can."

"Yes, sir. Thank you, sir."

***

179

Ben's heart burst with joy as he and Jason added the finishing touches. "What a wonderful story this is. I'm sure your teacher will love it."

Jason grinned. "Thanks, Dad. And I'm gonna add this picture of D. E. Harris when he was county clerk. Someone posted it on the Internet."

Ben studied the photo. Jason actually discovered what Daniel looked like! The man in the photo was probably about sixty when it was taken. Not much hair left, but a kind looking face. Ben studied it for family resemblance. Thinning hair, maybe. The shape of Ben's nose. Hard to say.

But Jason's enthusiasm for the man and his story made any effort Ben had put into tracking him down worthwhile.

"I'm proud of you, son," Ben said. "Want to go read it to Evan?"

"Evan!" Jason shouted in the general direction of the stairs.

Ben covered his ears. "I said *go* read it to Evan. He's in his room."

As Jason ran up the stairs in search of his brother, Ben wondered whether Daniel, too, had gradually transferred his mental and emotional energy to his work, and in the process learned to tune out his wife's distress and his children's need of their father. Did he ever shift more energy back into home life? Daniel's expression in the photo reminded Ben of the Mona Lisa, a pleasant smile that seemed to mask inner pain and loss. It was probably impossible to know what Daniel had gone through.

Well, Ben had his own uphill climb facing him. This weekend he and Lisa would talk with the boys. They had managed to agree that they were separating, not divorcing, at least not yet, and that they would get equal time with their sons, the logistics of which would be worked out when Lisa figured out where she would be moving. Most important, their problems were not the boys' fault, and both parents loved them deeply.

Maybe the space would give Ben and Lisa time to figure out how to reconcile. He did not want a divorce, he was sure about that. Lisa, though, he wasn't so sure of. She seemed to be more emotionally distant every day. Ben feared that their separation would enable her romance with this Gary fellow to move forward.

CHAPTER 15

SURPRISES

Darin Armstrong. Roxane wasn't sure how to think about lunch with him. Six months ago, Cypress View wasn't part of her consciousness at all, not even when she talked with Esteban. It was just a place on the map, a couple of freeway exits. Six months ago, vivid images of herself as a school superintendent did not cavort through her imagination. Back then, her professional world revolved around Taylor High School – its students, its staff, its challenges, and her victories large and small. That was the professional world she knew and loved. She hadn't craved something else.

Now this. What would Michelle Obama do if she were in Roxane's shoes? The former First Lady served Roxane as a touchstone in difficult situations. Would Mrs. Obama politely say "no thank you" to lunch with the school board president? Would she accept lunch but with no intention of accepting the job? Would she consider diving back into the emotional turmoil that considering it was bound to bring?

But Michelle Obama couldn't help her right now. For the time being, she was on her own.

She had agreed to meet Armstrong for lunch, although she couldn't imagine what he would say at this point that would draw her in. Rejection hurt. Scratching at a barely healed wound hurt. No thank you.

Cypress View's school board was probably wise to offer the job to someone with more administrative experience than she had. They could surely tell that she – what was the phrase? – had potential. Not quite ready, maybe in another few years, a little more experience under her belt. Not yet fully cooked.

Roxane hated the idea of being second choice – and that was clearly what she was. The fact that Harris, their first choice, backed out did not change that. The board should simply declare this a failed search and try again next year. No sense going back to the list, picking the one next in line, the one who has potential but isn't ready yet.

Apparently, Armstrong didn't see it that way. Why else did he want to drive all this distance just to talk with her? Couldn't he just do it over the phone? Wasn't that what they usually did? But she agreed to do him the courtesy of hearing him out. Armstrong probably just wanted to get the position filled. Maybe he figured a good compensation package, offered over a nice lunch, would do the trick.

But the only thing that actually could entice her was having support to shape the district's approach to curriculum, teaching, and relationships with families. She had a personal stake in the transformation of schooling, and she could envision that transformation in elaborate detail. Her main question for Armstrong had nothing to do with compensation, but rather how well he actually understood what she was about. She didn't expect much.

They had agreed to meet at a local restaurant. When she entered, she found him already seated.

She checked her watch. "You're not late, I'm early," Armstrong said, standing and pulling out a chair for her.

At first glance, Darin Armstrong reminded Roxane of a short-bearded Santa Claus. His appearance took her back to her childhood when a firefighter her father worked with, Mr. Mackey, would don a red suit every Christmas to visit homes, distributing small gifts to children. Roxane adored Mr. Mackey.

But Armstrong was not Mackey. It would be important not to let one bleed into the other.

"I'm so glad you decided to meet with me," Armstrong said. "After the debacle we've been through, I wasn't sure what you would think."

"I'm aware of some of what happened, but I'm probably missing many pieces," she replied. "I don't want to probe into what's not my business, but Cypress View is clearly facing some issues I hadn't known about."

"I'll fill you in, but let's order first and get that out of the way."

After they ordered, he folded his hands and looked directly into her eyes. "In a way, it's rather simple, really. And in a way, it's not. After the interviews concluded, you were our first choice. Some board members had concerns about your experience, particularly your lack of district-wide experience. But we figured you would be a quick study. What you bring that the other candidates lack is a deep and compelling vision for schooling, especially for the wide diversity of kids we serve and our collective failure to serve them well. Your vision is something others can't simply step into the position and learn, since it grew from your life and years of professional work."

"Thank you for telling me that." Her heart began to warm. She had actually been their first choice, and for the right reasons. "I assumed that in calling me, you were going down the list to second choice, after the first said no."

"Well, that isn't what I'm doing, but some might see it that way. When that news item was broadcast, you know the one I'm referring to, well, a few board members jumped ship on you. It wasn't so much because they were concerned about your politics, but they were worried about the white parent secession effort, which has been going on for a while. It comes and goes. As you know, a contingency of parents withdrawing their kids from our schools, whether to send them to private schools or somewhere else, that costs a district in more ways than one. We'd lose state funding as average daily attendance would drop. But the whole secession effort will also trigger more racial segregation in Cypress View than we already have. In other parts of the country, as I'm sure you are aware, some white neighborhoods have actually seceded from majority-minority school districts. Our board worries about that happening here."

Roxane mentally gave Armstrong credit for naming the racism the situation had evoked. And she was familiar with the possibilities board members feared.

He continued, "So, after an intense phone conference following TV airing of that interview, the board voted to offer the position to Dr. Harris. I don't mind telling you that I did not vote that way, but the majority prevailed. He is certainly well-qualified, no doubt about that. To several board members, he also seemed the safer choice. But he has since then decided not to take the job out of family considerations, as I understand it."

Roxane nodded.

"It didn't take long for us to identify who orchestrated that pathetic TV segment and gave that parent information about you to use as a weapon. That individual is no longer employed by Cypress View. We don't know whether Dr. Harris was involved at all. I certainly hope he wasn't, but that's no longer of concern to us. The point I want to emphasize is that you had been our first choice, and you were always my first choice. Now, as things have come to light, you are still the board's first choice."

Roxane felt herself flush. "Thank you. I greatly appreciate knowing that."

She gathered her thoughts as she took a sip of water. After the food server set their plates in front of them, Roxane continued, "I'm very gratified by your words. So, let me ask a couple of questions."

"Fire away."

"That mother in the TV interview, and group of other parents threatening the board with secession. That must still be a concern, I would think?"

Armstrong grinned for the first time since sitting down. "That mother, and others who make their voices heard periodically, they show up at board meetings now and then, and we do hear them out. They're worried about their kids' achievement levels, and complain about low expectations of the schools. In a community like this one, 'low expectations' is their code word for students of color. They're also critical of our teachers' attempts to shape the curriculum for a diverse student population. Too much political correctness, is how they put it. But when we press for specifics, they don't come up with much. The bottom line is that they're just not comfortable with the shifting demographics. Since the last board meeting, more than one contrite board member has apologized to me for giving in too easily to this vocal but very small minority of parents."

"Okay, that's fair," Roxane said. "Another question. I could tell some of the board members get what I'm about. You, I wasn't sure of, actually. But about three of them don't seem to have a very clear idea of what they'd be getting if they hire me. They engaged with me quite a bit about some things like contracts and budgets, but not about other things like student activism and community engagement. Can you tell me how much board support I would have?"

Roxane was surprised when Armstrong smiled broadly and his body seemed to relax. "Let me first tell you a little about myself," he said. "And please eat. No sense letting your plate get cold. Now, I'm not a teacher. I'm a nurse by training, semi-retired. I was a surgical nurse for most of my career. I became interested in schooling when my kids were small. They're grown now, with kids of their own. But as I cut back my work to half time and started looking around for other things I could do, I ended up volunteering in an elementary school down the street. Long story how that came about, and not relevant to this conversation."

Roxane nodded. "But you became interested in what teachers actually do."

"I did. Now this was back about eight years ago when funding for public services was being slashed, and schools bore much of the brunt of the economic downturn. I saw what teachers were up against as their class sizes grew, their salaries stagnated, and they had to buy many of their own teaching supplies. I started organizing fundraisers for schools in Cypress View, and that got me onto the school board."

Roxane was impressed. She hadn't expected to admire him.

He continued. "Now to your question. It was Esteban Ayala more than anyone else who, in a sense, reeducated me. I understand you and he have been friends for a while."

"Yes, we have."

"Well, you see, I came onto the school board with about as much understanding of race as the average white person, which isn't much. I kind of assumed that if we got our funding levels back up, if we made sure our teachers all had their credentials and taught what they were credentialed to teach, if we used the latest standards-based curriculum, and if we got some extra tutoring services, we'd be in good shape. It was Esteban, with the work he and others were doing with what he calls Raza Studies, I still think of it as Mexican American Studies, we get into interesting discussions about nomenclature. Anyway, it was their work that gave me an entirely different perspective. About three or four years ago when they were trying to get the district to adopt Raza Studies, I didn't follow what they were about. Esteban had me visit his classroom and classrooms of a few other teachers who were doing similar things. Then he took me through the data on the academic impact of their work. Well, I was amazed, I guess you could say. They were getting results that teachers who carefully followed the standards-aligned curriculum packages weren't getting."

Roxane nodded. She was familiar with research on the relationship between student ethnic identity, curriculum relevance, teachers' academic expectations, and student learning. Most people gave education research selective attention, if that. Interesting that an older white man who wasn't an educator did pay attention to it. She wondered if his medical experience inclined him in that direction.

He was saying, "So when I realized you take the same approach as Esteban and his crew, and you're getting the same kind of result, I knew you were the one we needed. Harris has a lot going for him, but not what you have. He can get the trains running on time, and he might be able to tackle problems like our scarcity of affordable housing. But you, Dr. Bedford, have the vision for getting our students to thrive intellectually, and that's what we need more than anything else."

That was all Roxane needed to hear, and she now understood why Armstrong wanted to talk with her personally.

"So back to my question about other board members," she said, "as well as members of the public who might not be too happy with changes I would want to make."

"Right. Here's what I learned to do to support Esteban," he said. "I've come to realize that he can explain why something makes sense to a bunch of white parents, let's say, but they might not listen. Some of them think he has some agenda that's strictly for Latino students. But if I say exactly what he said, they do listen. So he and I spend quite a bit of time together, usually with him getting me up to speed on what he's thinking about and why, and me talking him through the politics of the thing. Then we tag team, we plan who's going to say what to whom. Ask him about it. That process is what I propose to offer you."

"You plan to continue on the school board?"

"Until I get voted off, and so far people have been willing to put up with me. Being a damned good fundraiser helps." He beamed. "Now, what other questions do you have?"

Later, as they went their separate ways, Roxane felt gratified to know that Armstrong had seen and heard her for who she was. He had the vulnerability to admit ignorance, and to learn. That vulnerability allowed him to see beyond an applicant's resume and physical characteristics, and to recognize the values a person stood for. Yes, she could work with someone like that.

***

After dinner the following day, Roxane sat in the living room studying the Cypress View contract. One hundred seventy thousand with benefits seemed like a very good salary. Was this the same figure Harris had been offered, or was he offered more? Men often were, especially if they were white. She sighed. No way of knowing what his offer had been, short of asking Armstrong. And if Armstrong approved of the offer, unless she completely misread him, both were identical. She decided not to worry about it.

She looked up as Imani galloped down the stairs, waving her laptop like a bandana.

"Mama, Grandma, I just got something you'll want to see."

"Be careful with that, Precious!" Roxane grabbed at the flailing laptop that missed the wall by a hair.

"Where's Grandma?" Imani asked.

"Probably lying down," Roxane replied. "What's up?"

"What is it, Baby?" Ada entered the living room, a paperback she was reading in hand.

"You know the Dwyers in Chattanooga I friended on Facebook? Well, they don't all have the last name of Dwyer. One lady is named Celia Cobb. Her mom was a Dwyer."

Roxane and Ada exchanged glances. Ada said, "Are we supposed to recognize that name? 'Cause I sure don't."

"No. But Celia Cobb has looked through deeds records in the courthouse near where Edward and Maisie Dwyer lived, and she found some interesting stuff. She sent me one that's really funny. It was hard to read because of the old handwriting and how they talked back then. I had to study it for a while, but once I got it, it made me laugh."

"What is it?" Roxane asked as Imani perched herself on the edge of the couch and opened her laptop.

"Here, let me read it to you:

Trust deed, Edward Dwyer and D. E. Harris. I Edward Dwyer have this day for and in consideration of the sum of one dollar to wit bargained and sold, and do hereby bargain, sell, transfer and convey unto D. E. Harris two cows, one a jersey red cow about 6 years old, and the other a red muly cow same age. Said jersey cow will soon bring a calf which is included in this sale and transfer, also one sorrel horse about 8 years old to have and to hold ...

As Imani read, Roxane pictured her ancestor Edward, proud but in need of cash, being helped by someone, a neighbor perhaps, who loaned him the funds in a creative way. Clearly, Edward would not accept a handout. He would not have even mentioned the need if it were not critical. This Harris person found a way to help him without compromising his dignity, and without actually depriving him of the farm animals he depended on.

"Who was D. E. Harris?" Ada asked.

Imani shrugged. "I don't know."

Roxane recalled, "I seem to remember our Dwyers lived next door to some white Harrises in the census. Maybe this D. E. guy is one of them." Another Harris. They seemed to pop up like mushrooms. This one, though, seemed humane, caring, unlike the self-absorbed Harris whom Roxane met in the hospital, the one who seemed to feel entitled to whatever he wanted.

"Can you print me a copy?" she asked. "Maybe tomorrow I'll do a little digging and see what I can find out."

"Sure. I'll go print it right now."

"Before you do – have a seat, Mama. You, too, Imani," Roxane said. "I've been doing some checking on our finances, and poring through the contract Cypress View offered me, just to make sure I'm not missing anything."

"And?" Ada asked after a pause.

"I need to make sure both of you are behind me if I say yes."

Imani threw her arms around her mother's neck. "I'm proud of you Mama. I know you worry that I'll have to make all new friends, and that Sondra and I won't be able to see each other in person a lot, but I can deal with that. We'll see each other all the time on FaceTime and Instagram, anyway."

"I'm proud of you, too, Baby, and I'll be right there with you," Ada said, her voice choking with emotion. "Your father, looking down on you from heaven, must be so very proud, too."

"Okay. I love you both. Here goes." Roxane pulled out her cell phone and dialed Darin Armstrong.

***

Saturday afternoon Roxane was home working at her desk while Imani visited Sondra. Suddenly Roxane heard her mother hollering from the kitchen, "Baby, come look at this! I just figured out who D. E. Harris was."

Roxane dashed downstairs and found her mother waving something as if it were on fire.

"This man ..." Ada pointed to the item. "Remember when we couldn't figure out how this photo got into the Spencer Dwyer stuff? Well, this man is D. E. Harris, full name Daniel Ethan Harris, and former clerk of Monroe County. I was nosing around in Ancestry.com and found a picture of him that's almost identical to this one we have."

Roxane stared. "What on earth was a photo of the county clerk doing with Spencer Dwyer's records? Who put it there? There has to be more to it than that loan. Oh my, how was he be connected to our Dwyer ancestors? Could he have been a relative?"

Ada searched the kitchen counter for the 1880 U.S. census page Imani had printed a few days earlier, finding it buried under yesterday's newspaper. Just as Roxane had recalled, right next door to Edward and Maise Dwyer was a white Harris family, headed by Daniel E.

"So, he was a neighbor," Ada said. "But that still wouldn't explain why someone kept his photo with family records, even if he did make that loan to Edward Dwyer."

Eager to track down whatever clues could be found, Roxane sat down next to her mother to comb Ancestry's database. They quickly learned that Harris was born in Arkansas in the 1840s. No connection there – Edward Dwyer was born in Tennessee. The two were roughly similar in age, but they appeared to have grown up in different states. Exploring further, however, they learned that when he was a child, Daniel Harris had been sent to live with his grandparents in Monroe County, Tennessee after his father was killed in a duel. That meant Edward and Daniel did, in fact, grow up in the same county.

"But where were the Dwyers?" Roxane wondered. "I assume Edward's family had been owned by a white Dwyer family. Who were they? Friends of the Harrises, maybe?"

Suddenly Imani and Sondra bounded into the kitchen in search of something for lunch.

"I thought you were eating at Sondra's house, Baby," Ada said. "Let me see what I can toss together for you."

As her grandmother bustled around the kitchen, Imani shuffled through the papers on the table. "This is D. E. Harris?" she asked her mother as she looked at the photo.

"Yes, it appears to be. We're trying to unravel his relationship with Edward and Maisie Dwyer. We can't figure out why he would have arranged that loan, and then why the Dwyers would have hung onto a photo of him."

"He was county clerk," Ada added. "For him to do something like that, it seems like he and the Dwyers were on familiar terms."

"Maybe they hung out as kids," Imani offered.

"I doubt that," Roxane said. "Edward would have been a slave when he was a child. White boys didn't hang out with slaves, at least not past toddlerhood. Anyway, Daniel Harris was apparently raised by his grandparents. They might have lived near the Dwyers, and that could be how Edward and Daniel got to know each other. We were hunting for a white Dwyer family who might have owned Edward and his family, but we haven't found them yet. The closest Dwyers we could track down lived off in some other county."

Ada handed each girl a sandwich on a plate and a glass of sparkling water. "Clear yourselves a little space, but don't push the papers around too much."

Imani, hunched over her phone. "I'm contacting Celia Cobb. You remember, she's a Dwyer and lives in Chattanooga. She knows a lot about this stuff."

"Well, put your phone away so we can eat properly," Ada said. "Roxane, sit down and eat. I made you a sandwich, too."

A half hour later, lunch eaten and dishes cleared, Imani checked her phone for a response from Celia Cobb.

"Give her a chance to reply," Sondra said. "You get too impatient."

Imani's eyes widened. "She just did. She attached a copy of something. Let me open it and print it."

A minute later, all four were looking at a deed of sale. Jackson Harris – Daniel Harris's grandfather – had purchased four slaves, probably a family, from Robert Dwyer. In her note, Celia wrote, "Not sure why Harris left their name as Dwyer rather than changing it."

"Wow," Imani breathed. "D. E. Harris's grandfather actually bought our Dwyer family, and didn't bother changing their last name. Our Edward Dwyer grew up serving the Harrises."

Roxane was studying census records. "Edward Dwyer would have grown up in the same house as Daniel Harris, and then they lived next door to each other as adults, after the Civil War and Emancipation. Oh, my." Possibilities swirled through her head. Daniel Harris had descendants. Who were they and where had they gone? There couldn't be a connection between him and Ben Harris, could there? That would be too much of a coincidence.

"I need to know who Daniel Harris's descendants were. How easily can we find out?" she asked.

Using family trees posted on Ancestry.com, it took mere minutes to trace D. E. Harris's descendants up to the 1940s. After that, records thinned out and census data were unavailable to protect the privacy of the living. Did Dr. Ben Harris descend from D. E. Harris? It was possible, though highly improbable.

Since childhood, Roxane had been aware that someone bought and enslaved her ancestors, and that an indelible mark of bondage was the surname of an owner. She didn't learn much about that history in school, though. Most of what she learned about slavery and emancipation came from stories told at home and in church, then later when she studied Black history as an undergraduate. For years, Roxane had looked askance at any white person she met with a surname in her own family – Bedford, Dwyer, or Tower.

Now she added the name Harris. Harrises had never figured into the stories she learned about her ancestors, but obviously they were around. The census confirmed that. The census also confirmed that Harris was a common name. Roxane knew two Ben Harrises in college, one Black and the other white. Hundreds, maybe thousands, of Ben Harrises had lived.

Odds were that her competitor, Dr. Ben Harris, had no connection with the D. E. Harris who loaned Edward Dwyer twenty dollars, likely the same Daniel E. Harris who lived next door to him. Roxane couldn't tie Ben Harris to family trees she found because she had no idea where he was born and grew up, nor did she know names of his parents or grandparents.

Yet, she couldn't simply let go of the possibility that their histories were linked. Descendants of slaves rarely met descendants of the people who had owned their ancestors – and vice versa. People acted as though the histories of Black Americans and white Americans were separate. But they weren't, and this was one link she could actually look into. She said, "White and black histories in this country have always been connected. I have to know if Ben and I are part of the same past, and it looks like the only way I'm going to know is to go ask him."

"Does it matter?" her mother asked. "Is that worth finding out?"

"If his ancestors owned ours, unlikely as it is, I want to know," Roxane said. "Slavery might have ended a long time ago, but it has a long afterlife. Harris has said some things designed to elevate himself over me. His sense of entitlement didn't just spring from nowhere."

CHAPTER 16

BACK TO BEGINNINGS

Ben glared out the window. It was Saturday. He should be doing something with his sons. He should have thought to get tickets to a Giants baseball game. Instead, here he was, stewing alone, while Evan was out playing baseball, Jason was at a friend's house, and Lisa was – well, who knew where she was. She might be with Gary, that new heartthrob of hers. Ben shuddered. How was he going to win her back, especially now that it seemed she no longer liked what he had to offer?

He shut his eyes and lay back on the couch. His healing bones ached. No wonder. Earlier in the week he had returned to work fulltime, despite his doctor's advice. He couldn't just sit around anymore, waiting for his body to recover, waiting for someone else to give him a green light. He had lost control over most things, but he wouldn't give up his authority entirely. Before the accident he loved his work, and his work was the one thing that might restore him.

Ben was angry. He was angry that he spent so much of the past couple of months completely bored and useless, all because of that horrific car accident. Returning to work helped, although it did nothing to alleviate his anger with Mitchell. Growing up in quiet Ballard, how did Mitch become so dishonest, so devious? How had Ben's relationship with him – a relationship that had never been important – become so powerful and so poisonous?

Ben was angry that his family was falling apart, and he wasn't sure what he could do about it. Somewhere along the way, Lisa had changed. The joy she used to derive from creating a home and family with Ben had evaporated like a vernal pond in a drought. He still wasn't sure how or why. She said she had asked him to stay home more, to show the family more attention. But she hadn't really shared what she was feeling. She hadn't opened up to him. Or maybe she had simply stopped talking with him about things that mattered, assuming he didn't care or wouldn't listen. And maybe that was the problem – he didn't really listen.

And then there was that Bedford woman. Ben shouldn't feel anger toward her, but he did. At the very least, she had swooped in and grabbed from him the golden ring, the opportunity that should have been his. Somehow she had bewitched him, leading him to turn down the job offer because of the stain it left on his soul. By all rights, that job should still be his. How did someone far less qualified than he was manage to snatch it out from under him? Why had Darin Armstrong allowed that to happen? Armstrong could have persuaded Ben that he was needed in Cypress View, he could have helped Ben figure out a compromise with his family, he could have tamped down the sour taste Mitchell had poured over everything Cypress View. But he hadn't.

Bedford reminded Ben of the Black kids who were bussed into his school when he was a kid. They were bussed in so they would have more opportunity than their neighborhood schools afforded them. That opportunity was supposed to enable them to do better in life. It wasn't supposed to empower them to shove people like Ben out of the way.

Ben was angry.

The phone jerked his attention into the present.

"Ben, this is Roxane Bedford," came the voice over the line. "Do you have a minute?"

Was she clairvoyant? He couldn't think what to say. "Dr. Bedford. This is indeed a surprise," he finally muttered. "I guess I should congratulate you on landing the job. I hope it works out for you."

"Thank you," she said. "I'd like to see you on a different matter, if you don't mind. This one is personal. Would it be convenient to drop in, say, tomorrow afternoon sometime?"

"Okay," he said, hesitating. "How's one o'clock?"

***

Later that afternoon, Evan, Jason, and Lisa shuffled into the family room for the talk Ben and Lisa had been planning.

"What's up?" Evan asked. "You wanted to talk to us?"

"Yes. Sit down, both of you," Ben said. Lisa opened her mouth as if to begin the conversation, but Ben didn't want to give her a chance to direct it.

"Your mom and I have been going through a rough time. It doesn't have anything to do with you," he said. "It's our problem, but it will affect both of you."

Seeing the puzzled expressions on both boys' faces, Ben fished around in his mind for what to say next. He thought he had it all worked out, but the sentences he had rehearsed earlier in the day seemed to have vanished.

Lisa jumped in. "Your dad and I have decided to live apart for a while. We aren't getting a divorce, but we are separating until we can work out our problems."

Jason looked as though he were about to cry. "Why?"

"This doesn't have anything to do with you, sweetie," Lisa said as she stroked his shoulder. "We both want you around, we'll just be splitting our time with you."

Ben added, "Your mother and I have gotten on each others' nerves, and just need some time away from each other."

"I told you," Evan grumbled to Jason. "That's why Mom sleeps in the guestroom these days."

Ben and Lisa looked at each other.

"I'm going to stay here, and your mom is looking for a house to rent." Ben had stressed to Lisa that as long he stayed in their current house, they couldn't afford to buy a second house.

"Where?" Evan asked.

"I'm not sure yet, but I'd like the two of you to help me pick it out. I thought we'd take a look at some possibilities tomorrow," Lisa replied brightly.

"I don't want to move." Jason's face began to crumple.

"You aren't moving, exactly," said Ben. "You'll still have your room here, and you'll still be here a lot of the time. But you'll also have another whole room that you'll get to use as well."

Nothing felt satisfactory to Ben about the conversation, but at least he and Lisa confronted the issue with the boys as a team. It had been quite a while since they had last functioned as a team. Maybe it would make her wistful for the old days.

He gave both boys a firm hug. And he fervently wished Roxane hadn't called with the intent of seeing him the next day.

***

Roxane arrived on time the next afternoon. Ben explained his wife and boys were out doing some shopping. He didn't mention that what they were shopping for was a suburban house to rent.

As he poured her a glass of iced tea, Ben wondered why Roxane was here. She was just the person he did not want to see. He felt annoyed that she was disrupting his Sunday afternoon.

After a few pleasantries, Roxane explained the purpose of her visit. "My mother, the genealogist in the family, was digging around to locate information about some of our ancestors from Tennessee by the name of Dwyer. We started with a few names, a newspaper article, and some photos. The photo that puzzled us most was this one." She retrieved a photo from a large envelope and placed it in front of Ben.

Ben felt his stomach drop. "Where did you get that?" he stammered, blood draining from his face.

Roxane's eyes widened. "It was in some of my mother's things that were passed down from her mother. So you recognize this man?"

Ben's mouth went dry. He licked his lips before replying. "That's a photo of my ancestor Daniel Harris, I believe. It's almost identical to one someone posted on Ancestry.com." He felt as though a ghost he had only recently become aware of was beckoning him. As though Roxane, who shouldn't know a thing about Daniel Harris, had suddenly walked into Ben's present from his family's past.

Minutes passed as they stared at each other, or at least it felt that way. Finally, Roxane put the photo back in the envelope as she said, "I had wondered. It appears that Daniel Harris's grandparents – the people who actually raised him – they owned a family I descend from."

Ben was taken aback. "How can you know that?" he demanded.

She explained that she descended from Chattanooga Dwyers, and that her daughter had friended Dwyers in the Chattanooga area on Facebook. One of these friends supplied them with copies of two deeds from the Monroe County Courthouse: a transaction between D. E. Harris and Edward Dwyer, and the deed of sale in which Jackson

Harris purchased a family from Robert Dwyer, who lived in another county. She showed him the documents.

"I have a fragment of this one," he stammered as he fingered the farm animal deed of sale. He took a deep breath and tried again. "I had no idea. It caught my attention because his loan seemed like a nice thing to do for a neighbor. You're saying that neighbor had been Daniel's grandfather's slave? Daniel caught my interest because my life parallels his in some ways. We both almost died. But I never thought ..." Ben's voice trailed off. "Slavery was all so long ago. Generations ago. Is there something you want from me?"

Roxane studied him. "Just a chance to dialog with a descendent of the people who owned my ancestors. You never think about slaves in your family's past, do you? But I've always wondered who owned us. Imagine owning people. That you and I should be connected in this way might seem startling. But descendants of my family's owners are walking around every day, most of them, like you, probably oblivious to their family's history of owning people. Descendants of the people your family owned, like me, are also alive today. But the difference is that people like me are conscious that generations ago, somebody robbed our people of our humanity. Descendants of the owners airbrush the whole thing away, but we can't. And what's hard is that we don't usually know who robbed our ancestors unless we dig around. And then we might locate some clues, like my mother did."

Ben was floored. Even if his ancestors had owned slaves, what did that have to do with him, here and now? Was she trying to make him feel guilty? What could there possibly be to talk about?

He said, "Okay, maybe if you go back far enough, an ancestor of mine owned one of yours. But that was, what, over a hundred and fifty years ago. Are you here now to get back at me for that inflammatory news story about you? Trying to make me feel guilty for things I didn't have anything to do with? I didn't set up that interview, you know. That wasn't my doing." Ben felt like he was shaking, he was so angry.

"I'm not trying to get back at you for anything," she said. "But that news story was a good example of the violence white people use all the time to keep people like me in our so-called place."

He didn't respond. She continued, "All I want from you is an acknowledgement that your family, generations back, learned and then taught their children to believe that people like me are not fully human. And that this belief still exists, and it shapes a lot of white behavior, not to mention social policies like who gets access to health care."

What did health care have to do with Daniel Harris in Tennessee? She must want more than an admission from him that his ancestors had owned slaves. He stared mutely.

"Remember when I came to see you in the hospital?" she asked.

He nodded.

"Do you know why I came?"

"You were in the neighborhood for a meeting and June Washington asked you to drop some materials off on your way home."

"That's true. I could have left them at the information desk, but I was curious who you were. And when I met you, all I wanted to do was to give you my condolences on your accident," she said.

When he didn't respond, she continued, "The fact that we were competitors didn't bother me. What did bother me was your presumption, without ever having met me, that you would prevail and that an appropriate place for me might be to work *for* you, not *with* you. You also ignored the title that goes with my doctorate, something I encounter only from white people."

There she goes with the race card, he said to himself. "You're blowing things way out of proportion. Frankly, I had no idea why you were there. And I'm sorry I forgot to call you doctor. I thought maybe you came to gloat, thinking I was out of the running."

"No," she replied, "I only wanted to meet you and see how you were. That was my entire agenda."

Seconds passed. He squirmed. Finally, Roxane said, "Okay, I want to try something. But first, I want you to understand that I believe you and I can be colleagues. But there's a lot of garbage in the way, garbage that has its roots in our shared history. Can I try telling a story, based on the bits of our history I have, and my extended reading of U.S. history through the lens of Black people?"

Ben wished she would leave, but he was also curious to learn anything more about Daniel. He agreed to listen to her story, and then he would show her to the door.

***

It was a scorching mid-July day in 1851. Daniel pleaded, "Aw, come on, Edward. No one'll notice if you're gone a few minutes." Edward, the ten-year-old son of the slave family Daniel's grandfather owned, kept his eyes trained on the tomato plants he was tying up.

Daniel continued, "It's so hot today. We can just splash in the creek a little bit, then come right back. No one will ever know." He could go by himself, of course, but he preferred company, and the only one available was Edward. Neither of his younger sisters liked playing in water. The last time he hauled them along, they refused to get wet. His eighteen-year-old Uncle Ezekiel had gone into Madisonville with Grandpa, but Ezekiel didn't like to fool around with someone six years his junior anyway.

And it was a long walk to the nearest neighbor. So that left Edward. Daniel knew he wasn't supposed to play with him any more, but who would know?

Edward continued tying vines to their stakes and thinning tomato clusters while Daniel studied the damp spots on the back of Edward's shirt. One of Edward's jobs was to tend the vegetables, and when finished, he was supposed to help his father, his older brother, and a couple hired hands who were clearing brush for a road Grandpa wanted. But on a hot afternoon like this one, Edward took his time with the vegetables.

"I hereby order you to go swimming in the creek with Daniel," Daniel said in a childish parody of his grandfather's voice.

Edward jerked his head up and stared. Daniel could tell he was sorely tempted.

"C'mon, c'mon, c'mon. I won't tell anyone. Just come," he pleaded. "You're as hot as I am. You can come back to the tomatoes, all cooled off."

Edward jumped to his feet. "I bet I kin outrun you," he said as he dashed toward the path to the creek.

Once in the water, the boys reverted to the playful relationship of their childhood. Edward had been just five when Daniel and his two younger sisters had arrived from Arkansas to live with their grandfather and step-grandmother. Their father, trying to establish his cotton plantation, had been killed in a duel. A few days later, Daniel's grandfather and Uncle Ezekiel, both strangers to Daniel, had arrived in Arkansas to sell Pa's slaves and acreage in order to pay off his debts. Grandpa decided to take the three children back to Tennessee after realizing their mother, now destitute, was nonetheless responsible for three older children from her first marriage. She would need to remarry as quickly as possible. A bad situation with few choices. Tearfully, she agreed to hand Daniel and his sisters over to their grandfather.

When the children were settled in Tennessee, Daniel, who was seven at the time and furious at suddenly having lost both parents, gravitated toward Edward, the only male nearby within his age range. At the time, no one made a fuss about the slave owner's grandson playing with a slave child. In fact, the arrangement seemed to suit the adults – Daniel's grandparents, who had been concerned about their grandson's angry refusal to talk to them, and Edward's parents and older sister, who looked after both boys.

When Daniel turned ten, however, Grandpa began to instruct him on how to be a white man. Lesson number one: a white man never plays with the slaves. By then, Daniel's studies at school occupied so much of his time that the two boys naturally drifted apart. The boys' school was housed in a Methodist church in Sweetwater, the largest town in Monroe County. Daniel's teacher Mr. Lewis, only slightly older than Uncle Ezekiel, managed to inspire in Daniel a love of mathematics. Mr. Lewis told Daniel he had a knack for numbers and would become a first-rate bookkeeper when he grew up. Daniel spent many evenings working on problems his teacher sent home with him.

So he didn't see much of Edward. Except in summer when there was no school and Daniel's chores on the farm left him with stretches of free time. Like on this particular day.

Horsing around in Notchey Creek rekindled their childhood friendship, if only for a sliver of a blazing afternoon. They wrestled, they splashed and dunked each other, they whooped and hollered. Finally, thoroughly drenched, they made their way back up the trail that cut through dense foliage, laughing and slapping each other as they went.

As they emerged from the bushes, Edward froze.

"What's wrong – oh." Looking up the house, Daniel saw Grandpa, apparently back from Madisonville. He stood on the porch like a statue, watching them approach, the switch in his hand.

"Grandpa," Daniel stammered.

His grandfather glared. "Boy," he nodded toward Edward, "I think your ma'am wants you. I'll deal with you later. Daniel, you come with me."

"Grandpa, don't use that thing on us." Daniel pointed at the switch. "It was so hot today we just needed to cool off. So we could do our work better."

Grandpa trained a steely glare on Daniel. "Come inside with me."

"You're not gonna beat Edward, are you?" Daniel's voice shook. "It wasn't his fault, he went because I told him to."

"You told him to," Grandpa repeated.

Daniel stared at the floor, his mind whirling. What if he caused Edward to get a beating? He had never seen his grandfather actually whip one of the slaves, but he had seen him take the switch to their shoulders or the backs of their legs.

Seared into Daniel's memory was witnessing his father lash a slave. His pa didn't realize Daniel was nearby, but that might not have mattered anyway. Pa ripped the slave's shirt off and tied his hand to a pole over his head. Daniel had never seen the man's back before; the skin was all rippled and gouged like an angry hillside after a fire.

He hadn't expected the first lash to crack so loudly. The man didn't cry out right away, not until the lashes dug deeply into his skin and blood coursed down his back. Before it was over, Daniel had run into the house, hands over his ears to block the sound of the man's suffering and his father's whip.

201

His father returned to the house when it was over. When he discovered Daniel sobbing on his bed, he sat down next to the boy and gently asked what was wrong. When he learned that is son had witnessed the lashing, Daniel's father sighed. "Son, you have to understand that those people aren't like you and me. They don't feel pain the same way you and I do. And from time to time, I just need to remind them who's boss. That boy Jim, he was caught trying to run off. I just can't have that. Paid good money for that boy, and he's a strong worker. He'll be okay in a day or two. You understand?"

Daniel nodded as if he understood, but he didn't. Pa stood. "Son, you're gonna need to toughen up. One of these days, you'll be one keeping the slaves in line. I didn't like it either at first, but you get used to it."

But Daniel never did get used to it.

As far as he knew, Grandpa didn't whip his slaves. He owned just this one family, and farms in this part of Tennessee weren't like the plantations in Arkansas. On his pa's plantation, the slaves had lived in little huts away from the family's house. His pa supervised their work, but never actually worked with them. The only slave Daniel remembered getting to know was Bertha, who cooked and cleaned for the family. Here, there was only one slave family and Daniel was on easy terms with all four members. This part of Tennessee was too hilly for big plantations. While farmers grew crops like wheat, their farms were small. Daniel knew only a couple of farmers who owned many slaves; most didn't own any. People like Grandpa were more likely to hire single white men as hands than they were to buy slaves. And, they often worked right alongside the help, whether white or Black.

But still, Daniel didn't doubt that Grandpa knew how to use a whip, and would do so if he thought it was needed.

"Grandpa, I told Edward to come to the creek with me. He didn't want to do it at first. But I get so tired of being by myself sometimes. The girls are no fun at the creek, they won't even get wet. So I talked Edward into going with me."

After a minute, Grandpa said, "Sounds like you don't have enough work to do around here. We'll fix that. I have some business dealings tomorrow in Sweetwater and I'm taking you with me.

But you need to realize that you put Edward in a fix. He knows he needs to obey us, and I guess that includes you. I told him to tend the garden. Then you told him to run off with you. You shouldn't have given him an order contradicting mine, and he shouldn't have listened to you."

"I won't do it again, Grandpa. You're not gonna beat Edward, are you?"

Grandpa picked up the switch and waved it. "I should use this on the both of you." He dropped it to the floor as he continued.

"Something else you need to understand. It was okay for you and Edward to play when you were little, but he's not all that different from a dog. As a baby, you and the dog were on the same level, but as you grew up, you outgrew the dog. Same with the Negroes. Your mind keeps developing, but theirs doesn't. Your sense of right and wrong develops, but theirs doesn't. The only way you can act like equals is to lower yourself down to their level. They're never going to come up to your level. God didn't make them that way."

"I understand, Grandpa," Daniel said. The switch let him know it would be best not to argue. So he didn't.

But he wondered. During the half hour splashing around in the creek, he felt as though Edward was a boy just like him – the same way he had felt when they played together as youngsters.

But then, Daniel thought, if Negroes were actually as smart as white people, wouldn't someone have noticed? Wouldn't they be reading the Bible, maybe writing letters to each other like white people did? Wouldn't they keep track of their money in ledgers? Maybe the owners didn't pay slaves because they were incapable of keeping track of cash.

That Sunday in church, Daniel noticed for the first time that all the pictures of God and Jesus looked an awful lot like Grandpa and Uncle Ezekiel, and not one whit like Edward and his pa. That had to mean that God created white people in his image. Daniel wasn't sure whose image God created the slaves in, but it couldn't have been in God's image. No, white people were the ones closest to God, except the angels of course. All other forms of life were created at lower levels, and that was just the nature of things.

***

"So even if Daniel wasn't one of the ones whipping his Black workers, he still learned to accept a system that dehumanizes people like me," Roxane concluded. "All I want from you is your recognition of that system and how it benefits you, and if at all possible, your commitment to changing it."

Ben sensed she expected him to understand what her story from back in the 1800s had to do with him, here and now. He didn't condone white violence against African Americans. But hadn't he tacitly condoned Mitchell's attack on Roxane? Was that what she was digging to find out more about?

"You're a good storyteller," he said finally. "But even if things happened just the way you imagined – well, that was very long before you and I were born. You can't just recreate a story from generations ago and assume it explains what happens today."

"Ben, that history isn't dead," Roxane said. "That past is still with us, and we need to come to grips with it. I still live it every day, and you do too, even if you don't recognize it. Our lives and our histories are braided, don't you see? Edward experienced trauma when your ancestors treated him as less than human. Daniel also experienced trauma when he was forced to learn to see someone he cared about as not quite human. That trauma hasn't gone away. Every time a young Black man gets shot by an officer, or a Black kid in school gets punished for something white kids get away with, or the creations of Black artists are ignored while white artists are celebrated, we relive centuries-old trauma."

Ben wasn't sure how to respond, so Roxane continued. "For a white person, learning to see a childhood friend as not human because of the color of his skin must have been traumatic. I have to believe it was. This is important because what's at stake is your recognition of my humanity. A white kid grows up connecting with someone, regarding that person as a friend and as very much like himself, and then the kid's parents, the people he trusts the most, drum into him that this person, this childhood friend has no more humanity than a farm animal. Who do you trust? Who do you believe? Your parents or your experience with that person? I would think having to choose would be traumatic."

"It might have been," Ben conceded. "It probably was. But as I said, that was generations ago."

"But trauma gets passed on. We know that parental trauma affects offspring physiologically. There's even a theory that trauma changes the DNA, and gets passed on that way. That's what they found in some research on Union prisoners during the Civil War, and how the trauma of starvation they experienced in prison camps affected their DNA."

Ben started. "You're saying I've inherited some of the trauma Daniel Harris experienced in war at a genetic level?"

"I'm not familiar with trauma he experienced, and I'm not a geneticist. I don't know," Roxane said.

"You're suggesting he passed on at least three traumas to me. Starvation, near-drowning, and learning to see his playmate as inhuman and deserving of cruelty," Ben said.

"Well, I'm not sure what to think about genetic research," Roxane repeated. "It's out there, but as I say, I'm not a geneticist. However, I do see trauma as passed on, at least through the world we construct for the next generations. Daniel certainly had to grapple with a moral issue. Either his family acted immorally by enslaving human beings, or the people they enslaved really were less than human. I have no idea how Daniel would have made sense of that as a kid. But then, as an adult, what did he pass on to his children? After all, even though slavery was abolished, the people who had been enslaved were still kept down with violence. Most white people teach their kids to believe they're superior, and to think the people they are holding down get what they deserve."

"Roxane, you're painting things too – too – well, there are all kinds of shades of gray," Ben protested. In his own family, after all, it was Lisa, not him, who taught prejudice to their sons. Roxane even seemed to be attacking Daniel, a good man who treated his Black neighbor with respect. "If what you say is true, then tell me why Daniel helped your ancestor with that loan. It seems he still had some regard for Edward as a fellow human being."

"Yes, he probably did. He probably went through life with an unresolved tension between what he was taught about Black people, and what he actually experienced," Roxane agreed. "But I wonder whether, as county clerk, he ever did anything to challenge the growing virulent racism around him. That racism constantly thwarted Edward while benefiting Daniel. I wonder if Daniel ever recognized what all Edward and his people were up against, and how much it would matter if white people like him actually stood up and did something."

"There's no record one way or the other. I don't think he was one of those people who went out on the street with protest signs," Ben felt exasperated. What did she expect of Daniel – and of him, for that matter?

"No, and if he did, you'd probably know about it," Roxane pressed him. "He would have been regarded as a traitor of sorts. Treating Edward humanely isn't the same as challenging the system that continued to dehumanize Edward, and his son Spencer, and Spencer's son Porter, and on and on. Don't you see? Daniel was what you might think of as a good white person, but he never challenged the racial order. He was part of it, it worked for him. But Edward, and then the rest of us, we spend our lives challenging that system. And what do we get for it? I get called a Black radical troublemaker who a school board shouldn't hire into a leadership position. My daughter's father got treated as a dangerous Black radical and criminal. My father, a Black Panther, was seen as part of a dangerous gang that wants to overthrow the system and kill the cops. That's just because we take on a system designed to keep us down. What I need from you is recognition that both of us inherited a system designed for people like you and not for people like me. It's a system that can be changed, but you need to be part of that work."

Ben felt as though all that had been building up inside Roxane for the last few weeks had just found release, and he was the target. He didn't know what to say. She seemed to want a response from him, but what? He couldn't simply sweep away the decades of racism that had impacted her ancestors, and he couldn't see the point of apologizing that Daniel didn't become an antiracist crusader. And how could he undo today's racism? The problems seemed too big, he seemed too small.

But he couldn't say that. It would be like brushing her off.

Roxane seemed to be waiting for a response, but Ben couldn't think of one. Not yet, anyway.

Presently, she stood and thanked him for seeing her. He mumbled a reply. Then, to his relief, she left.

CHAPTER 17

UNRAVELING BRAIDS

As she drove home, Roxane pictured Ben trying to make sense of their conversation. She had left him speechless. A deer in the proverbial headlights. She had hoped he would engage with her, but she probably expected too much. She was like the child trying to shake down a cat who was perfectly content up in a tree, right where it was. Best left alone?

No. History had woven their lives together. Many people think race separates us, but in a way, Roxane thought, it also links us, and we need to follow those links. Throughout human history, people have harmed others they regard as different due to religion, culture, or geographic location. But race – the idea that we can be divided and ranked hierarchically based on biology – belief in that idea added a deep layer of insidiousness. There would be no such thing as race if European landowners – which probably included some of Ben's ancestors – hadn't latched onto the idea four hundred years ago, as a way of dividing people from different parts of the world whom they sought to control. Give status and privileges to the patchwork multitudes from Europe in exchange for their languages and their love for the homeland – unite them as white – and they would help keep everyone else in line. She hoped that sooner or later, Ben would come to terms with how that history continues to play out.

Roxane thought about the direct line connecting the long history of white violence against Black people with police brutality today. Whites justified violence with racial stereotypes, while using violence to maintain control. Just a few days ago, a photo on the internet showed a man taking a knee during the national anthem at the White House's "Celebrate America" event. That event replaced what would have been a White House visit by the Super Bowl victors, the Philadelphia Eagles, which the president had canceled after most players refused to come. They refused because of his demand that players stand during the national anthem. Missing in most news accounts was much discussion about why Black athletes chose to kneel. Kneeling had become a form of peaceful protest against state-sanctioned police brutality toward people of color, particularly African Americans. The brutality itself has such a long, ugly history. The real problem was how to confront that brutality, rather than how to get Black athletes to remain standing.

But like so many white people, Ben seemed unable to participate in a conversation about race – to dig into issues, analyze experiences, ask questions. He knew stock phrases – *slavery was so long ago, that doesn't have anything to do with me, my ancestors were good people*. But he punctuated them with silence. She had poured out her heart, wishing to hear what was in his heart. But no, he was polite and brief, about as responsive as a store clerk who didn't have an item she was looking for.

Roxane recalled a recent Southern Poverty Law Center report that documented a rise in hate crimes for the fourth year in a row. Almost nine thousand had been reported to the FBI the previous year. Over one-fourth of them were directed against Black people because of race. Anti-black hate crimes were followed by those targeting people for sexual orientation or gender identity, then by those targeting white people. Hate crimes based on religion followed, but were far fewer than those based on race.

She had hoped that personalizing how Ben's ancestors learned to see themselves as the most evolved and, therefore most deserving, might draw him into considering how that view continued to be taught generation after generation. She wanted him to recognize the present as built on the past, a past constructed by people not much different from us today. She wanted him to see her as a person he was connected to rather than a category of people he was distinct from – to see their histories as well as their destinies as woven together. And she wanted him to be willing to unravel the racist power dynamic, and to help create a new braid of respect and solidarity.

Daniel and Edward's relationship set the template for Ben's relationship with Roxane, and hers with him. That template scripted lives within a system that elevated one at the expense of the other,

Daniel over Edward, Ben over Roxane. And just like Roxane resented Ben assuming an air of superiority over her, he probably resented the lengths she went to in order to get him to listen. The system of racism bred resentments. In order to move forward, we would need to recognize pain and trauma we have been hauling around from one generation to the next.

But it wasn't Ben per se that was the problem. No, it was the social rules that positioned them unequally. If they worked at it, she believed they could become allies, although they would have to confront a chasm that lay between them. Funny thing, race – it doesn't even exist at a biological level. Humans created the idea, then built a huge apparatus around it. As allies, Roxane and Ben could confront that human-created system that pushed him forward and her back.

Maybe she hoped for too much. But no. She thought of Frank Roberts in the history department, who was beginning to work with her as she leaned on his commitment to teaching. She thought of Darin Armstrong, the former nurse who allowed his defenses to drop and his relationships with people of color to deepen. She thought of Henry Louis Gates' TV show *Finding your Roots*, in which every story complicated simplistic portraits of who we think we are and who we come from, many revealing long-hidden braids woven across racial, ethnic, and geographic ancestries.

She sighed. As long as Ben wanted status and recognition, he would probably continue to cast himself as an expert who could figure out everything by himself, and to view white power brokers and opinion creators as his touchstone, his role models to emulate. To become useful to urban education as she understood it, he would need to turn away from the pedestal of recognition that drew him like a moth to a candle. He would need to learn humility. Seemed unlikely.

***

"Everyone babysits, Mama." Imani thrust out her lower lip. "I'm almost fourteen. I'm old enough."

Roxane had just walked in the door after returning from Ben Harris's house when Imani accosted her.

"We'll be moving to Cypress View in a few weeks, who would you babysit? By the time you drum up business here, we're gone and we don't know anyone yet in Cypress View. Besides, what do you know about babysitting?" Roxane asked, wondering where this idea had come from. Imani, who had never shown an interest in young children, now thought she could care for them?

"How can I learn if you don't let me try?"

Roxane cringed as she pictured her daughter holding a screaming baby, clueless about what to do.

"Has one of our neighbors approached you about it?" Roxane asked.

"No, not yet. I could make little fliers and put them on doors, like the pizza companies do," she replied.

"Well, maybe when we get to Cypress View, there will be a class or something for young people to learn babysitting. It isn't something you can just do without some training," Roxane said, hoping to end the conversation.

"Sondra's babysitting this summer," Imani persisted as she trailed her mother into the kitchen. "Her mom helped her get started. Her mom said it's a good way for a girl to earn extra money and learn responsibility. I don't know why you won't help me like that."

Roxane's shoulders tightened as she recognized Imani's use of guilt to try to get her way. Extra money, now there was a motivator. And Sondra was the instigator. Roxane didn't oppose the idea of Imani learning to babysit, but the girl had no training or experience, and the family was about to move. How could she get her stubborn daughter to face reality?

"Who is Sondra babysitting for?" she asked, suspecting Imani's friend was probably helping a relative.

"The Wellingtons. They're a rich white family with a big fancy house. They usually hire Megan, a girl in our class, but Megan got sick and she recommended Sondra. Sondra's been over at the Wellingtons when Megan was babysitting, so she kind of knew what to do. And her older sister went with her the first time."

Images of Black women caring for white babies throughout U.S. history flooded Roxane's mind. Her female ancestors had given

212

over their time to caring for Ben's ancestors when they should have been able to devote that time to their own families. Many slave women had to spend more time with white children than with their own. Roxane thought of the generations of white mothers who were able to take jobs while their kids were cared for by underpaid Black domestic workers. Work with no benefits, no retirement, no security. As though reflected in those shards of history, nowadays one saw young women of color – like Sondra and Megan – pushing strollers of white babies.

No way could she allow her daughter to jump right into that stream of history. She said, "Baby, do you have any idea how many Black women through the ages have skimped on taking care of their own in order to earn money to feed their families by caring for someone else's white children?"

Imani regarded her mother as if she had sprouted weeds. "Mama," she said, "I'm thirteen. I don't have children and I'm not trying to feed the family. I want to learn responsibility and make a little extra money for myself. I don't even know what you're talking about."

Imani was right, of course. She didn't have to work and she didn't have children of her own. But Roxane couldn't shake the image of Black women feeding, bathing, consoling, rocking, telling stories to white children, and the exploitation such images evoked.

She sighed. "Let's at least get ourselves moved to Cypress View. It wouldn't make any sense to hire yourself out here, then move just as you land a first job. We'll look into baby sitter training as soon as we get there. I promise." Another idea struck Roxane. "You'd be a great tutor for young people. After we get ourselves moved, how about going to one of the community centers to see if there are kids you can help with schoolwork?"

Imani shrugged. "I guess. But I don't want to become a teacher."

Roxane countered, "You can tutor kids without becoming a teacher, although you'd be good at it."

Out went the lower lip again. "Mom, I'm really proud of you, but I don't want to be just like you. I was thinking about maybe going into fashion design, something like that."

Imani's announcement shouldn't have come as a surprise. Since she could walk, the girl had created striking looks with clothing and accessories. Roxane recalled finding her daughter at age three, digging through her drawer of scarves, tossing them on the floor as she sought the largest red scarf to wrap around herself like a sarong. At the moment, sporting a shirred white top under a denim jacket with slim jeans and a white head wrap, Imani could grace a magazine cover.

But it did come as a surprise. "Fashion design," was all she could think to say.

"You're disappointed in me," Imani said accusingly.

"No, Baby, I'm never disappointed in you." Roxane threw her arms around her daughter. "Just surprised, that's all. Maybe we can find out if any of the designers in San Francisco's Garment District is hiring interns for the summer."

The ring of her cell phone intruded. Roxane glanced at it. Esteban! Must be something going on in the Cypress View Unified School District.

"María Ximena Ayala just arrived," he announced in response to her greeting. "I'm about to text you a couple of pictures.

Who was María Ximena Ayala? Then the penny dropped. "Oh my god, your daughter!"

"Two hours old. I'm calling family right now. Godparents are family. She's so tiny and beautiful, she's just perfect." His voice choked.

"Esteban, I'm so excited! Congratulations, and when can I come see her?" Roxane realized she was dancing around the room.

"Whenever you want. Maybe give us a day or so. Brenda's exhausted."

Looking directly at Imani, Roxane said, "My daughter and I will come to welcome her into the world late tomorrow afternoon. I think you'll be needing a babysitter as she gets older, and Imani can't wait to help out."

To Imani's puzzled expression, Roxane said, "Baby, you now have a little godsister in Cypress View. Her name is María Ximena Ayala." Roxane's phone pinged as Esteban's photos came through. She opened them, them showed them to Imani. "Meet your godsister. You're about to become one of the most important people in this precious child's life. You'll learn to babysit, and to tutor and to love. You're a big sister now."

CHAPTER 18

SHARDS OF HISTORY

A tumult of emotions assaulted Ben as the door clicked shut behind Roxane. How dare she enter his home and accuse him of racism. She barely knew him; this was only their second meeting. At their first meeting, despite her protest to the contrary, she had seemed gleeful, anticipating that he would drop out of the applicant pool. He didn't, but in the end, she still managed to be the one who got the job. She had what she wanted. What did she have to gain by coming into his home and diminishing not just him, but his whole ancestral lineage?

His hands were shaking with anger. Maybe there was something to Mitchell's accusations about her after all. Maybe she was a troublemaker.

Ben turned on the TV and flicked through channels until he landed on a baseball game. The Dodgers versus the Pirates. He didn't care which team won, but watching it would distract him while he calmed down.

Presently, Lisa and the boys returned home.

"Found just what I was looking for," Lisa announced as she kicked off her shoes in the entryway. "A nice little three-bedroom in a quiet neighborhood on the north side of Morgan Hill."

"In a gated community?" Ben asked with condescension as she walked into the family room.

"No, it isn't," she replied matter-of-factly. "But it feels safe."

Her code for a white neighborhood, Ben thought to himself.

"I put a deposit on the lease. We take possession of the house July 1. You two like it okay, right?" She looked at Evan and Jason.

Evan mumbled, "It's okay, I guess." He turned to his dad. "Mom likes the schools there better, but I wish it was in San Jose. Jason got his bike back, you know."

"His bike?" Lisa asked.

Evan turned back to his mother. "Well, isn't that the main reason you want us to move to Morgan Hill, because you think people around here steal things?"

Ben was surprised he brought it up. Evan had been just as adamant as Lisa about the "apartment" kids stealing things. He must have changed his mind when his mother took the accusation seriously, which instigated an unwelcome change in his life.

Jason, ever the optimist, ran upstairs after his brother, yelling, "Hey, Evan, I'll beat you at *Fortnite*."

In Lisa and Ben's tug of war over where to send the boys to school in August, Ben had won a concession on behalf of Jason. While Lisa insisted on enrolling Evan in the best high school in Morgan Hill, she agreed to let Jason attend the middle school his elementary school fed into, mainly so he wouldn't lose the few friends he had.

But both boys would still be spending about half their time in the predominantly white neighborhood Lisa favored. Ben could just picture Roxane's reaction to him condoning his sons growing up surrounded by white people.

But he hadn't condoned it. He didn't agree with Lisa. He didn't equate whiteness with safety and honesty as she seemed to do.

As he listened to Lisa rattling around in the kitchen, he thought about how Roxane had accused Ben (and white people in general) of feeling entitled to the best, of fighting to protect systems that work for them but not for everyone. Take selective schools, for example. Designed to prepare kids for elite universities, a predominantly white school in an affluent neighborhood like the one Lisa had selected would wrap Evan in a bubble with other kids like himself, keeping him away from kids who were of various shades of brown. Away from the majority, really.

Would his sons grow up assuming, as he had done, that Americans of different backgrounds had separate histories, lead separate lives? As a kid in predominantly white Ballard, Ben learned to regard the people from other parts of Seattle as being from some other world. Even when the schools he attended were desegregated, he regarded the bussed in Black inner-city kids as interlopers he avoided, and he didn't remember anyone helping him to see things differently.

It wasn't until that summer in San Diego, after graduating from the university and landing in a Boys and Girls Club, that Ben finally started getting to know people like those he had earlier only viewed from a distance. Antwon's thirst to learn computers had surprised him, conflicting with what he thought African American youth might find interesting. As Ben got to know Antwon, then Antwon's friends, some of his assumptions gradually dissipated. Or at least, his preconceptions became more nuanced, more textured, less absolute.

Were his sons now learning to see people like themselves as separate and superior, as he had done? Maybe without realizing it, he and Lisa were playing a role similar to Daniel's grandfather when they used their own racial privileges to prepare their children to take up a life of power and authority. With the country's demographics more diverse now than they had been when Ben was young, perhaps his sons were starting to feel as though they were under siege. Maybe they would fight to become part of the elite, an elite that felt the need to barricade itself from everyone else. Was that the future he envisioned for them, the shards of history he and Lisa would now pass on to them? He could blame her, but to be perfectly honest, as their father, there was a lot more he could be doing.

Ben didn't see Lisa return to the family room. "You're pensive," she said, startling him. "Is there something else we should talk about?"

"I was just thinking about how complicated life is. I know you want to protect the boys, but by cocooning them, Evan especially, you're cutting them off from other people they share the planet with," he replied.

"I think we've already discussed that. I'm not cutting them off from people, as you put it. I'm just being more selective about the people they associate with." She turned to leave.

"Roxane Bedford was here while you were out," Ben said.

Lisa turned. "Here? In our house? What on earth did she want?"

"She and I share a history I didn't know about. Apparently, neither did she until recently. You might have heard me talk about my ancestor Daniel Harris."

"The one who survived the boat explosion?" Lisa asked. "You helped Jason write a story about him, I think it involved loaning money to someone."

217

"Not just someone. Roxane Bedford's ancestor," Ben said.

"What a coincidence, if it's true," Lisa said after a pause. "She came all the way over here to tell you that?"

"It's true, alright. She had a copy of the same loan document we used for Jason's paper, and a photo of Daniel. It seems Daniel Harris's grandfather owned some of her ancestors."

Ben took a deep breath. "People I descend from believed they had a right to own people, force them to work, then keep the earnings. Just think about that. I've been thinking about it all afternoon."

Lisa sat down opposite him, looking puzzled. "Roxane Bedford came here to do a guilt trip on you, it sounds like. She must resent you for having been offered the job first. Well, slavery ended generations ago. Why are you sitting here dwelling on it? You can't feel guilty for something you didn't have anything to do with."

"Guilt isn't what I feel," he said. "I'm realizing that my family passed down, generation after generation, a way of relating to people. When I was a kid, I learned to keep my distance from people who didn't look like me, to regard them as different. Maybe our school desegregation program wasn't supposed to teach that, but it did, simply by expecting us all to pretend we were colorblind when we were anything but. And I learned to make sure people who looked like me stayed in control. Even to this day when I vote, how often do I vote for a person of color? I can think of only a very few instances. Here we are now, doing it all over again with our own kids. Instead of just learning to be human, we learn to be white, to think of ourselves as superior and to act as if we were. Does that make any sense to you?"

Lisa stared at him as though he had suddenly begun speaking Chinese. Then she stood. "I don't know about you, but all I'm doing is protecting our kids and their future. They are white. Both of us are. I don't see why you're making a big deal of it. I just want to make sure our boys have the full range of opportunities and support available to them. That's what any parent would do, and if some parents aren't doing the same thing for their kids, well, it isn't my responsibility."

As she stalked out, sorrow washed over Ben. Not so much sorrow about her biases – heaven knew, we all have them. No, the sorrow was for their inability to talk about it. Not only were they not planning together for their future, but the basis on which they used to plan and communicate seemed to have vanished. Sometimes Lisa felt almost like a stranger to him. Ben realized that this must be what it feels like when a marriage dies.

As though Roxane were standing beside him, he recognized how Lisa went to battle to protect her sense of entitlement in order to pass it on to their sons. Maybe he hadn't seen this drive in her when they first married because they had no offspring then. But they did now, and she seemed to fear the hoards she believed were ripping away advantages she saw as due her family by dint of their hard work. The disappearance of Jason's bike had been one among many small incidents over the years in which she put faces to the people she feared. What they had in common was that most of them were not of European descent.

And hadn't Ben done the same thing most of his life? His experiences as a teacher and now as a school administrator had gradually created cracks and ripples through that worldview, but Ben began to wonder if he still clung to a presumption of superiority. That seemed to be Roxane's main message to him.

For the past few weeks, as he delved into his family history, he had found himself asking about this or that problem: *What would Daniel have done?* But perhaps the wisdom he imagined his ancestor would give him had unintentionally solidified a view of the world that took white supremacy for granted. What had Roxane said about Daniel? As nice as Daniel seemed to be, he had never done anything to challenge the racism right around him. He probably complained about the Klan, but he didn't take them on. As county clerk, he gathered data about people, but as far as Ben knew, he had never used that data to make racist systems in housing and employment visible, nor had he challenged those systems.

Would Roxane say the same thing about Ben? If so, would she be right? Now, all these decades later, Ben had a chance to do more than Daniel had done. But what?

It could be that he actually wasn't the best qualified candidate to lead Cypress View schools. For his entire professional life, he had equated qualifications with credentials, as well as breadth and depth of experience running classrooms, schools and school systems. Managing the details, creatively solving what was solvable, and not getting bogged down by problems that had no real solutions. But he didn't have a larger vision, at least not the way Roxane had, of what schooling should do for the young people of Cypress View, of California, of the nation. Maybe in a way he hadn't considered before, Roxane actually was better qualified.

Dinner was subdued. Afterward, Ben sat with the boys as they watched their favorite TV shows. He offered to make popcorn, but they declined. They went to bed early.

He flicked the channel to a history documentary. He didn't actually watch it, but by feigning interest, he could avoid talking with Lisa as he burrowed into himself. He had prided himself on making public education work for a wide diversity of kids. Now he wondered whether that was what he had actually been doing. He thought about the way he had enforced Richford's no hat policy. Kids had become used to it, but some of the Black students found it racially discriminatory. Maybe it was, and he hadn't listened.

As a math teacher, he had become known and respected for his students' high success rates, and for teaching in a way kids found fun and comprehensible. He had prided himself on teaching urban students well. He had wrapped his understanding of his own reputation around those successes. But there had been students he didn't reach, like Thomas and Carolyn, both very bright African American students who missed class routinely, and the Valdez twins who could have earned A's but spent class time competing for the attention of their peers. How many students had he excised from his memory in order to support the story he told himself about his successes as an urban teacher?

What would Roxane think of the way he handled the district's requirement that high schools offer ethnic studies? A group of Taylor students wanted what he considered a radical version that would focus on racism and community activism, while he and his administrative team favored teaching about diverse cultural contributions. He thought the class should emphasize the positive rather than delving into sticky and painful issues. His side won. Now he wondered if he had dismissed an opportunity to engage the school's students of color more deeply.

Just like he had missed cues from Lisa that they were drifting apart. Evan might have been more observant about family dynamics than he had been.

He needed to change.

As he drifted off to sleep, the history documentary playing softly in the background, Ben thought about Richford's security officer Chad Hernandez. A few months ago he had told Ben about being stopped by the police for failing to use a turn signal to change lanes. Chad said he was used to it, police stopped him all the time. Ben couldn't remember when the police had last stopped him, and thought Chad must be exaggerating. What if Chad was simply telling the truth? What if his experiences really were different from Ben's simply because of his brown skin?

CHAPTER 19

AFFIRMATION

It was Friday morning, the last teacher workday of the year. Roxane's palms felt moist as she walked toward the cafeteria. The kids now gone, teachers had a day to wrap up paperwork and departmental planning for the coming academic year. Taylor had a tradition of a staff lunch in the cafeteria, with the principal offering a few closing words. Her nervousness surprised her, since addressing the staff was nothing new. It must be anxiety about how they would react to what she planned to say.

Then too, there was her anxiety about the new job. She had been acting as though she had everything under control, but she felt as jittery as a teenager on a first date. Would she actually be able to do the work expected of a superintendent? There was so much she didn't know. She had no idea, for example, how to think about district-wide student transportation, or a district-wide plan for homeless and transient students. These were things she paid attention to with respect to her own school, but not for a whole school district. And what did she know about primary-level education? No more than the average parent. What was the best way to teach spelling, for instance? Of course, she wouldn't need to know exactly what primary grade teachers did, but she would need to make sure their work was supported. There was special education, rather different in elementary schools than in high school.

And then there was the matter of how she would get back to Oakland. After all, Oakland was her home. Her dream was to work with the schools there. Cypress View had never been part of that dream.

And what if she turned out to be a big flop in Cypress View?

Not a chance. She had already mastered many hurdles in her life, this was just one more. Stand tall.

"Any exciting plans for the summer, Dr. Bedford?" someone asked, coming up behind her. It was Margarita Rendón, the Spanish teacher.

"Not exactly." Roxane said, thinking about what lay ahead. "What about you? Don't you spend part of every summer in Spain?"

Margarita grinned. "I leave for León next Monday."

"Why León?"

"Friends there," Margarita replied. "We'll hang out a few days, then go take in some touristy stuff in Bilbao and Salamanca. Then I'm participating in a six week literature institute in Madrid."

Roxane smiled wistfully. She had never spent a summer out of the country, nor one doing "touristy stuff." She was usually either working or taking classes. The summer ahead of her, she would be moving. Margarita didn't know that yet, so Roxane simply wished her *buen viaje*.

The cafeteria buzzed. Teachers who often seemed harried when kids were around now laughed and joked with each other. Counselors and administrators chatted with teachers rather than sticking together. Teachers mingled across department lines; fences dissolved, at least for the moment.

When everyone was seated, food in front of them, Roxane walked to the podium.

"I will miss all of you," she began. Surprise registered on many faces. She continued, "Earlier this week, I signed a contract to become the next superintendent of Cypress View Unified School District."

People glanced around, unsure how to react. While a few knew she had interviewed at Cypress View, most didn't. She saw expressions of surprise, even shock. A ripple of murmurs grew. She could see people wondering whether applause would convey congratulations or good riddance. Several staff members looked as though they were trying to figure out if some already knew about her departure, or if this was news to everyone.

Frank Roberts leapt to his feet. Roxane's stomach clenched; what was he about to do?

"I think I speak for many of us here when I say ..." he paused, glanced around, and continued, "when I say this is a damn shame for us and a coup for Cypress View. Just speaking for myself, you've been a challenge. When you first came here, Dr. Bedford, I found you hard to take. I thought you were completely wrong for this school, too pushy with ideas we didn't need. But I've come to realize that you've been the challenge we needed. You've pushed me in directions I hadn't intended, but I'm glad you did. You've been exactly the right person for this school, and, well, you leaving us is such a surprise, I can't imagine who will be able to fill your shoes." Emotion washed across Frank's normally implacable face.

Applause broke out, with shouts of "Hear, hear!" Not everyone clapped, and some did so tepidly, but the spontaneous warmth from the majority brought tears to Roxane's eyes. She looked at Frank, and for the first time she could remember, he gave her a genuine smile. Her throat clenched.

She took a deep breath and continued. "Thank you. I didn't expect that. Thank you so much. I want to leave with just a few words about how proud I am of all of you, the team here at Taylor, and the work you do here. I know you're aware of tremendous challenges facing public education these days. The browner the average complexion of kids in the public schools, the greater the struggle for funding. This isn't simply a matter of poverty, either. The greater the proportion of kids of color in a district, the weaker the funding. And since our kids will continue to come to us more and more diverse, less and less white, we have a lot of work to do making sure funding supports us rather than drying up."

Several heads nodded.

"While our average class size here in San Jose Unified is 25 students, Palo Alto's is 23. Our district spends about twelve thousand dollars per year on each student, while Palo Alto spends a little over twenty thousand. Our students are almost ninety percent students of color, while Palo Alto's are about sixty percent students of color, the largest non-white group being Asian. Depending on local property taxes for about a third of our budgets creates huge inequities. Imagine what we could do if resources were spread equitably."

As she looked around, she saw heads nodding. Good. They were with her.

"Public education, the work you do here day in and day out, is foundational to this democracy. Our kids might be valued and provided for quite unequally, which is fundamentally wrong, but the country itself depends on a well-educated populace. And diverse as our future citizens are, that well-educated populace must be able to collaborate on solutions to issues that face all of us. Those same disparities we experience in education funding run through most of our social institutions, and need to be addressed. When I think about public health, for example, some communities have access to high quality care while others don't. But public health affects all of us, and to deny quality care to some people because of the kind of work they do brings down the quality of health we all experience. Now, what does this have to do with your work here at Taylor High?"

She was beginning to lose a few. Three teachers had drifted back to the drinks table for refills, a handful were whispering or signaling to each other, a few more were checking their phones.

"P.E. and health teachers, what I'm speaking about goes right to the heart of your work, and I was thrilled by the new public health unit you added to your curriculum this last year." Two health teachers who had been buried in their phones looked up in surprise. "Kudos to you," Roxane said warmly. Her applause directed toward these two departments initiated a wave of claps and cheers.

"History and social studies, over the years I've been here, your engagement of our kids in thinking and in analyzing social issues has become legendary. I've been so impressed by your willingness to adapt your deep expertise to our kids and their concerns." With broad smile, she sent a wink to Brian Sandoval. Sure, she exaggerated their accomplishments, but praise always worked as an effective motivator.

"Science teachers, well what can I say, I hear from kids all the time how much they appreciate your linking of science concepts with experiences they have every day. I'd venture to say that fewer of our kids engage in risky behavior with drugs because of your teaching, and more of them will enter science fields as they go on in higher education." More applause.

"And our Taylor Cougars sports teams are not only tough out on the field, but also demonstrate the best teamwork in this district. You've seen me at games. I know what I'm talking about. You do yourselves proud. So, whether you think of yourself as a cougar or a panther – they're much the same thing, you know," Roxane grinned wickedly as she brandished her Taylor Cougars T-shirt, "you, the faculty and staff of Taylor High School, do the work of bringing our diverse populace together so they can learn to solve our common problems in a supportive, thoughtful and equitable fashion. Just think of it, what else brings together young people from different walks of life as effectively as public education? As the eminent philosopher John Dewey said, 'We only think when confronted with a problem.' I commend all of you on your work getting our youth to think, to learn, and to work together. I'll miss you, but I'll take what I've learned from you into the next phase of my work. Thank you and have a wonderful summer."

Roxane had not expected the standing ovation. For most, it was heartfelt; for a few, she knew it was peer pressure. But in that moment, she understood that her vision for Taylor had finally prevailed. Her constant pushing of the teachers, and now her public affirmation of the value of their work, enabled all but the most reluctant to express appreciation for what she stood for. She would indeed miss this group of professionals.

***

"How was your last day, Baby?" Roxane's mother greeted her at the door with a kiss on the cheek. "You look radiant."

Roxane dropped her purse and book bag on a chair. "Mama, you know all the worrying and fretting I've been doing ever since I got this job? The days I come home and dump my problems on you?"

Her mother nodded.

"Well, it was all worth it. I wish you would have been there today. My staff gave me such an outpouring of appreciation that, well, I was blown away."

"I always knew you could succeed when you set your mind to it."

Roxane looked past her mother to the kitchen table, which as usual was strewn with papers. "More research?" she asked.

"No," her mother replied. "I've spent all day trying to pull this family history stuff together. My last memoir class session is tomorrow and I'd like to present it as done rather than in progress. This isn't exactly a memoir because it isn't about my life, but the instructor loves what I'm doing. After I finish it, I want to get it bound all nicely to give Imani for her birthday. I'll make you a copy, too."

"Imani will love, it, Mama," Roxane said, thinking about her daughter's interest in Black history.

"Now, here's what I have." Ada sat down at the table and picked up a printed two-paged stapled document. "Here's the story I told you and Imani about Edward finishing his cabin right after emancipation. I realize now that the neighbor's grandson was your Ben Harris's ancestor Daniel."

"*My* Ben Harris?" Roxane asked as she sat down.

"Well, you know, it's such a common name. No, of course he's not yours, but that's a way to differentiate him from all the other Ben Harrises out there."

Roxane laughed. Her mother certainly had creative ways to keep track of people.

Ada continued, "Now, that story, along with this family tree …" she picked up her most recent rendition of the Dwyers – "starts the family history off quite nicely."

While Roxane studied the family tree, her mother retrieved another printed document. "And here's the story about Spencer and how he became an activist. At the end, I included this photo of Spencer's son Porter. Nice looking man, I think."

Roxane smiled. "Indeed he was. And you have the story I wrote down for you about Daniel and Edward when they were adolescents."

"Oh, yes. That's very important," Ada said. "It shows how white people taught their young that our people aren't fully human. Maybe not exactly the same as how they do it these days, but the same general idea would still pertain."

Ada picked up another printed document. "This is Ben Harris's son's story. Thank you for getting it from Dr. Harris."

"Ben offered it," Roxane said. "I didn't know about it, but after I went to his house a couple of weeks ago, he emailed it to me in case I wanted to read it."

"Very nice of him," Ada said. "Now, what I don't have is a story about Daniel himself. We know something about where he came from and how he grew up, and we know something about his life later on when he was county clerk, but what happened in between? I bet your Ben Harris has some information."

Roxane laughed. "He's not ..."

"I know, I know. But can you ask him? The point I want to make in this little book is that, different as our backgrounds and experiences might be in this country, white people and Black people have always been interconnected, and those interconnections haven't gone away."

"I'll email him right now," Roxane said. "You might not get anything before tomorrow morning, though"

"Thank you, Baby, that's alright. I'll appreciate whatever he can send, whenever he can send it. Tell him I'll send him a copy of the whole thing when I'm done." Ada paused as a thought hit her. "No, tell him I'll bring it to him personally. I don't like this email stuff anyway, it makes things too impersonal. Now, can you help me think of a title?"

CHAPTER 20

A BETTER PLACE

The first day of school in August found Ben standing next to Chad Hernandez at the main entrance to Richford High School as kids swarmed up the steps.

"Summer sure flew, didn't it," Ben remarked between surges of kids.

"Yeah. It seems like just yesterday we were standing here," Chad replied.

Just yesterday. Or a lifetime ago, Ben thought. Lisa and the boys had moved to the rental house in Morgan Hill. After Ben helped them get settled in, then returned home alone, he felt as though his life had died. Certainly his marriage seemed beyond life support. Although he and Lisa hadn't yet planned to divorce, that outcome seemed inevitable. He couldn't be the husband she seemed to want now, and the hard-edged, overly protective white mom fleeing "the hoards" who she had become was no longer the wife he wanted.

What kind of wife did he want? He wasn't sure. At present, he had no interest in hunting for one. But he did know that if he were to marry again, any future wife would need to support the person he was rather than someone she wished him to be. She would also need to believe that the best way to support his sons was to help them learn to connect with the world rather than sheltering them from it.

Ben had spent much of the summer helping the boys navigate the transition in their lives. He had feared Evan would resist the high school in Morgan Hill, but his resistance evaporated when Evan discovered that it was better equipped than the schools he had attended in San Jose – more and newer computers, better science labs, and most importantly to Evan, a bigger and newer sports stadium. Jason was happy remaining in a San Jose school he was already familiar with.

Jason now attended both the San Jose taekwondo studio and one in Morgan Hill. Evan tried to continue playing baseball in San Jose, but hated the long bus ride, so he reluctantly signed up for a new team. Ben was right there with each of them. The boys seemed subdued, but Ben figured they were resilient. They stayed with him every other week, although as school was starting, he and Lisa would need to develop a rhythm for getting the boys to and from schools in two different districts.

Ben made more of an effort than he had in a long time to attend as many of their sporting events as possible, and to think up enjoyable things to do with them. There would be no taking of his sons for granted. He discovered a community center not far from his house that offered quite an array of activities for a very diverse population of kids. He wasn't sure why he hadn't noticed it before. It reminded him of the Boys and Girls Club in San Diego where he first got to know some urban youth. One of the activities was chess, something Evan had expressed interest in learning a few years back. Two Mexican American kids, local chess stars, regularly won tournaments. The first time Ben took the boys there, Evan tried to look bored, but as they were leaving, he asked if he could sign up for lessons. Jason, in the meantime, discovered a guitar class he might like to try. Ben felt optimistic that any friendships the boys developed here might counter whatever sense of white exclusivity they were getting from their mother.

His relationship with Lisa was cool and strained, almost polite. How weird it felt to ring her doorbell rather than just walking in. Would it always feel that way? Sometimes images of the old Lisa filled him with loss. Other times he couldn't quite remember what those days felt like.

An unexpected bright spot of the summer had been Roxane Bedford's mother. Not long after he had sent Roxane his story about Daniel's life, her mother had contacted him, saying she wanted to bring him something. He had been floored when she presented him with a bound copy of a book she had written, entitled *Family History in Black and White*. The book contained five chapters, including Jason's story about Daniel and Edward, and his own story about Daniel's survival of the Sultana explosion. When Roxane had asked him for any information he had about Daniel's life, she had mentioned that her mother was working on a project, but he had no idea what a fine project she had in mind. Once the boys settled into their own routines, he planned to give each of them a copy. After all, it chronicled a part of their own family history equally as much as Roxane's.

Ben realized that he was barely listening as Chad, between groups of kids arriving, described a trip his family took in July. Suddenly it hit Ben that he had never had a serious conversation with Chad about school. Or about anything else, for that matter. How often had Ben let his mind wander as Chad talked? He knew nothing of Chad's experiences as a kid in San Jose's schools, but his life had been much like that of many current Richford students, Ben suspected. How did Chad view the kids, from the point of view of an adult whose main role was to keep law and order in the school? What did he think about the school's disciplinary code, or its policies? Maybe Ben would become a better principal if he learned how to learn from people like Chad – people whose lives were more like the students' than his own. It came to him that he had never intentionally initiated a conversation with any person of color at Richford specifically about race or how racism might be manifest in the school.

He wanted to make the school a better place for kids and staff, and he had presumed himself to have more answers than anyone else. After all, he was the one with the administrative credential and doctoral degree. But now he realized there were teachers in the building he had never spoken with except about routine matters. Maybe even a few he hadn't directly spoken with at all. And there were students with ideas he had never really listened to, like that group who tried to explain what they wanted for the ethnic studies class.

Well, he could begin by actually listening to Chad. After greeting a cluster of girls arriving, he took a deep breath, turned to Chad and said, "I've been thinking about how we can make this school a better place for all the kids. The students of color as well as the white students. Being white myself, it might be easier for me to see what the white kids need. Would you mind dropping by my office later this morning? I'd like to pick your brain about how this school could be improved for all of the kids here, especially kids whose backgrounds are not like mine."

Chad scratched his head. "Gee, Dr. Harris, no one's asked my opinion about that before. Sure, I'd be glad to. Just off the top of my head, one thing is that I might want a few more teachers who speak Spanish. My parents didn't understand English very well, especially my mom, so there wasn't much communication between them and my teachers. They felt embarrassed coming into the school, they felt too uneducated. So they hardly ever came. I've noticed the same thing here."

Chad quickly turned to some boys entering the building, addressing them in rapid-fire Spanish. Then he turned back to Ben. "They pay attention when I talk to them like their parents do."

Ben nodded. He realized that facility with Spanish wasn't a skill he paid much attention to. It was a plus, of course, in a school like this that served so many Spanish-speaking families, but probably not one he had prioritized.

Ben scanned the parking lot and walkway. "Looks like we have a full house. By next week, we'll have bunches of late stragglers, but no one wants to start the year off on the wrong foot. Well, I look forward to our conversation later this morning."

Ben was about to turn toward his office when Chad asked, "Ever heard of some lady named Diane Ravitch?"

"Sure," said Ben. She was a well-known author and former Assistant Secretary of Education.

"I've been listening to some of her podcasts. They're pretty interesting, I like her take on education," Chad said.

"I've read some of her work, but haven't listened to her podcasts," Ben replied. "What do you like about them?"

"Well, she's really critical of Secretary DeVos, and I've learned more about DeVos's background by listening to her. She's critical of how wealthy people use their wealth to reshape public education. Stuff I hadn't exactly thought about, but when I listen to her, I think, well, yeah, that's true."

Ben had read some of Ravitch's writings while in graduate school. He said, "I'll tune into one of her podcasts sometime."

"Let me know what you think. Well, I'm gonna hang by the door here in case a few more straggle in. Have a good day, sir."

As he walked to his office, Ben wondered why Chad was attracted to Diane Ravitch and her podcasts. Ravitch was a historian and writer who ended up specializing in education, but – just like David Brooks – she had never been a schoolteacher or a principal. He felt his stomach churn. He had the day-to-day expertise, she didn't. Maybe he should start his own podcast.

Now, there was an idea.

As he entered the main office, Carmen alerted him that a Mrs. Whittier was in his private office for a brief conversation. She wouldn't say what it was about.

As he entered, he took in a large woman in a bright red dress. "Dr. Harris, I'm Thelma Whittier, and I'm so glad to meet you," she said. "I'm representing Campbell Union High School District, where we're about to launch a search for a superintendent. I'm here to try to convince you that Campbell would be a better place for you than here, because you would get to apply what you know to a whole system of schools rather than just one. The district is so close that you probably wouldn't even have to move. I hear you'd be an outstanding candidate, and want to chat with you about applying for the position."

Ben blinked in surprise as his mind whirred. She thought he would be outstanding. She recognized his expertise as an urban education leader. This could be his chance to gain the visibility and experience he sought. And he wouldn't have to move, he could remain active in the boys' lives. On the other hand, being a superintendent would probably require longer hours than the roughly sixty plus he logged per week as a high school principal, and it would probably consume more evenings and weekends. He might have to be more selective about which of the boys' activities he became involved in.

But why did people have to listen to pundits like Ravitch and Brooks, rather than true experts like himself? This could be his chance.

Gathering his wits, he cleared a pile of folders from a chair. "Have a seat. I'm not sure I'm interested, but I'll hear you out."

SUGGESTED DISCUSSION QUESTIONS

1. How would you characterize what Ben wants? What Roxane wants? How does what they want shape the kind of leader each becomes?
2. By alternating chapters between Ben's and Roxane's points of view, readers see each character experiencing leadership in an urban high school differently. To some extent, those differences derive from their personalities and interests. How does racism factor into their different experiences and perspectives? Sexism?
3. Roxane and Ben had two quite different visions for the purpose of schooling. How would you characterize each of their visions? Do you know people who have similar visions for schooling? To what extent can their visions be combined or merged?
4. Roxane's belief in Black self-determination is reflected the pride she expresses for her father's work with the Black Panthers. What stories have you heard about the Black Panthers? To what extent are they similar to or different from Roxane's? Why do you think the Panthers provoke very different kinds of responses in people?
5. Parenthood is very important to both Roxane and Ben, and both have to grapple with implications of raising children in a racist society. How do those implications play out similarly and differently for each of them?
6. Ben and Lisa have grown apart. What were the main factors behind the differences that drove them apart? To what extent do you think those differences were there all along, but below the surface? What caused them to become magnified?
7. Why does Ben have so much difficulty discussing race and racism with Roxane? Why does Roxane want him to be able to do so? How difficult do white people in your experience find discussing race? What kinds of things seem to help open up the conversation?
8. Some readers may think the historical relationship between Roxane and Ben is contrived or too coincidental. What do you think and why?

9. Roxane argues that all of us have inherited trauma from the nation's centuries of experience with slavery. To what extent to you agree with her? Can you give examples of ongoing trauma that you have witnessed or experienced?

10. The historical sections of the novel turn out to have been written by Roxane's mother Ada. Were you surprised? Could another character have been the author?

11. Which character do you think grows or changes the most through the novel? Why do you think so?

12. The novel ends on an inconclusive note when Ben is presented with an opportunity much like the one that launched the story. What do you think he does and why?

AUTHOR'S NOTE

Although this is a work of fiction, the historical sections are based on extensive research into my own family's history. The present-day sections grew from my imagination, drawing on actual events as well as data on San Jose's schools. Cypress View doesn't exist except in the pages of my fiction, but I drew from on small bay area cities to construct it.

Three of the historical characters are based on real people: Daniel Ethan Harris, the Union soldier, is based on Dewitt Edwin Harris, and Jackson Harris, his grandfather, is based on George C. Harris, both of them my ancestors. I based Edward Dwyer, the enslaved boy who became a sharecropper, on the tiny bit of information I could find about Ellis Coffin, a Black sharecropper who lived near Dewitt Harris on one census record.

To gather data, I made use of the census and other well-known genealogy tools, and I traveled to Monroe and McMinn Counties in east Tennessee in 2009. In the Monroe County courthouse, I combed through old deeds records. One that I unearthed is the deed of sale (or loan) between Harris and Dwyer, which is worded exactly as written in this novel. I also found a photo of D. E. Harris hanging in the courthouse, along with photos of other former county clerks.

To develop Daniel Harris's roots in Arkansas, I used census data as well as the archives of the *Arkansas Gazette News* (1819–1930); No. 17 – Whole No. 1369, March 30, 1846; and Orville W. Taylor's *Negro Slavery in Arkansas*, University of Arkansas Press, 2000.

For background on life in east Tennessee during and after the Civil War, I consulted F. A. Bailey's "Class and Tennessee's confederate generation," *The Journal of Southern History 51*(1), 1985, 31–60; Reba Bayliss Boyer's *Monroe County, Tennessee records, 1820–1870*. Southern Historical Press, 1970; Noel C. Fisher's *War at Every Door: Partisan Politics & Guerilla Violence in East Tennessee 1860–1869*, University of North Carolina Press, 1997; M. A. Grant's unpublished Master's thesis, "Internal Dissent: East Tennessee's Civil

War, 1849–1865," East Tennessee State University, 2009; Oliver Perry Temple's *East Tennessee and the Civil War*, The Robert Clarke Co., 1899; The Monroe County Heritage Book Committee's *Monroe County Tennessee Heritage 1819–1997*, Don Mills, Inc., 1997; and Melanie Greer Story's "Heroic Courage and Unfaltering Devotion, Gathering of East Tennessee veterans" *Tennessee Historical Quarterly* 68(2), 2009, 174–197.

For background on Cahaba Prison, I used the unpublished doctoral dissertation of José O. Díaz, "To Make the Best of Our Hard Lot: Prisoners, Captivity and the Civil War," The Ohio State University, 2009. For background on the Sultana explosion, I turned to Jerry O. Potter's *The Sultana Tragedy*, Pelican Publishing Co, 2000.

Although the character Spencer Dwyer is fictional, I tried to construct him and the context of Chattanooga as authentically as possible. I consulted Michelle R. Scott's *Blues Empress in Black Chattanooga*, University of Illinois Press, 2008; and Samuel Roderick Jackson's unpublished Master's thesis, "An Unquenchable Flame: The Spirit of Protest and the Sit-in Movement in Chattanooga, Tennessee," Georgia State University, 2008. I based *The Voice* newspaper on *The Blade*, a newspaper that was run by Randolph Miller of Chattanooga.

The present-day sections of this novel owe most of their existence to my imagination. I drew some of my inspiration for Ben Harris from the historical figure Benjamin Franklin Butler, whose physical characteristics, early childhood, and later ambitions formed the basis of Ben's character. I drew this inspiration from works such as Dick Nolan's *Benjamin Franklin Butler: The Damnedest Yankee*, Presidio Press, 1991; and Chester G. Hearn's *When the Devil Came Down to Dixie*, Louisiana State University Press, 1997.

I drew freely on various general news sources about teacher strikes and other issues. In Chapter One, the article by David Brooks entitled "Good Leaders make Good Schools" was actually published in the *New York Times*, but in March of 2018 rather than December of 2017. In invented the two letters to the editor in Chapter 2, but based them on my reading of similar letters in California newspapers, as well as Sarah Holder's "Why are so many people fighting housing for teachers?" *CityLab*, October 17, 2018. The news article that introduces Chapter 6 is fictional, but based on reading similar articles in California newspapers. The report by the Southern Poverty Law Center, mentioned in Chapter 9, is Swathi Shanmugasundaram's "Hate Crimes, Explained," April 15, 2018, available at www.splcenter. org/20180415/hate-crimes-explained #targets. In Chapter 16, Roxane refers to an article about inherited trauma; that article is Olga Khazan's "Inherited trauma shapes your health," from *The Atlantic*, October 16, 2018; my thinking was also informed by Resmaa Menakem's *My Grandmother's Hands*, Central Recovery Press, 2017. For detailed analysis of the historic roots of racial housing segregation, I consulted Richard Rothstein's *The Color of Law*, Liveright, 2017; and the *U.S. News and World Report* by Joseph P. Williams, "Segregation's Legacy," April 20, 2018.

I am greatly indebted to my community of readers who offered their encouragement as well as many insightful and critical suggestions for improving earlier drafts of the manuscript. Deep thanks go to Linda Turner Bynoe, Dudley Bynoe, Taharee Jackson, Luanna H. Meyer, Leslie Patiño, Noni Mendoza Reis, Dorothy Vriend, and Bonnie Wirfs. And to my wonderful developmental editor Ronit Wagman, I am very grateful for helping me tighten and polish my manuscript.

ABOUT THE AUTHOR

Christine Sleeter is Professor Emerita in the College of Professional Studies at California State University Monterey Bay, where she was a founding faculty member. Sleeter is an internationally recognized leader in social justice multicultural education and teacher education. She is author of several non-fiction books, including *Power, Teaching and Teacher Education* (Peter Lang, 2013), *Un-Standardizing Curriculum* (2nd edition with Judith Flores Carmona, Teachers College Press, 2015), *Culture, Difference & Power* (Teachers College Press, 2001), *Doing Multicultural Education for Achievement and Equity* (with Carl A. Grant, Routledge, 2011), and *Transformative Ethnic* Studies (with Miguel Zavala, Teachers College Press, 2020). *Family History in Black and White* is her third work of fiction. Her two previous novels include *White Bread* (Brill Sense, anniversary edition, 2020), and *The Inheritance* (self-published, 2018). Sleeter's work has been translated into several languages. In 2020, she was inducted into the National Academy of Education. In 2009, the American Educational Research Association honored Sleeter with its prestigious Social Justice in Education Award. She currently resides in Monterey, California. For more information, please visit www.christinesleeter.org

Printed in the United States
By Bookmasters